(Under)Represented Latin@s in STEM

Critical
Studies of
LATINXS
in the
Americas

Margarita Machado-Casas and Yolanda Medina
General Editors

Vol. 19

The Critical Studies of Latinxs in the Americas series
is part of the Peter Lang Trade Academic and Textbook list.
Every volume is peer reviewed and meets
the highest quality standards for content and production.

PETER LANG
New York • Bern • Berlin
Brussels • Vienna • Oxford • Warsaw

(Under)Represented Latin@s in STEM

Increasing Participation Throughout Education and the Workplace

EDITED BY Timothy T. Yuen,
Emily P. Bonner,
AND María G. Arreguín-Anderson

PETER LANG
New York • Bern • Berlin
Brussels • Vienna • Oxford • Warsaw

Library of Congress Cataloging-in-Publication Data

Names: Yuen, Timothy T., editor.
Bonner, Emily P., editor.
Arreguín-Anderson, María G., editor.
Title: (Under)represented Latin@s in STEM: increasing participation throughout
education and the workplace / edited by Timothy T. Yuen,
Emily P. Bonner, María G. Arreguín-Anderson.
Other titles: (Under)represented Latinos in STEM
Description: New York: Peter Lang, [2018].
Series: Critical studies of Latinxs in the Americas; vol. 19
ISSN 2372-6822 (print) | ISSN 2372-6830 (online)
Includes bibliographical references and index.
Identifiers: LCCN 2018024909 | ISBN 978-1-4331-5171-2 (hardback: alk. paper)
ISBN 978-1-4331-5175-0 (pbk. : alk. paper) | ISBN 978-1-4331-5176-7 (ebook pdf)
ISBN 978-1-4331-5177-4 (epub) | ISBN 978-1-4331-5178-1 (mobi)
Subjects: LCSH: Hispanic Americans—Education.
Hispanic Americans in science.
Science—Study and teaching—United States.
Classification: LCC LC2669 .U48 2018 | DDC 371.829/68073—dc23
LC record available at https://lccn.loc.gov/2018024909
DOI 10.3726/b13022

Bibliographic information published by **Die Deutsche Nationalbibliothek**.
Die Deutsche Nationalbibliothek lists this publication in the "Deutsche
Nationalbibliografie"; detailed bibliographic data are available
on the Internet at http://dnb.d-nb.de/.

Dedication

We hope that this book will contribute to the improvement of STEM opportunities and education for Latin@ students and, ultimately, all learners. We hope to not only recognize, but also provide kernels of solutions to the social, educational, and institutional challenges that contribute to persistent inequities in educational settings for Latin@ students. As such, we dedicate this book to those students and teachers who are working every day in the fight for equity within a system that is inherently inequitable.

Table of Contents

Figures and Tables

Figures

Tables

Foreword: Identity Formation as a Spiraling Process

BELINDA BUSTOS FLORES

As a young child, I recall the launching of Sputnik and the subsequent push toward the sciences and mathematics fields. We were introduced to new ways of approaching mathematics and science and these subjects became part of the daily curriculum. Our young President Kennedy challenged our imaginations that one day we would travel into space and land on the moon. We marveled with the space flights and eventual landing on the moon. Families all over the country gathered around their television sets to witness these events and this resulted in much pride for our country. I remember looking into the night sky and wondering what new life we might discover. While somewhat scary, I thought, could I be an astronaut? Yet, while these advances brought opportunities for some, it was clear from the images we saw that this was a White male's world. During this period, ongoing civil rights struggles were fraught with tensions across the country; much of the south was racially segregated. In the case of Latino children, across the country, linguistic segregation occurred with the denial of their heritage language and the proliferation of Mexican schools in south Texas. These actions were clearly intended to subjugate the Latin@ population to schools with limited resources, thereby resulting in inequitable schooling and relegating them to the lower income strata (San Miguel, 1987). Now, almost 50 years later, while landmark legal battles over civil, educational, and linguistic rights have been won (e.g., *Mendez vs. Westminster*, 1947; *San Antonio ISD v. Rodriguez*, 1973; *Lau vs. Nichols*, 1974) and legislation has been passed (e.g., Elementary Secondary Education Act; Bilingual Education Act), we continue to see the underrepresentation of Latin@s pursuing Science, Technology, Engineering, and Mathematics (STEM) fields and in the workforce.

As Yuen, Bonner, and Arreguín-Anderson in this volume point out, it is in our nation's best interest that we find pathways for preparing Latin@ youth for the STEM professions. Beyond a demographic imperative, it is a matter of social and equitable justice. Yuen *et al.* situate their work within science identity formation and posit that other lenses do not consider how the individual experiences science as a worthy enterprise that encompasses who they are. In this comprehensive volume, we note how the formation of an affirmative identity as a scientist is critical.

My colleague, Ellen Riojas Clark, and I (Clark & Flores, 2001; Flores & Clark, 2017) speak to the importance of personal and professional identities. While our research has focused on Latin@ teachers, this research is pertinent to the discussion on STEM identity formation. We have maintained that teachers who understand their identity formation can assist students in their identity development. We suggest that a positive ethnic/cultural identity responds to the quintessential question, "Who am I?" We also posit that having a firm identity of self, in particular, a cultural/ethnic identity, is linked to the individual's efficacy beliefs, which responds to "What can I do?" and in turn enhances the individual's motivation.

To see the interrelationship among identity, efficacy, and motivation, we can use the spiral as a heuristic model to understand identity and knowledge formation. As a geometric symbol, the spiral was understood and used across ancient cultures to signify natural growth and evolution. Lavodnas (2017) posits that "nature uses this shape [spiral] (among others) to build living and non living structures from microscopic unicellular organisms to galaxies that encompass billions of planets" (p. 7). Interestingly, each galaxy as each human being is unique. If you imagine the individual at the center of the spiral, and then consider that with each experience, the spiral expands as the individual's understanding of self, knowledge, and skills increases. Hence, as a starting point, it is important to see oneself as an ethnic/cultural being and then develop other identities, for example, a STEM identity. In the case of Latin@s, their heritage language, which is a reflection of their ethnicity/cultural identity, is linked to their persistence in STEM. Stevenson *et al.* (2017) observed that in maintaining their native language, Latin@s were able to form supportive networks, which boosted their resiliency and academic success. These researchers surmise: "With a solid sense of pride in who they are, our Latina participants negotiated meanings, facilitated interactions, and re-affirmed their cultural identities, thereby facilitating the enactment of the resiliency that has enabled their success in STEM fields" (p. 123).

Relationships and experiences in which the individual's identities, affirmation, and recognition occur are crucial in expanding one's identity. As such, family as a support system and role models (faculty, teachers, and peers) enhance the development of an individual's STEM identity. Parental engagement is also key in supporting Latina's STEM persistence (Brkich, Gallard Martínez, Flores, Claeys, & Stevenson, in press).

Beyond being supportive, it is important that families recognize a child's tendencies and curiosity toward STEM. Such interests should be encouraged and nurtured. Verdín and Claeys (2017) noted that successful Latina scientists pointed to playing with blocks, mathematical games, chemistry sets, and role-playing (doctor, engineer) as young children promoted their scientific thinking. Play as an authentic activity assisted these Latin@s in meaning making, encouraged their curiosity, and supported their identity formation.

The important role that educators (preschool–college) play in the Latin@s STEM identity formation and knowledge cannot be underscored. Educators must provide students with the recognition that affirms students' identity and identity formation through the curriculum and instructional activities (Jenlink & Townes, 2009). This volume speaks to the importance of having well-prepared teachers who are confident and competent in the teaching of STEM concepts to English learners (ELs). STEM thinking does not only occur in English. Authentic tasks must also have linguistic considerations and opportunities to learn the discourse of science. Through a project entitled Accelerated Teacher Education Program for preparing culturally efficacious STEM teachers, the importance of allowing students to use their heritage language or translanguaging practices was emphasized and promoted (Flores, Claeys, Gist, Clark, & Villarreal, 2015). As a result, we observed classrooms in which there was high interaction and engagement among ELs and non-ELs. Engaging ELs in STEM activities, anchored on their linguistic and cultural knowledge, promotes their interest, knowledge, and identity. In turn, this expands students' learning opportunities while affirming their identity as scientists.

Further compounding the issue that teachers are often not well prepared to teach STEM concepts, they often approach the teaching of these concepts as if these are free of bias (Tolbert, Stoddart, Lyon, & Solís, 2016). We must consider that too often the school curriculum promotes hegemonic discourse in which only Western knowledge is considered as premium (Apple, 2004). Classroom discourse and lessons must disrupt majoritarian myths about the STEM field, who has contributed to the STEM field, and who can be a scientist. Educators must move beyond Western knowledge and consider other ancient, indigenous, and cultural groups' contributions to science. Students should not find themselves as wanting to shed their ethnic self because the curriculum fails to recognize their identity and cultural group. These critical discussions must also engage students in understanding how issues of culture, gender, race, and positionality intersect with educational, employment, and economic opportunities. Dialoguing about these issues is essential in identifying the sociopolitical forces at play that often serve to perpetuate the status quo (Sloan, 2009). In dissecting this discourse, students will develop agency to counter such majoritarian tales and likely continue in their path toward a STEM degree and career.

Furthermore, enriching experiences should provide Latin@s opportunities to engage in STEM research. It is important to move beyond rote learning as is discussed in various chapters in this volume. The classroom must become a living laboratory that allows students to develop science literacy, such as hypothesizing, testing, writing-up, and presenting results. One such exemplar:

> Project-based pedagogy engages children in textual and experiential inquiry about authentic questions, and so can be considered discourse enabling. That is, project-based pedagogy affords students and teachers' opportunities to investigate, talk, read, and write about questions of interest to them. (Moje, Collazo, Carrillo, & Marx, 2001, pp. 469–470)

The Project-Based Approach, which employs authentic problem solving, student-centered tasks within an interdisciplinary setting, has demonstrated positive academic outcomes for EL, low-income, and diverse learners (Capraro, Capraro, & Morgan, 2013; Han, Capraro, & Capraro, 2014; Moje *et al.*, 2001). These authentic experiences further augment Latin@s' STEM identity.

Additionally, as indicated in the volume, Third Spaces can also provide students opportunities to learn and grow. As a formal setting, the classroom can become a third space (Moje *et al.*, 2001) in which differing discourses (home versus school) can be explored and intersected to enhance STEM learning and literacy. Informal learning within third spaces can afford learners opportunities to engage in problem solving without the pressure of high-stakes testing. Through the Academy for Teacher Excellence informal learning Robotics clubs, Schuetze, Claeys, Flores, and Sczech (2014) observed that children's STEM interest and confidence was promoted. Similarly, field trips are powerful experiences in promoting interest in the STEM fields as noted in this volume. However, often schools do not have funds for field trips. An alternative is bringing the experience to students. For example, a nonprofit organization, SASTEMIC, provides a Geekbus, a high-tech mobile STEM experience promoting problem-based learning and design thinking, to children in low-income schools (2017). The goals are to promote STEM interest as learners use authentic tasks to solve real-life problems in their daily lives and in their communities. Over the last five years, hundreds of schools have been served. These types of efforts must be supported through private and public funding in order to increase children's opportunities, interests, and identities in STEM.

In sum, as addressed in this volume, STEM identity formation requires familial support, role models, and opportunities to engage in science through formal and informal experiences. In order to see oneself as a scientist, certain support systems and structures must be in place. As a community, we must also invest in our Latin@ youth by providing STEM opportunities. Supportive contexts in which individuals are given opportunities to act and think like scientists, essentially a recognition of their STEM identity, promotes their self-efficacy and augments their motivation. Further, as Jenlink (2009) purports: "When recognition is enacted that intends to shape identity and affirm an individual, it is a step to realizing the aim of democracy through embracing difference as a defining quality of a democratic society" (p. 209). Returning to the spiral analogy, each STEM experience generates and foments the growth of the individual resulting in an expansive spiral that continuously affirms a STEM identity. Hence, STEM experiences as described in this volume are key in countering the achievement gap and in ensuring that Latin@s persist, graduate, and are employed in the STEM fields. I congratulate the authors for using identity formation as a lens to understand STEM engagement.

References

Apple, M. W. (2004). *Ideology and curriculum* (5th ed.). New York, NY: Taylor & Francis.

Brkich, K., Gallard Martínez, A. J., Flores, B. B., Claeys, L., & Stevenson, A. (in press). Latina parental involvement: Contributions to persistence in STEM fields. In B. Polnick, B. Irby, & J. Ballenger (Eds.), *Girls and women of color in STEM: Navigating the double bind*. Charlotte, NC: Information Age Publishing.

Capraro, R. M., Capraro, M. M., & Morgan, J. R. (Eds.). (2013). *STEM project-based learning*. Rotterdam: Sense Publishers.

Clark, E. R., & Flores, B. B. (2001). Who am I? The social construction of ethnic identity and self- perceptions of Latino preservice teachers. *The Urban Review, 33*(2), 69–86.

Flores, B. B., Claeys, L. C., Gist, C. D., Clark, E. R., & Villarreal, A. (2015). Culturally efficacious mathematics and science teacher preparation for working with English learners. *Teacher Education Quarterly, 42*(4), 1–31.

Flores, B. B., & Clark, E. R. (2017). *Despertando el ser: Transforming Latino teachers' identity, consciousness, and beliefs*. New York, NY: Peter Lang Publishers.

Han, S., Capraro, R., & Capraro, M. M. (2014). How science, technology, engineering, and mathematics (STEM) project-based learning (PBL) affects high, middle, and low achievers differently: The impact of student factors on achievement. *International Journal of Science and Mathematics Education, 13*, 1089–1113.

Jenlink, P. M. (2009). Coda: Recognition, differences, and the future of America schools. In P. M. Jenlink, & F. H. Townes (Eds.), *The struggle for identity in today's schools: Cultural recognition in a time of increasing diversity* (pp. 207–210). Lanham, MD: Rowman & Littlefield Education.

Jenlink, P. M., & Townes, F. H. (2009). *The struggle for identity in today's schools: Cultural recognition in a time of increasing diversity*. Lanham, MD: Rowman & Littlefield Education.

Lavodnas, B. (2017). *The intelligent universe and the nature of reality*. Retrieved from Academia.edu

Moje, E. B., Collazo, T., Carrillo, R., & Marx, R. W. (2001). "Maestro, what is 'quality'?": Language, literacy, and discourse in project-based science. *Journal of Research in Science Teaching, 38*, 469–498.

San Miguel, G. (1987). *Let all of them take heed*. Austin, TX: University of Texas Press.

SASTEMIC. (2017). *Geek bus: A mobile makerspace*. Retrieved from https://geekbus.com

Schuetze, A., Claeys, L., Flores, B. B., & Sczech, S. (2014). LCM as a community based expansive learning approach to STEM education. *International Journal for Research on Extended Education, 2*(2), 1–19.

Sloan, K. (2009). Dialoguing toward a racialized identity: A necessary first step in a politics of recognition. In P. M. Jenlink & F. H. Townes (Eds.), *The struggle for identity in today's schools: Cultural recognition in a time of increasing diversity* (pp. 30–48). Lanham, MD: Rowman & Littlefield Education.

Stevenson, A., Gallard Martínez, A. J., Brkich, K., Flores, B. B., Claeys, L., & Pitts, W. (2017). Latinas' heritage language as a source of resiliency: Impact on academic achievement in STEM fields. *Cultural Studies of Science Education*, 1–13. doi:10.1007/s11422-016-9789-6

Tolbert, S., Stoddart, T. S., Lyon, E., & Solís, J. (2014). The next generation science standards, common core state standards, and English learners: Using the SSTELLA framework to prepare secondary science teachers. *Issues in Teacher Education, 23*(1), 65–90.

Verdin, C., & Claeys, L. (2017). Latina and *Mexicana* STEM Educators' *Concientización: Desterrando los Motivos para Ensenar*. In B. B. Flores & E. R. Clark (Eds.), *Despertando el ser: Transforming Latino teachers' identity, consciousness, and beliefs*. New York, NY: Peter Lang Publishers.

Preface

TIMOTHY T. YUEN, EMILY P. BONNER, AND MARÍA G. ARREGUÍN-ANDERSON

The need to grow a diverse and competent workforce in science, technology, engineering, and mathematics (STEM) becomes paramount as our society endeavors to develop creative and innovative solutions to today's complex problems brought forth by technological advances. Educators at all levels are tasked with developing students who can be active contributors to a technology-rich society in which STEM knowledge and skills are key. A diverse workforce draws in multiple perspectives and strengths; thereby enabling meaningful creativity and innovation leading to societal advancement. One of the major educational obstacles in meeting this goal is equitable access to STEM opportunities for students of color. In the U.S., the lack of opportunities for students of color in the STEM fields is notable and must be addressed by the all stakeholders in the education pipeline. Specifically, Latin@s, the fastest growing population in the U.S., are severely underrepresented in the STEM fields in college and the workforce.

At 17.8% of the U.S. population, Latin@s are the largest minority group (U.S. Census Bureau, 2106) in the nation, and that number is expected to grow over the next few decades. As such, Latin@s are expected to make up over 70% of the growth in the U.S.'s workforce by 2020. It has been reported, however, that only about two-thirds of Latin@ students in the U.S. have access to high-quality, advanced course offerings in STEM areas. Where these programs or courses are available, they are not widely publicized (PCAST, 2012). While current statistics show that Latin@s constitute 25% of students enrolled in K–12 public schools (National Council for Education Statistics, 2012), this racial/ethnic distribution is not reflected in STEM field occupations. Recent NSF statistics show that Latin@s represent only 6% of the science and engineering workforce (National Science

Foundation, 2016). Although Latin@s have an equitable representation in earning bachelor's degrees across all fields, only 10–11% of science and engineering degrees are earned by Latin@s (National Council for Education Statistics, 2012; National Science Foundation, 2016). Also, a small number of institutions, which are limited geographically and demographically, graduate the majority of Latin@s in STEM (National Council for Education Statistics, 2012). At the graduate level, 8.8% of master's degrees and 6.6% of doctoral degrees in science and engineering were earned by Latin@s.

As a result, Latin@s are less likely to obtain employment in higher paying jobs in STEM fields. These statistics illustrate the crucial role that STEM educators play in adequately preparing and connecting Latin@ students to the increasing number of jobs in related fields. Without explicit support for Latin@ students, the marginalization of this population will continue to be exacerbated. Thus, the motivation for this edited volume is to bring attention to the issue of underrepresentation of Latin@s in STEM and highlight the work that is being done by educational researchers and practitioners around the country to increase Latin@ participation and achievement in STEM.

The following chapters explore a broad range of historical and contemporary issues surrounding Latin@ underrepresentation in STEM, and span multiple contexts including grade levels, learning environments, and specific STEM disciplines across the nation. Readers should not only gain a deep understanding of how underrepresentation of Latin@s in STEM is manifested in society, but also how this issue is promulgated throughout the education pipeline and into the workforce.

Additionally, research-based educational programs, initiatives, strategies, and techniques that seek to enhance participation of Latin@s in STEM are presented. The chapter authors present research on evidence-based programs aimed at increasing Latin@ participation and success in STEM throughout the education pipeline. More specifically, each author speaks through the lens of teacher preparation, family and community involvement, and/or student engagement. These foci are congruent with the idea of providing a forum to showcase stories of success as well as narratives that encapsulate struggles and lessons learned as individuals and entities embark in the quest of actively challenging and changing the status quo. Furthermore, the research-based ideas and strategies presented in these chapters should guide readers in driving toward transformative practices as well as educational policy-making and decisions.

As the chapters will show, broadening participation of Latin@s in STEM requires a multipronged approach that empowers Latin@ students, prepares STEM teachers of all levels in critical and culturally responsive pedagogies, and brings support from the home and community. The work will also show how it is essential that all stakeholders involved must take an active role in building strong STEM identities among Latin@ students at all levels of the education pipeline.

This book is organized into four sections with each section focusing on a critical component of increasing Latin@ participation and success in STEM in the education pipeline: (1) understanding the sociohistoric context of Latin@ underrepresentation; (2) preparing teachers to address the linguistic and cultural needs of their students; (3) creating strong family and community programs that support student participation; and (4) educational programs and initiatives that engage students.

Part 1—Latin@ Underrepresentation in STEM explores sociohistoric contexts that have contributed to the underrepresentation of Latin@s in STEM across the education pipeline, which provides the historical and contemporary contexts for the work presented in subsequent chapters. These authors outline implications of this type of systemic exclusion in the education system, the workforce, and society at-large. Postsecondary education is a critical time between formal education and the workforce and it is where underrepresentation of Latin@s in STEM is well documented in terms of degrees earned. This discussion begins with Herrera, Kovats Sánchez, Navarro Martell, and Zeledón-Pérez's study on the role of Hispanic Serving Institutions (HSIs), particularly at the community college level. Although two-year HSIs have been shown to be critical access points for Latinx as well as female students in STEM, their analysis also points out that more work in supporting and preparing minority students in STEM must be done before and throughout college. Against this backdrop of Latin@s in STEM at the postsecondary education level, the next chapter presents an intersectional comparison of case studies conducted by Lu and Rodriguez wherein each author examined the ways in which STEM identities are developed among students, and how those identities may differ according to gender at the undergraduate level. Their research shows the importance of providing Latin@ students positive and authentic STEM experiences, which in turn have a positive impact on their STEM and academic identities. The last chapter in this section by Villa, Hampton, and Hsu investigates issues related to engineering and computer science: major selection, persistence, and retention in Latinas. Their multiple case study reveals the everyday challenges three Latinas faced in engineering and computer science with respect to gender biases, institutional and societal racism, and home/life responsibilities throughout their career and how their own STEM identities were shaped as they navigated through these challenges. This study re-asserts the need for creating more inclusive and positive

STEM learning environments for Latin@ students throughout the entire education pipeline.

Part 2—Teacher Preparation and Professional Development presents research on programs that prepare pre-service and in-service educators to work with and motivate Latin@ students to become interested in and, ultimately, enter the STEM fields. Teachers play a crucial role as gatekeepers and facilitators of STEM, especially early in the education pipeline where children's only STEM experiences may come from schools. This section emphasizes the need for educators to be inclusive, culturally responsive, and engaged in transformative practices in increasing Latin@ participation in STEM. In the first chapter of this section, Barrera and Webb reported on a simulated language experience that places pre-service elementary teachers in the role of English Language Learners (ELLs) in which they had to work on science activities in an unfamiliar language (French) with and without language supports. Placing pre-service teachers in the roles similar to what their future students will experience was shown to be transformative: their findings indicated that they became more aware of the need for language supports in science learning for ELLs and empathetic towards the needs of diverse learner populations. Next, Solís, Bravo, and Mosqueda report the outcomes of preparing bilingual pre-service teachers through the Integrating Science and Diversity Education (ISDE) framework, which brings language and literacy together in science. Their findings show the importance of contextualization and language play/translanguaging (and the intersection of two) in creating high-quality science experiences for bilingual learners as well as the need for teacher educators to prepare pre-service teachers in such practices. In continuing with the theme of transformative teaching practices, Torres and Razfar studied the impact of a professional development workshop for K–8 science teachers in which they reflected on their own ideologies on the intersection of language, gender, and race in STEM learning and teaching. Teachers were also required to draw from their students' funds of knowledge as part this work. In broadening teachers' awareness of how language, gender, and race affect STEM learning and teaching, the authors make a case for action research that would engage teachers in ongoing reflection of their perceptions on what is being taught and how it is being presented to their students.

Part 3—Family and Community Involvement looks beyond the formal school environment by investigating the ways in which STEM education can become a part of students' and communities' everyday lives. This section showcases examples of successful partnerships between schools, universities, and communities, and between STEM and non-STEM fields that work together to broaden participation in STEM. First, Claeys, Lima, and Bhounsule studied a postsecondary service-learning program that engages both STEM and non-STEM majors as mentors to children in robotics/STEM clubs in communities with high populations of low socioeconomic Hispanic students. Their findings reveal that through this robotics club, STEM major participants enhanced their own engineering preparation while also increasing young Latino learners' access to STEM education. Thus, opportunities for such informal STEM experiences are beneficial to Latin@ and minority students who could potentially enter the STEM field as well as those who are currently in it. The next chapter by Argus-Calvo, Saldaña Corral, and Kosheleva discuss the outcomes of a community-based program that brings music and art together with STEM for elementary Hispanic students. The collaboration between the local orchestra, art museum, and university serve as a bridge between the STEM content learned in the classroom and what students experience in the real world; thereby enabling other pathways to STEM. The last chapter in this section by Campbell and Trevisan describes an ethnographic study of an outreach program aimed at increasing Latin@s in STEM through informal and formal education in rural areas with a specific aim at integrating families into children's STEM experiences. Additionally, this program was done in collaboration with STEM industry, government and non-profit agencies, and school districts. The impact of this program resulted in parents having greater awareness of science and resulted in a successful number of Latin@ students going onto university and pursuing STEM degrees. These programs bring STEM out of the classroom and into Latin@ students' everyday and home lives and vice versa.

Part 4—Student Engagement includes research on learner-centered initiatives and approaches such as innovative learning environments that facilitate Latin@ success and interest in STEM. Throughout this section, these learning environments have empowered Latin@s to become active participants in STEM as well as engaged them to reflect on their own STEM identities. First Hsu's study explores cogenerative dialogues between high school students and other stakeholders, such as teachers and scientists, within the context of internships. The cogenerative dialogue model provided a successful, active, and empowering learning environment for low socioeconomic students. Next, Davis and Rivera present a behavioral phenomenological study to investigate how maker experiences can increase computer science interest among Latin@ students. Their study highlighted the importance of active participation in communities, within computer science and makerspaces, in developing self-efficacious computer science identities in Latin@ students. The third chapter by Buenrostro investigates the impact of critical mathematics instruction at the high school level. This critical approach infused math knowledge and skills into students' everyday lives in order to empower them to become leaders and advocates in their community. The outcomes Buenrostro reports show how critical mathematics instruction led her primarily Latin@ students to feel a greater connection to social issues through math in which they were empowered to address them. Next, Hite, Midobuche, Benavides, and Dwyer present issues of STEM access within the context of middle school, formal schooling environments, and rural populations. The authors use Third Space theory as a lens to discuss the design of experiences within a STEM club that focuses on informal agricultural experiences. In the final chapter of this section, Esquinca and Villa report on an ethnographic study that explores how communities of practice can empower Latin@s to become engineers and leaders in engineering. This study emphasizes the need for such communities to provide underrepresented groups with opportunities to access STEM and actively engage in and support structures and models. Each of the learning environments presented in this section was designed to make STEM accessible and meaningful to Latin@ students. The positive outcomes on student affect and achievement show that supportive learning environments must be planted throughout the education pipeline starting from early childhood and well into post-secondary education.

Throughout this book, the need to support Latin@ students in constructing positive STEM identities, preparing teachers to be culturally responsive in STEM, and creating inclusive and engaging STEM learning environments is evident. While providing access to STEM opportunities to underrepresented and underserved populations is important for broadening participation, it is also essential that educators actively and intentionally support Latin@ students in becoming engaged and successful participants in STEM communities. Further, we must create unique STEM opportunities that have historically not existed for these students, encouraging all stakeholders to reenvision what it means to be a professional in a STEM field. To increase and sustain the participation of Latin@s in STEM, Latin@ students must experience was it is like to be STEM worker, think of themselves as STEM workers, and believe in their abilities to be successful STEM workers.

Latin@ students' competence, performance, and recognition of themselves as "scientists" are key to the development of a positive STEM identity (Lu, 2015). As this book exemplifies, an affirmative STEM identity does not emerge by accident. It is the result of systematic efforts to form competent STEM students motivated to eventually become professionals, equipped with vast knowledge and skills to understand, question, and potentially transform the STEM fields. This ability to navigate and successfully perform as a member of a STEM community can only trigger more creative and diverse responses to the increasingly complex challenges facing the world today.

As the authors of these chapters suggest, context, pedagogy, and student engagement are critical in process of STEM identity formation. The seeds must be planted in the fertile soils of schools, family interactions, community spaces, and teacher preparation programs. These are the contexts in which expectancies and values begin to influence career choices and perceptions of self-efficacy in STEM. We hope that educators, administrators, policy makers, and educational advocates will be able to take the proven strategies from these chapters to inform their own work in increasing Latin@ participation and success in STEM throughout the education pipeline.

References

Lu, C. (2015). Finding los científicos within: Latino male science identity development in the first college semester. *Journal of College Student Development, 56*(7), 740–745.

National Center for Educational Statistics. (2017). *Racial/ethnic enrollment in public schools.* Retrieved from https://nces.ed.gov/programs/coe/indicator_cge.asp

National Council for Education Statistics. (2012). *Higher education: Gaps in access and persistence study.* Washington, DC: US Department of Education.

National Science Foundation. (2016). *Women, minorities, and persons with disabilities in science and engineering.* Retrieved from https://www.nsf.gov/statistics/2017/nsf17310/

President's Council of Advisors on Science and Technology (PCAST). (2012). *Engage to excel: Producing one million additional college graduates with degrees in science, technology, engineering, and mathematics.* Washington, DC: Executive Office of the President.

U.S. Census Bureau. (2016). *USA QuickFacts from the US Census Bureau.* Retrieved from http://quickfacts.census.gov/qfd/states/48/4865000.html

Acknowledgments

It was our intent to create a strong collection of research-based chapters that will help educators and administrators increase Latin@ participation in STEM. To maintain a high level of rigor, all chapters underwent an intense peer review process both internally among the chapter authors and the editors, and externally through a panel of expert reviewers. We would like to acknowledge the following experts who served as the external peer reviewers for this edited volume: Melanie Bertrand, Zulmaris Diaz, Isaura J. Gallegos-Webb, Lucia Ganendran, Gabriela Gonzalez, Trevor A. Pickering, Monica Ridgeway, Re-Anna S. Roby, and Jessica Wilson. Lastly, we would like to thank the chapter authors for sharing their work on broadening participation in STEM.

Part 1: Latin@ Underrepresentation in STEM

1. Latinx Students in STEM College Pathways: A Closer Look at Diverse Pathways through Hispanic Serving Institutions (HSIs)

Felisha A. Herrera, Gabriela Kovats Sánchez, Melissa Navarro Martell, and María-José Zeledón-Pérez

Community colleges and Minority Serving Institutions (MSIs)—Hispanic Serving Institutions (HSIs), in particular—serve as key access points to postsecondary education for Latinx[1] students and provide several pathways for pursuing STEM (Science, Technology, Engineering, and Mathematics) degrees. Nearly 40% of all undergraduate students of color are enrolled in MSIs (Cunningham, Park, & Engle, 2014). HSIs, specifically, are federally defined as institutions with a Latinx student population of 25% or greater (Contreras & Contreras, 2015). However, unlike other MSIs, HSIs do not have a written mission or vision to serve or recruit Latinx students (Núñez, Hurtado, & Galdeano, 2015). Considering 60.8% of all Latinx students are enrolled in HSIs (Hispanic Association of Colleges and Universities, 2016) and nearly 50% of HSIs are two-year colleges (Excelencia in Education, 2014a), the overlapping institutional contexts of community colleges and HSIs are particularly important environments that impact the postsecondary experiences of Latinx students.

Forty percent of all Latinx undergraduate degrees are awarded by HSIs (Dowd, Malcom, & Macias, 2010), which are among the top 25 institutions of higher education that award degrees to Latinx students (Santiago, 2012). Given the potential that HSIs provide in terms of retaining Latinx students, it is important to consider how these institutions can better support Latinx students pursuing STEM degrees. This chapter provides a summary of current literature and empirical research on Latinx students entering STEM fields through diverse college pathways. Additionally, this chapter highlights national trends among Latinxs in STEM at HSIs and specifically focuses on the community college context. The role of two-year HSIs is closely examined through an exploratory descriptive analysis of the most recent longitudinal nationally representative data available through the National Center for Education Statistics (NCES).

Literature Review

Hispanic Serving Institutions

HSIs are federally defined by the Higher Education Opportunity Act (HEOA) as accredited, degree-granting, public or private nonprofit institutions of higher education with 25% or more full time equivalent undergraduate Latinx students (Contreras & Contreras, 2015). Colleges and universities designated as HSIs are eligible to apply for federal grants through Title V also known as Developing Hispanic-Serving Institutions Program (Santiago, 2006). According to the Hispanic Association of Colleges and Universities (2016), there are 435 HSIs in the US serving more than 1.8 million Latinx undergraduate students, with 83% of HSIs concentrated in California, Texas, Puerto Rico, New Mexico, Florida, and New York. Forty six percent of HSIs are public two-year colleges, and 3.9% are private two-year institutions (Excelencia in Education, 2014a). In total, two- and four-year HSIs represent 12.9% of all nonprofit higher education institutions and enroll 21.9% of all students (Hispanic Association of Colleges and Universities, 2016).

Furthermore, higher education institutions with an undergraduate Latinx enrollment between 15 and 24.9% are identified as emerging HSIs (Excelencia in Education, 2015; Hispanic Association of Colleges and Universities, 2015; Santiago & Andrade, 2010). As of 2016, there are 33 states with at least one emerging HSI (Excelencia in Education, 2016). According to the U.S. Department of Education, there are 310 emerging HSIs; 34.5% of which are two-year institutions (Hispanic Association of Colleges and Universities, 2016). Thus, the number of designated HSIs is expected to grow significantly within the next ten years as the Latinx population continues to grow (Excelencia in Education, 2015; Hispanic Association of Colleges and Universities, 2015).

Community College Context

Between 1993 and 2014, Latinx enrollment in higher education increased 13 percentage points, from 22 to 35% (Pew Research Center, 2016). This rise is attributed in part to the growing number of students of color enrolling specifically in community college (Provasnik & Planty, 2008). Latinxs, in particular, are more likely to attend community college than any other ethnic group (Balassone, 2013; Long, 2016). Almost half of all Latinx students, nearly 7 million, are enrolled in community colleges across the U.S. (Pew Research Center, 2016). In 2013, 22% of students enrolled in public community colleges were Latinx (Pew Research Center, 2016). Nationally, among Latinxs that attained STEM bachelor's degrees, 61% attended a community college at some point in their educational trajectories and 18% earned an associate's degree prior to obtaining their bachelor's degree (Malcom, 2010). Community colleges play a vital role in STEM education as they provide key access points to higher education for Latinxs (Hagedorn & Purnamasari, 2012; Packard, Gagnon, LaBelle, Jeffers, & Lynn, 2011; Provasnik & Planty, 2008; Salzman & Van Noy, 2014; Wang, 2013).

Underrepresentation in STEM

While literature on STEM students at the community college level is still emerging, empirical studies demonstrate that underrepresented students of color aspiring STEM degrees at community colleges are at a disadvantage when compared to students at four-year institutions (Grandy, 1998; Wang, 2015). Although Latinx students enter community colleges at higher rates, only a small percentage successfully transfer to a four-year university (Bailey, Jenkins, & Leinbach, 2005). These low transfer rates have been attributed to numerous factors: lack of support on behalf of the institution (Ovink & Veazey, 2011), high student to counselor ratios, ineffective advising, and remedial coursework (Crisp, Nora, & Taggart, 2009; Hagedorn & Purnamasari, 2012; Ovink & Veazey, 2011). Specifically, Crisp *et al.* (2009) found that a disproportionately large number of Latinx students are assigned or incorrectly placed in developmental or remedial courses. Lee, Flores, Navarro, and Kanagui-Muñoz (2015) also found a direct correlation between self-efficacy beliefs and persistence among students who were placed into remedial coursework. Further, Wang (2015) argues that community colleges have yet to develop pathways for STEM degrees in the same way that four-year universities have.

Among four-year institutions, the challenge of underrepresentation in STEM remains. Although historically underrepresented students enter college with interests in STEM fields at equal rates to their White and Asian counterparts, too few of these students successfully graduate with STEM degrees from four-year institutions (Bailey *et al.*, 2005; Huang, Taddese, &

Walter, 2000; Malcom, 2010). For example, Hurtado, Eagan, and Hughes (2012) analyzed data on the entering freshmen cohort of 2004 and found that only 29% of Latinx, 21.8% of African American, and 24.9% of American Indian students compared to 43% of White students, who intended to major in STEM actually completed a STEM four-year degree within four years. Latinx, African-American, and American Indian students only accounted for 14.7% of the total STEM degrees awarded in 2010 (Estrada *et al.*, 2016).

While academic preparation impacts student retention in STEM majors at the four-year level, educational settings and STEM climate are also central to the experiences of underrepresented students of color (Engberg & Wolniak, 2013; Garcia & Hurtado, 2011; Ong, Wright, Espinosa, & Orfield, 2011; Ovink & Veazey, 2011). Similar to the community college context, Latinx four-year STEM students are faced with a lack of institutional support (Hurtado *et al.*, 2007; Hurtado & Carter, 1997; Ovink & Veazey, 2011). Feelings of isolation, invisibility, and tokenism within predominantly White environments are common experiences among underrepresented students of color in STEM at four-year institutions (Byars-Winston, Gutierrez, Topp, & Carnes, 2011; Hurtado *et al.*, 2007; Hurtado, Newman, Tran, & Chang, 2010; Ong *et al.*, 2011; Orom, Semalulu, & Underwood III, 2013). Moreover, the traditional competitive nature of STEM programs also negatively impacts underrepresented students of color's adjustment to campus (Hurtado *et al.*, 2007, 2010) and hinders their persistence in STEM majors (Seymour & Hewitt, 1997).

In their study of four-year institutions, Hurtado *et al.* (2010) found that perceptions of hostile racial campus climates and highly competitive environments negatively impacted the academic adjustment of underrepresented students of color pursing STEM majors during their first year. Ong *et al.* (2011) define STEM disciplines as "meritocratic in nature and [their] focus on grades, classroom performance, and research results" ignores the "social realities of racism and sexism in science environments" (p. 183). As a result, underrepresented students of color, both undergraduate and graduate, commonly experience issues related to ethnic and gender discrimination, which impacts their sense of belonging on campus. Similarly, Orom *et al.* (2013) found that underrepresented medical students of color received less support and exposure to positive learning environments, experienced discrimination, and were more likely to perceive their race as having a negative impact on their medical school experience in comparison to their White peers.

The literature also identifies a positive link between supportive educational spaces and the persistence of underrepresented students of color in STEM (Cole & Espinoza, 2008; Hurtado *et al.*, 2007). Precollege summer programs have been found to improve retention rates of student of color in STEM (Palmer, Maramba, & Elon Dancy Ii, 2011). For community college students in particular, strong support systems, engagement in introductory STEM courses, hands-on research, and faculty mentorship have been found to increase student retention in STEM (Morgan & Gerber, 2016; Myers, Starobin, Chen, Baul, & Kollasch, 2015; Wang, 2015; Wang, Sun, Lee, & Wagner, 2017). Similarly, college support STEM programs and research/ laboratory opportunities for undergraduates at the four-year institutional level have proven to encourage STEM participation among underrepresented students of color (Byars-Winston *et al.*, 2011; Chang, Sharkness, Hurtado, & Newman, 2014; Hurtado *et al.*, 2007; Ong *et al.*, 2011). Lee *et al.* (2015) also found that Latinx students' participation in hands-on engineering opportunities led to greater self-efficacy, which increased confidence and intentions to persist in college.

Student relationships with faculty are also important predictors of STEM persistence (Byars-Winston *et al.*, 2011; Hurtado *et al.*, 2010; Ong *et al.*, 2011; Ovink & Veazey, 2011). Faculty that foster collective learning (Byars-Winston *et al.*, 2011) and validate students' identities as emerging scientists are instrumental in promoting STEM persistence (Ong *et al.*, 2011). Ovink and Veazey (2011) also draw attention to the role of academic advisors within college support programs. The hands-on mentoring approach of these advisors helps keep underrepresented students of color motivated and "on track" while providing them with social and cultural capital that allows them to pursue specific STEM careers (Ovink & Veazey, 2011). For community college students, faculty and academic advisors provide crucial psychological and instrumental support among underrepresented students pursuing STEM majors (Archuleta-Lucero, 2015; Packard *et al.*, 2011).

In their extensive examination of HSIs, Núñez *et al.* (2015) found these institutions more likely to have supportive campus climates with fewer incidents of racial and ethnic discrimination reported. Specifically, the greater visibility and representation of Latinx students, faculty, and administration at HSIs foster the possibility for creating supportive campus climates and increasing academic self-concept for Latinxs (Núñez *et al.*, 2015).

HSIs and STEM

Through a brief examination of the most recent nationally representative data, this chapter underscores the importance of understanding the role of HSIs as STEM pathways for Latinx students. A descriptive analysis will highlight the role of HSIs in STEM entrance and persistence and provide a national profile of STEM students attending HSIs. The data presented are derived from the 2004–2009 Beginning Postsecondary Students Longitudinal Study (BPS:04/09) available through the NCES. This data set is designed to investigate factors relevant to student success in college (e.g., enrollment, persistent, attainment). The BPS:04/09 is a nationally representative sample of approximately 16,100 first-time, first-year beginning students, conducted through three waves of data collection. The first wave in 2003–2004 and two follow-up surveys collected additional data in three-year interviews, 2006 and 2009 (Cominole, Riccobono, Siegel, & Caves, 2010). Through descriptive statistics computed using NCES PowerStats, we outline the role of two- and four-year HSIs in STEM access.

STEM Entrance

Table 1.1. STEM[1] entrance by race/ethnicity at HSIs[2]

	Two-year HSIs	Four-year HSIs	All HSIs
White	5.3	1.3	2.9
African-American	8.3	3.5	5.7
Asian American/Pacific Islander	26.4	5.9	12.1
Latinx	49.8	44.9	47.4
All Students	14.6	6.3	9.7

[1] STEM fields include mathematics, sciences (including physical sciences and biological/ agricultural sciences), engineering/engineering technologies, and computer/information sciences
[2] Federally designated Hispanic Serving Institution
Source: U.S. Department of Education, National Center for Education Statistics, 2003–2004 Beginning Postsecondary Students Longitudinal Study, Second Follow-up (BPS:04/09). Computation by NCES PowerStats Version 1.0

First, we examine the distribution of students entering STEM fields through HSIs in Table 1.1. We define STEM students as those that declare a major in mathematics, sciences (including physical sciences and biological/ agricultural sciences), engineering/engineering technologies, and/or computer/information sciences at any point during the six-year college enrollment period. Among all beginning postsecondary students who entered a STEM field at some point over a six-year period, only 9.7% start at an HSI. Larger proportions of two-year versus four-year STEM students begin at HSIs, with 14.6% of STEM students starting at two-year HSIs (public and private nonprofit) compared to 6.3% of STEM students starting at four-year HSIs (public and private nonprofit).

Across racial groups, we see that two-year HSIs are key STEM access points, not only for Latinx students, but for other students of color as well. Two-year HSIs enroll 49.8% of Latinx, 26.4% of Asian/Pacific Islander, and 8.3% of African-American students in comparison to their White peers with only 5.3% enrolling at HSIs. Considering that HSIs contribute to nearly half of the Latinx STEM entrants at two-year institutions, it is imperative to look toward two-year HSIs as an underutilized opportunity for addressing under-representation in STEM for Latinx and other students of color.

HSI STEM Student Profile

Reflective of the significant institutional stratification by race/ethnicity and by income in the US educational system (Carnevale & Strohl, 2013), HSIs are disproportionately less selective four-year institutions and/or community colleges and Latinx postsecondary students are concentrated within HSIs (Núñez, 2017). In particular, HSIs educate a large proportion of students of color from urban school districts as more than 50% of these institutions are community colleges located in urban settings (Excelencia in Education, 2014b). Therefore, we need to better understand the undergraduate profiles of those who enter STEM fields through HSIs. Table 1.2 highlights student characteristics among STEM entrants across two-year HSIs and non-HSIs.

Table 1.2. Profile of 2003–2004 beginning community college students who entered STEM[1] fields through 2009 at HSIs[2] and Non-HSIs, by selected student characteristics

	Two-year HSI	Two-year Non-HSI
Gender		
Male	64.6	70.7
Female	35.4	29.3
Parents' highest education		
High school diploma or less	45.5	37.9
Some college/voc. training but no degree	19.7	18.0
College degree	34.9	44.2
		(Continued)

Table 1.2—Continued

	Two-year HSI	Two-year Non-HSI
Income group 2003–2004		
Lowest quarter	47.6	22.6
Middle two quarters	38.4	52.4
Highest quarter	14.0	25.1
High school GPA		
Below B	15.4	22.0
At least B	84.6	78.0
Remedial education		
Remedial course 2004: Any	36.3	27.0
Remedial course 2004: Math	30.6	20.2
Enrollment 2003–2004		
Full-time	42.1	55.9
Part-time	38.2	29.4
Mixed	19.7	14.6

[1] STEM fields include mathematics, sciences (including physical sciences and biological/agricultural sciences), engineering/engineering technologies, and computer/information sciences
[2] Federally designated Hispanic Serving Institution
Source: U.S. Department of Education, National Center for Education Statistics, 2003–2004 Beginning Postsecondary Students Longitudinal Study, Second Follow-up (BPS:04/09). Computation by NCES PowerStats Version 1.0

While many studies point to the low representation of women in STEM fields (Starobin & Laanan, 2008), we find through disaggregation that the proportion of females to males is higher among HSI STEM entrants in comparison to non-HSI STEM entrants. While the number of women entering STEM at two-year HSIs does not reach parity with the proportions of men, the percentage of women in STEM at HSIs (35.4%) is six percentage points higher than the proportion of STEM women at non-HSIs (29.3%). The socioeconomic backgrounds of students are an important consideration as literature has posited that HSIs, particularly community colleges, disproportionately serve first-generation, low-income, and nontraditional students

(Núñez, Sparks, & Hernández, 2011). Among HSI STEM entrants, only 34.9% of students had parents who had attained a college degree, equating to nearly 10 percentage points less than their STEM counterparts beginning at non-HSI two-year institutions. Similarly, the income distributions of STEM students at HSIs were concentrated in the lowest income bracket with almost half falling within this category and only 14% in the highest income bracket, which compares with 25% of students at non-HSIs who fall within the highest income bracket.

Precollege preparation is one of the most commonly cited factors influencing the postsecondary attainment among low-income and underrepresented students (Chang *et al.*, 2014; Crisp *et al.*, 2009). Two-year colleges and HSIs face the challenge of students entering with varying levels of access to the high-quality precollege learning experiences that prepare them for STEM undergraduate programs. There is a measureable difference of over six percentage points in the proportion of HSI STEM students who earn at least a B in high school (78%) as compared to the proportion of STEM students within this grade range (84.6%) attending non-HSI institutions. STEM students who enter postsecondary education at HSIs require remedial intervention at a much higher rate than their non-HSI STEM peers. The proportion of STEM HSI students requiring at least one remedial course in any subject is over 10 percentage points higher than their non-HSI peers, with 36.3 and 27%, respectively. Similarly, in math the proportion of STEM HSI students (30.6%) requiring at least one remediation course is over 10 percentage points higher than that of non-HSI STEM students (20.2%). Lastly, in terms of full-time enrollment, the proportion of HSI STEM (42.1%) who were enrolled full-time in 2003–2004 is over 13 percentage points less than the proportion of STEM students attending non-HSIs (55.9%).

STEM Persistence

We examined STEM persistence over a six-year period for those who started postsecondary education in 2003–2004. We concentrated on students whose first institution was a two-year HSI or two-year non-HSI, with a specific focus on Latinx students. Differences across these institution types were observed. At both two-year HSIs and two-year non-HSIs, Latinxs have significantly lower STEM persistence rates in comparison to their non-Latinx peers. Latinx students at HSIs have the lowest proportion of students who were retained in STEM (12.5%) overall, which is over 23 percentage points lower than their non-Latinx peers (35.2%) at these same institutions. Interestingly, we found similar gaps in STEM persistence at non-HSIs, but these differences are not as profound at HSIs with 21 and 33.2% STEM persistence among Latinx and non-Latinx respectively. In addition, there are larger proportions of Latinx students who leave postsecondary education entirely (35.9% compared to 28.7% for non-Latinx students) and who persist in college but switch out of STEM majors (51.7% compared to 36.2% for non-Latinx students). Our findings confirm previous studies suggesting that graduation rates for Latinxs at HSIs are not equitable to non-HSIs.

Figure 1.1. STEM[1] persistence as of 2009 for 2003–2004 beginning two-year students by first institution HSI[2] status.

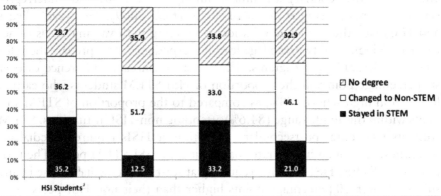

₁ STEM fields include mathematics, sciences (including natural, physical sciences and biological/agricultural sciences), engineering/engineering technologies, and computer/information sciences

₂ Federally designated Hispanic Serving Institution

₃ HSI students includes race categories: White, African American, Asian American/Pacific Islander, American Indian, Other & more than one race

Source: U.S. Department of Education, National Center for Education Statistics, 2003-04 Beginning Postsecondary Students Longitudinal Study, Second Follow-up (BPS:04/09). Computation by NCES PowerStats Version 1.0

Source: Authors

Discussion

Our findings demonstrate that two-year HSIs are critical access points in the STEM pipeline for Latinx students and other students of color. While community colleges overall enroll women in STEM at higher rates, two-year HSIs are vital in broadening participation for women in STEM. In addition, we observed larger proportions of low-income, first-generation college students, and part-time students are concentrated within two-year HSIs. Socioeconomic factors are important considerations as they may require students to work full-time, which can inhibit the academic and social adjustment of STEM students (Hurtado *et al.*, 2010). While academic preparation has been cited as one of the most important factors impacting STEM access and retention (Chang *et al.*, 2014; Crisp *et al.*, 2009; Engberg & Wolniak, 2013; Garcia & Hurtado, 2011), we found that two-year HSIs admit slightly larger proportions of STEM entrants with high GPAs (B or higher) in comparison with two-year non-HSIs. However, two-year HSIs had higher rates of students requiring remedial coursework, particularly in math. Early interventions in math and other STEM core courses are important for STEM advancement, especially within two-year colleges (Wang, 2015).

Unfortunately, our analysis of national data confirms that outcomes for Latinxs at HSIs are not equitable to their peers at non-HSIs (Contreras, Malcom, & Bensimon, 2008). STEM retention rates for Latinxs at two-year HSIs are 23 percentage points lower than their non-Latinx peers at two-year HSIs and nearly nine percentage points lower than their Latinx peers at two-year non-HSIs. While the literature we reviewed identifies the potentially positive educational features of and opportunities for HSIs to promote Latinx STEM persistence and attainment, scholars continue to call for more research to determine the role of HSIs in ensuring equitable outcomes for Latinx STEM students (Crisp *et al.*, 2009; Garcia & Hurtado, 2011). As Garcia (2017) argues, being a Hispanic "Serving" Institution goes beyond the metrics of Latinx persistence and attainment, but includes providing community engagement opportunities, positive campus climate, and support programs. Clearly there is an opportunity for HSIs, particularly two-year HSIs, to play a critical role in increasing Latinx representation in STEM and more work is needed to harness the potential of these unique contexts.

Acknowledgments

This material is based upon work supported by the National Science Foundation under NSF DUE-1644990. Any opinions, findings, and conclusions or recommendations expressed in this material are those of the authors and do not necessarily reflect the views of the National Science Foundation.

Note

1. Latinx is used in place of Latino/a. Latinx serves as a gender-neutral term that is not limited by the gender binary ("Latinx," 2016).

References

Archuleta-Lucero, A. (2015). *Faculty and student interactions at the community college: An examination of the interaction order.* Retrieved from http://digitalcommons.utep.edu/dissertations/AAI10007407/

Bailey, T., Jenkins, D., & Leinbach, T. (2005). Community college low-income and minority student completion study: Descriptive statistics from the 1992 high school cohort. *Community College Research Center.* Retrieved from http://eric.ed.gov/?id=ED484355

Balassone, M. (2013). *Report: Despite graduating from CA's best schools, Latinos choose community college.* Retrieved from http://universityofsoutherncalifornia.createsend1.com/t/ViewEmail/j/E763C590AAAF8000/F8861AAD58372902C68C6A341B5D209E

Byars-Winston, A., Gutierrez, B., Topp, S., & Carnes, M. (2011). Integrating theory and practice to increase scientific workforce diversity: A framework for career development in graduate research training. *CBE-Life Sciences Education, 10*(4), 357–367. https://doi.org/10.1187/cbe.10-12-0145

Carnevale, A. P., & Strohl, J. (2013). *Separate and unequal: How higher education reinforces the intergenerational reproduction of white racial privilege.* Washington, DC: Georgetown University Center on Education and the Workforce. Retrieved from http://www.voced.edu.au/content/ngv:57695

Chang, M. J., Sharkness, J., Hurtado, S., & Newman, C. B. (2014). What matters in college for retaining aspiring scientists and engineers from underrepresented racial groups. *Journal of Research in Science Teaching, 51*(5), 555–580. https://doi.org/10.1002/tea.21146

Cole, D., & Espinoza, A. (2008). Examining the academic success of Latino students in science technology engineering and mathematics (STEM) majors. *Journal of College Student Development, 49*(4), 285–300.

Cominole, M., Riccobono, J., Siegel, P., & Caves, L. (2010). 2007–08 National Postsecondary Student Aid Study (NPSAS:08) Full-scale Methodology Report (NCES 2011–188). U.S. Department of Education. Washington, DC: National Center for Education Statistics. Retrieved from http://nces.ed.gov/pubsearch

Contreras, F., & Contreras, G. J. (2015). Raising the bar for Hispanic serving institutions an analysis of college completion and success rates. *Journal of Hispanic Higher Education, 14*(2), 151–170. https://doi.org/10.1177/1538192715572892

Contreras, F. E., Malcom, L. E., & Bensimon, E. M. (2008). Hispanic Serving Institutions: Closeted identity and the production of equitable outcomes for Latino/a students. In M. Gasman, B. Baez, and C.S.V. Turner (Eds.), *Understanding Minority Serving Institutions* (pp. 71–90). Albany: State University of New Your Press.

Crisp, G., Nora, A., & Taggart, A. (2009). Student characteristics, pre-college, college, and environmental factors as predictors of majoring in and earning a STEM degree: An analysis of students attending a Hispanic serving institution. *American Educational Research Journal, 46*(4), 924–942.

Cunningham, A., Park, E., & Engle, J. (2014). *Minority-serving institutions: Doing more with less*. Washington, DC: Institute of Higher Education Policy. Retrieved from http://www.voced.edu.au/content/ngv:62293

Dowd, A. C., Malcom, L. E., & Macias, E. E. (2010). *Improving transfer access to STEM bachelor's degrees at Hispanic Serving Institutions through the America COMPETES Act*. Los Angeles, CA: University of Southern California.

Engberg, M. E., & Wolniak, G. C. (2013). College student pathways to the STEM disciplines. *Teachers College Record, 115*(1), 1–27.

Estrada, M., Burnett, M., Campbell, A. G., Campbell, P. B., Denetclaw, W. F., Gutiérrez, C. G., Zavala, M. (2016). Improving underrepresented minority student persistence in STEM. *CBE-Life Sciences Education, 15*(3), es5. https://doi.org/10.1187/cbe.16-01-0038

Excelencia in Education. (2014a). *Black + Brown: Institutions of Higher Education*. Washington, DC: Excelencia in Education. Retrieved from http://www.edexcelencia.org/hsi-cp2/research/black-brown-institutions-higher-education

Excelencia in Education. (2014b). *Hispanic-Serving Institutions (HSIs): 2012–13*. Retrieved from http://www.edexcelencia.org/gateway/download/27244/1492141463

Excelencia in Education. (2015). *Hispanic undergraduate enrollment at HSIs by sector, 1994–95 to 2013–14*. Washington, DC: Excelencia in Education. Retrieved from http://www.edexcelencia.org/hsi-cp2/research/hispanic-undergraduate-enrollment-hsis-sector-1994-95-2013-14

Excelencia in Education. (2016). *Excelencia in education reports more Hispanic-serving institutions overall, but growth remains concentrated*. Excelencia in Education. Retrieved from https://www.edexcelencia.org/sites/default/files/click_download/2016%20HSI%20News%20Release%201.27.16.pdf

Garcia, G. A. (2017). Defined by outcomes or culture? Constructing an organizational identity for Hispanic-serving institutions. *American Educational Research Journal, 54*(1_suppl), 111S–134S.

Garcia, G. A., & Hurtado, S. (2011). Predicting Latina/o STEM persistence at HSIs and non-HSIs. In *American Educational Research Association Annual Conference, New Orleans, LA*. Retrieved from https://heri.ucla.edu/nih/downloads/AERA%202011%20-%20Garcia%20and%20Hurtado%20-%20Predicting%20Latino%20STEM%20Persistence.pdf

Grandy, J. (1998). Persistence in science of high-ability minority students: Results of a longitudinal study. *Journal of Higher Education, 69*(6), 589–620.

Hagedorn, L. S., & Purnamasari, A. V. (2012). A realistic look at STEM and the role of community colleges. *Community College Review*, 91552112443701.

Hispanic Association of Colleges and Universities. (2015). *HACU legislative agenda*. Washington, DC: Hispanic Association of Colleges and Universities. Retrieved from http://www.hacu.net/images/hacu/govrel/2015_Legislative_Agenda.pdf

Hispanic Association of Colleges and Universities. (2016). *Fact sheet: Hispanic Higher Education and HSI*. Retrieved from http://www.hacu.net/hacu/HSI_Fact_Sheet.asp

Huang, G., Taddese, N., & Walter, E. (2000). Entry and persistence of women and minorities in college science and engineering education. *Education Statistics Quarterly, 2*(3), 59–60.

Hurtado, S., & Carter, D. F. (1997). Effects of college transition and perceptions of the campus racial climate on Latino college students' sense of belonging. *Sociology of Education, 70*(4), 324–345.

Hurtado, S., Eagan, M. K., & Hughes, B. E. (2012). *Priming the pump or the sieve: Institutional contexts and URM STEM degree attainments.* Presented at the Annual Forum of the Association for Institutional Research, New Orleans, LA.

Hurtado, S., Han, J. C., Sáenz, V. B., Espinosa, L. L., Cabrera, N. L., & Cerna, O. S. (2007). Predicting transition and adjustment to college: Biomedical and behavioral science aspirants' and minority students' first year of college. *Research in Higher Education, 48*(7), 841–887.

Hurtado, S., Newman, C. B., Tran, M. C., & Chang, M. J. (2010). Improving the rate of success for underrepresented racial minorities in STEM fields: Insights from a national project. *New Directions for Institutional Research, 2010*(148), 5–15. https://doi.org/10.1002/ir.357

Latinx. (2016). *OxfordDictionaries.com.* Retrieved from https://en.oxforddictionaries.com/definition/Latinx

Lee, H.-S., Flores, L. Y., Navarro, R. R., & Kanagui-Muñoz, M. (2015). A longitudinal test of social cognitive career theory's academic persistence model among Latino/a and White men and women engineering students. *Journal of Vocational Behavior, 88,* 95–103.

Long, A. (2016). *Overcoming educational racism in the community college: Creating pathways to success for minority and impoverished student populations.* Sterling, VA: Stylus Publishing, LLC.

Malcom, L. E. (2010). Charting the pathways to STEM for Latina/o students: The role of community colleges. *New Directions for Institutional Research, 2010*(148), 29–40.

Morgan, M. V., & Gerber, M. M. (2016). Utilizing factor analysis to inform the development of institutionally contrived experiences to increase STEM engagement. *Community College Journal of Research and Practice, 40*(3), 204–218.

Myers, B., Starobin, S. S., Chen, Y., Baul, T., & Kollasch, A. (2015). Predicting community college student's intention to transfer and major in STEM: Does student engagement matter? *Community College Journal of Research and Practice, 39*(4), 344–354.

Núñez, A.-M. (2017). Commentary: centering the "marginalized majority": How Hispanic-serving institutions advance postsecondary attainment. *American Educational Research Journal, 54*(1_suppl), 135S–139S.

Núñez, A.-M., Hurtado, S., & Galdeano, E. C. (2015). *Hispanic-serving institutions: Advancing research and transformative practice.* New York: Routledge.

Núñez, A.-M., Sparks, P. J., & Hernández, E. A. (2011). Latino access to community colleges and Hispanic-serving institutions: A national study. *Journal of Hispanic Higher Education, 10*(1), 18–40. https://doi.org/10.1177/1538192710391801

Ong, M., Wright, C., Espinosa, L. L., & Orfield, G. (2011). Inside the double bind: A synthesis of empirical research on undergraduate and graduate women of color in science, technology, engineering, and mathematics. *Harvard Educational Review, 81*(2), 172–208-390.

Orom, H., Semalulu, T., & Underwood III, W. (2013). The social and learning environments experienced by underrepresented minority medical students: A narrative review. *Academic Medicine, 88*(11), 1765 1777.

Ovink, S., & Veazey, B. (2011). More than "getting us through": A case study in cultural capital enrichment of underrepresented minority undergraduates. *Research in Higher Education, 52*(4), 370–394. https://doi.org/10.1007/s11162-010-9198-8

Packard, B. W.-L., Gagnon, J. L., LaBelle, O., Jeffers, K., & Lynn, E. (2011). Women's experiences in the STEM community college transfer pathway. *Journal of Women and Minorities in Science and Engineering, 17*(2), 129–147. Retrieved from http://www.dl.begellhouse.com/journals/00551c876cc2f027,123ee04f5c874ba3,3044733424dcb71a.html

Palmer, R. T., Maramba, D. C., & Elon Dancy Ii, T. (2011). A qualitative investigation of factors promoting the retention and persistence of students of color in STEM. *Journal of Negro Education, 80*(4), 491–504.

Pew Research Center, J. M. K. (2016, July 28). *5 facts about Latinos and education*. Retrieved December 11, 2016, from http://www.pewresearch.org/fact-tank/2016/07/28/5-facts-about-latinos-and-education/

Provasnik, S., & Planty, M. (2008). Community colleges: Special supplement to the condition of education 2008. Statistical Analysis Report. NCES 2008–033. *National Center for Education Statistics*. Retrieved from http://eric.ed.gov/?id=ED502349

Salzman, H., & Van Noy, M. (2014). *Crossing the boundaries: STEM students in four-year and community colleges*. Retrieved from https://rucore.libraries.rutgers.edu/rutgers-lib/49393/

Santiago, D. (2006). *Inventing Hispanic-Serving Institutions (HSIs): The basics*. Excelencia in Education. Retrieved from http://eric.ed.gov/?id=ED506052

Santiago, D. A. (2012). *Finding your workforce: The top 25 institutions graduating Latinos*. Retrieved from http://www.edexcelencia.org/hsi-cp2/research/finding-your-workforce-top-25-institutions-graduating-latinos

Santiago, D. A., & Andrade, S. J. (2010). Emerging Hispanic-serving institutions (HSIs): Serving Latino students. *Excelencia in Education (NJ1)*. Retrieved from http://eric.ed.gov/?id=ED508202

Seymour, E., & Hewitt, N. M. (1997). *Talking about leaving : Why undergraduates leave the sciences*. Boulder, CO: Westview Press.

Starobin, S. S., & Laanan, F. S. (2008). Broadening female participation in science, technology, engineering, and mathematics: Experiences at community colleges. *New Directions for Community Colleges, 2008*(142), 37–46.

Wang, X. (2013). Modeling entrance into STEM fields of study among students beginning at community colleges and four-year institutions. *Research in Higher Education, 54*(6), 664–692.

Wang, X. (2015). Pathway to a baccalaureate in STEM fields are community colleges a viable route and does early STEM momentum matter? *Educational Evaluation and Policy Analysis, 37*(3), 376–393.

Wang, X., Sun, N., Lee, S. Y., & Wagner, B. (2017). Does active learning contribute to transfer intent among 2-year college students beginning in STEM? *The Journal of Higher Education,* 88(4), 593–618.

2. Increasing the STEM Pipeline by Strengthening Latin@ Science Identity Development

Charles Lu and Sarah L. Rodriguez

STEM (Science, Technology, Engineering, and Math) is the future. According to the U.S. Department of Commerce (2010), technological innovation accounted for over half of U.S. economic growth within the past 50 years. The 30 fastest-growing occupations in the next decade will require at least some background in STEM (National Science Foundation [NSF], 2017). In fact, STEM occupations grew by 17% from 2008 to 2018, compared to 9.8% growth for non-STEM occupations (U.S. Department of Commerce, 2010). Of the 4.7 million STEM workers in the U.S., 68% of them held a bachelor's degree, 23% held an associate's degree, and 9% have a high school diploma or less. As expected, the STEM workforce is a highly educated one. Two-thirds of all STEM workers possessed a bachelor's degree in a STEM discipline, demonstrating that it may be more challenging to enter a STEM career without a STEM degree in hand (Toldson & Esters, 2012).

Simultaneously, American business leaders are concerned about the supply of STEM employees coming through the education pipeline. Less than 40% of all graduating high school students are prepared to take a college-level science class and that number is significantly lower (25%) for underserved groups (American College Board, 2014). A study by the National Science Foundation (2017) showed that the U.S. has one of the lowest STEM to non-STEM degree rates in the world. If this critical shortage of the STEM labor force continues to increase, American businesses will find it difficult to remain competitive in an increasingly global and technologically advanced marketplace (NSF, 2017; U.S. Department of Commerce, 2010).

At the same time, American demographics are changing. Data from the 2010 U.S. Census indicated that more than half of the growth in the total population of the U.S. between 2000 and 2010 was due to the increase in the Hispanic population, and this growth is expected to continue. The country is expected to become "majority minority" by 2050, and one in three U.S. residents is expected to be of Latin@ descent (U.S. Census Bureau, 2010). Data from the 2010 U.S. Census indicated that 37.9% of the Hispanic population is below 19 years of age, demonstrating that a substantial portion of the Latin@ population is, and will continue, to be moving through the educational pipeline for years to come.

Given the economic and demographic imperatives of STEM as well as the growing Latin@ population, it is vital that the U.S. ensures STEM success for Latin@s. Current trends indicate that Latin@s are interested in pursuing a STEM major, but are attaining STEM degrees at lower rates than their White and Asian peers (NSF, 2017). Furthermore, prior research has shown that over half of all STEM degree pursuers change majors within the first two years and that the first few weeks of college are critical for Latin@ students (Higher Education Research Institute, 2010).

Most relevant studies focusing on minority students in STEM fields have used some form of capital theory, critical race theory, or resistance theory as a conceptual lens (Carlone & Johnson, 2007). Even though these theories provide a starting point for research in STEM education, they also possess two substantial limitations. First, studies that used some form of capital theory, such as STEM success being related to intrinsic motivation, perseverance, family support, and strong precollege science experiences, can be applied to almost any successful student (Carlone & Johnson, 2007). Utilizing science identity as a theoretical framework can provide a deeper exploration of how race, ethnicity, and/or gender complicate these factors.

Another limitation of the theoretical models used in most studies is the lack of student agency in these studies (Carlone & Johnson, 2007). This may be seen by the factors that are used to explain success or lack of success, all of which are extremely static. For example, a student either has strong parental support or precollege science experiences, or she does not (Carlone & Johnson, 2007). While these explanations are well documented in the literature, they also place students as passive recipients of learning with little consideration as to how she may be able to creatively position herself against those barriers (Carlone & Johnson, 2007). Further, these frameworks lock the student's experiences into a snapshot rather than looking at a gradual evolution of how the experiences have grown, changed, and developed. The field needs critical and innovative explanations for promoting or accounting for the experiences of Latin@s in STEM. This chapter addresses this critical area by considering student professional identity development as an analytical lens and technique for promoting educational change within today's social context.

This chapter sets the context and provides a call to action for scholars, administrators, and policymakers alike to focus on Latin@ science identity to increase success and retention in the STEM disciplines. The book chapter will consist of four sections: (1) an overview of science identity development; (2) a description of two studies of Latin@ science identity development; (3) an analysis of common themes between these two studies; (4) a discussion of implications for future research, practice, and policy.

Science Identity Development Model

Scholars in science education have posed three compelling arguments for the use of identity as an analytical lens (e.g., Brickhouse & Potter, 2001; Carlone & Johnson, 2007; Lemke, 2001). First, scholars who use social theories of learning (e.g., Cobb, 2004; Lemke, 2001; O'Neill & Polman, 2004) make the argument that studying identity allows for multiple vantage points for the science teaching and learning environment. According to Cobb (2004), exploring identity permits us to ask questions about the kinds of people promoted and marginalized by science teaching and learning practices; the way students come to see science as a set of experiences, skills, knowledge, and beliefs worthy (or unworthy) of their engagement; and the possible ways that students' emerging identities in science might eventually involve changes in their more enduring sense of who they are and who they want to become.

Another argument advocating for the use of identity as an analytical lens involves the investigation of how women and underrepresented minorities are socialized and enculturated into the predominantly Anglo-masculine norms and discourses of science (Brown, 2004; Kelly, 2007; Varelas, House, & Wenzel, 2005). While sociological studies have been done on the topic, identity construction may be even more helpful in understanding how students, particularly women and underrepresented minorities, beginning their study in the sciences may be drawn to, pushed away from, and/or forced to negotiate aspects of their identities with the cultural norms of the scientific community.

Lastly, the utilization of identity as a theoretical lens advocates for a more equitable and evolving science education (Carlone & Johnson, 2007). Traditionally, the way that science is taught in schools implies that science is a clear-cut set of definitions and tasks, and is a finished and complete body of knowledge. As a result, this education promotes a lack of creativity, innovation, and narrow science identities (Carlone & Johnson, 2007; Gilbert & Yerrick,

2000). Carlone (2004), for instance, found that girls in a traditional physics curriculum, which emphasized lectures and verification labs, embraced the certainty of knowledge because it allowed them to earn good grades. However, they did not develop science identities because the nature of the tasks deemphasized scientific thinking, talking, and tool use (Carlone, 2004). In other words, the cultivation of short-term knowledge and interest are not enough to develop a sustained interest in science, especially in higher education. Therefore, a strong need remains to look beyond the interest levels and grade performances of STEM students. Rather, the exploration of science identities provides a deeper understanding of why STEM students persist or falter in their majors.

The two studies explored within the second section of this chapter utilized Carlone and Johnson's (2007) model of science identity which combines elements of development with understanding the complex way that intersecting identities influence the science identity development process. Carlone and Johnson's study sought to make sense of the scientific experiences that 15 successful women of color had over the course of their undergraduate and graduate studies in science. In creating their model of science identity, Carlone and Johnson considered one primary question: How would people with a strong science identity be described? First, they must not only be competent in their own scientific knowledge and abilities, but also must be motivated and curious to understand the scientific world. Second, they must have the confidence and adequate skills necessary to perform those skills in front of other people. For example, they must be able to utilize scientific tools correctly, discuss topics with proper scientific literacy, and interact with professionals in the scientific community in formal as well as informal scientific settings.

Also, they must not only recognize themselves as "science people," but also must be recognized as a science person by others and as a contributing member to the scientific community. As a result, Carlone and Johnson captured those three aspects of the science identity in three interrelated dimensions of their model: competence; performance; and recognition. The three aspects of the science identity previously discussed—competence, performance, and recognition—overlap. Perhaps the most obvious example might be a scenario where someone is extremely competent in his knowledge of science material and can perform with peers in a small group, but still does not get recognized by others as a science person. A case like this was discovered in a study examining women who were extremely competent and performed very well in an engineering program, but were still not recognized as legitimate engineers by their professors or potential employers (Tonso, 1999).

Another ethnographic study by Tonso (2006) discovered that some of the engineering students at elite U.S. universities who were the most valued and highly recognized in their program had the lowest competence in reality. As a result, it is critical that these regions of overlap between performance, recognition, and performance are considered when utilizing science identity as a theoretical lens.

Lastly, this model of science identity assumes that other aspects of one's identity, such as gender, race, and ethnicity, intersect to influence an individual's science identity. Applied here, the concept of intersectionality asserts that an individual's position within the STEM environment is simultaneously gendered and raced (Collins, 2008; Crenshaw, 1991; hooks, 1992; Noddings, 1992). These considerations are a call for stakeholders to consider both the micro and macro level systems of social domination and inequality that may exist within this environment (Collins, 2008; Crenshaw, 1991). However, this model also argues that identity theory is unique in that it "takes into consideration the complex interplay between structure and agency and the way these tensions play out over time" (Carlone & Johnson, 2007). Unlike the other theoretical frameworks relevant to this topic that primarily focus on the constraints institutions place on individual possibilities, identity also accounts for agency. For instance, rather than thinking of race and gender as something that we are, identity construction considers race and gender as something that we do (Brickhouse, Lowery, & Schultz, 2000).

In this chapter, we argue that framing studies through identity construction will allow for the study of Latin@s in STEM across time and in different contexts rather than a static moment in an individual's life (Gee, 2000; Lemke, 2001). In addition, the consideration of gender, race, and ethnicity within that development addresses the need for a more nuanced approach to understanding the experiences of Latin@ STEM students.

Two Studies of Latin@ Science Identity Development

This chapter presents two separate studies regarding Latin@ science identity development at the same research university in the southwest region of the U.S. by Lu (2013) and Rodriguez (2015). The studies were conducted at different times and neither of the authors participated in the other's initial study. The authors' collaboration and ultimately this chapter emerged after data collection was completed. This ongoing dialogue among authors was meant to connect and corroborate findings between the two studies as well as create a space for exploring future work in this area and providing recommendations for action.

The purpose of the study conducted by the first author (Lu) was to examine science identity development in Latino men during the first semester of college. Data were collected over four months through two individual, semi-structured interviews with 12 Latino men majoring in diverse STEM disciplines. To obtain a representative sampling group, each discipline (science, technology, engineering, and math) had at least one student. Out of the 12 participants, 5 of the participants were the first in their families to attend college. In addition, three of the participants were born and attended a portion of their K–12 schooling in Mexico. The sample was also socioeconomically diverse; four participants grew up in households with less than $15,000 family income and four participants grew up in households with more than $75,000 family income. The duration of all interviews ranged from 60 to 90 minutes.

The study conducted by the second author (Rodriguez) interviewed 16 undergraduate Latina students (juniors and seniors) majoring in the STEM disciplines at a at a Predominantly White Institution research institution in the southwest. Each student participated in two 1-hour, semi-structured interviews. The study centers upon the perspectives of Latina juniors and seniors because their persistence through the college experience yields an enhanced understanding of STEM identity development experiences across multiple years within the discipline and at the research site. Out of the 16 participants within this study, seven of the participants were the first in their families to attend college. Fourteen of the 16 participants possessed Mexican family origins while 11 of the 16 participants within this study grew up in households with between $15,000 and $75,000 family income. The duration of all interviews ranged from 60 to 90 minutes.

Despite conducting two separate studies on Latino and Latina students, the authors asked similar research questions, such as "How do Latin@s make meaning of their formal and informal STEM experiences?", "How do they develop their science identities during their college experience?", and "What is the relationship between their science identity and other aspects of their identities (e.g., gender, race, socioeconomic, etc.)?" The participants responded to these questions in the two studies in relatively similar ways, which we compare and discuss in further detail in the findings section later in this chapter.

For this chapter, we used an open coding procedure to establish initial concepts and categories within each study (Strauss & Corbin, 1998). Afterward, we merged categories based on common themes regarding STEM identity development that we saw between both studies. Throughout the analysis process, we exchanged our analyses of the data on several occasions, which allowed us to affirm and challenge each other's interpretations of the data. Ultimately, we arrived at a set of shared interpretations that were grounded in the data.

To minimize the perceived power imbalance between the researchers and students, we both employed appropriate strategies to limit the influence of power on their interactions with the participants, such as dressing casually, offering to conduct the study in a neutral location or a place of the participant's choosing, and sharing informal pieces of our own lives. Although we both made efforts to reduce power inequities during our studies, we acknowledge that some disparity was unavoidable due to our positionalities as researchers with certain levels of education. Furthermore, there were inherent limitations in both of our studies. Latino freshmen were participants in the study conducted by the male researcher. Latina juniors and seniors were participants in the study conducted by the female researcher. Therefore, the participants are in different stages of their college careers and some of the responses may have been influenced by gender dynamics between the researcher and participant. The male researcher is also Asian-American, and the participants in his study may have been less forthcoming about some of their challenges due to stereotypes about the "model minority" myth, particularly when discussing topics about science and math. Finally, we do not disaggregate the findings by generational status in the U.S. or by parents' educational level, although we acknowledge that these differences heavily influence the construction of one's science identity.

Findings

Several common themes emerged from both studies, which separately explored science identity development in Latin@s majoring in STEM at a research institution. Lu's (2013) study on Latino men majoring in STEM disciplines found that students equated competence in the STEM disciplines primarily with testing; in other words, if you are good at science and math, you will test well. Many of the participants in the study identified themselves as "science people" as early as elementary school because they tested better in science and math than in reading or writing. This notion of test scores as a reflection of science competency became conflicting for many of them after they failed to perform on their first round of exams.

Rodriguez's (2015) study on Latina women majoring in STEM fields examined how students made meaning of their STEM experiences and developed their STEM identities. This study found that science identity recognition from professors, peers, and family played an important role in the science identity development of Latinas in STEM. In addition, this study found that Latinas negotiated that recognition and their science identities through the lenses of their gender, racial, and other intersectional identities.

Although these are two individual studies, we synthesized findings in order to further our understanding of STEM experiences and identity development for undergraduate Latin@ students. We focus on three themes that cut across both studies: (1) engaging with STEM material and research early builds science identity; (2) science identity recognition essential to identifying as a scientist; (3) intersectional identities influence science identity development.

Engaging with STEM Material and Research Early Builds Science Identity

Participants in both studies reflected on and discussed the importance of being engaged with STEM-related communities, material, and research early on in their college careers. Being involved in a very practical way with the research of faculty members allowed both male and female participants to understand the STEM culture and gain necessary technical skills; however, the male participants tended to be overconfident in their abilities and the female participants were more likely to doubt themselves, particularly in their first-year science courses. In addition, Latinas within this study "performed" their identities explicitly by using technical terms and integrating science and a feeling of exploration into their daily lives, whereas the Latino male participants did not overtly think about or feel the need to perform their science identities.

For Latinas, engagement provided an opportunity to demonstrate or perform their competence in STEM subjects and be recognized as a valuable member of the STEM community. Latinas within this study performed their science identities through their engagement with STEM contexts, such as internships with faculty or industry companies, and their produced deliverables, such as research presentations or computer programming. One participant, Esperanza, remarked, "They had a national conference of all the people who were doing research and they picked me to represent the earth sciences…I was up there with everyone else presenting and…so it was validating, encouraging." The acts of researching within her discipline and presenting her findings validated her place within the STEM college environment and made her feel as though she was a scientist. Reinforcing Carlone and Johnson's (2007) model, this study demonstrates that the three elements of science identity development (competence, performance, and recognition) overlap for Latinas in the STEM fields.

For Latino men, engagement with these contexts mean defining and re-defining for themselves what it meant to be a scientist. Jordan, commented on how his eyes were opened to the economic and political side of the scientific world. Before the seminar, he wanted to be a scientist because he did not enjoy business or politics. Then, he heard from a scientist who worked for a governmental agency who exposed him to the political atmosphere for acquiring grants, publications, and compliance issues. Jordan said, "I was…mad when I heard this. That's when I realized I'll never be able to escape [business or politics], even as a scientist." As such, early engagement with science communities, material, and research allowed students to meet and interact with professional scientists and helped develop important pieces of science identity. These findings support previous literature which has suggested that engagement with the field might influence the emerging identity of the student (Cobb, 2004) and that science identities may have to be negotiated within various contexts and other identities or beliefs (Carlone & Johnson, 2007).

Science Identity Recognition Essential to Identifying as Scientist

Science identity recognition also played an important role in the identity development of Latin@s in STEM. Recognition from professors, family, and peers (both STEM and non-STEM) was key to students feeling like a STEM "person." Self-identifying as an "engineering person," a "scientist" or more generally as an "explorer" reflected the ability of participants to feel a connection to the scientific inquiry mindset and the STEM community.

For Latinas, recognition of their science identities was crucial to a sense of validation and persistence within these fields. One participant, Victoria, said, "it all culminated in this moment where I gave a presentation and a faculty member came up to me and was like, 'I was very impressed by your presentation.'…It really validated and justified all those years of hard work." Particularly for Latina women, who so often encountered peers who doubted their abilities or a STEM context which considered them gender and racial/ethnic outsiders, recognition of a science identity established their place within this community.

Like their female counterparts, Latino men also sought validation from experts within the field. Mateo enthusiastically explained how his science identity completely changed after meeting a famous evolutionary scientist in his seminar, one that he had learned about in middle school. Through this interaction, Mateo realized he had access to some of the most famous names in the industry and felt more encouraged in his ability to become successful in the field. Nonetheless, many of the Latino men in this study discussed that the transition from high school to college was challenging for their science identities because they were no longer recognized as "the smartest guy." One third of the participants no longer saw themselves as scientists and largely felt that way because they were not acknowledged by their peers and teachers as science people. They described the feeling as "becoming invisible" during the first semester of college. Such findings for Latino men in this context may relate to greater issues related to male gender role conflict, including the need for control, the drive for competition, and the pressure to achieve (O'Neil, 1981; Saenz, Bukoski, Lu, & Rodriguez, 2013).

Intersectional Identities Influence Science Identity Development

Latin@s within both studies discussed the intricate relationships between their various intersectional identities and their STEM identity development. Latin@ students are often marginalized within STEM contexts as a result of their racial/ethnic identities. Furthermore, these contexts often further marginalize Latina women as a result of simultaneous racism and sexism that results from these historically masculine and predominantly White spaces (Collins, 2008; Crenshaw, 1991; hooks, 1992; Noddings, 1992).

The Latinas experienced subtle and blatant racism, particularly from their peers. However, they also experienced sexism and lowered expectations because of their presence within a predominantly masculine space. One participant, Ashley, explained: "I mean even as a woman in computer science, you do feel the sense of not being perceived as smart...and I mean you throw in the whole minority thing." In identifying as a first generation college student, several students also felt a sense of pride in their accomplishments and family support, yet also experienced feelings of uncertainty about how to navigate the college environment. As a result, the relationships between these identities and the STEM experience influenced identity development. The identities that these women held, as students of color, women, first-generation students, and more influenced the way in which they navigated the STEM community and the way in which others interacted with them. For these students, it was not enough to describe how their racial and ethnic identities influenced their experiences

The Latino men also revealed aspects of their gender in the study but through more subtle elements of masculinity. For example, many of them enjoyed the fact that the scientific community held a sense of elitism and was perceived as difficult to enter. One of the students discussed that he thrived off of the "cut-throat nature of the scientific community where only the truly smart people are able to survive." This may confirm some of the literature about Latino masculinity, specifically the cultural and social constructions of competition (see, for example, Torres, Solberg, & Carlstrom, 2002). Participants told stories about peers or friends that they knew who were not achieving at high levels in STEM courses, and the level of satisfaction they got from knowing that the scientific community was not accessible by everyone. Ironically, some of the participants who emphasized the inaccessibility of the scientific community as a primary motivator for being in the field were also the lowest performing students in the study.

Future Practice, Policy, and Research

Practitioners, policymakers, and scholars alike can do more to support Latin@ students as they build their professional identities and successfully attain a STEM degree. Policymakers can support these environments by encouraging learning communities and communities of practice focused on STEM pathways to enhance opportunities for science identity development. College practitioners may ensure that all students majoring in STEM are placed in a science learning community. Research has shown that Latin@ students who are acknowledged, validated, and encouraged in their first year of college are more likely to succeed in STEM courses, build STEM identities, and go on to attain a STEM degree (Aschbacher, Li, & Roth, 2009; Lu, 2016).

Administrators and faculty members may also find a way to incorporate more hands-on inquiry to supplement their science and math courses. As such, universities should partner with organizations in the local community, such as teaching hospitals, technical laboratories, museums, clinics, and private practices to provide accessible opportunities for students to experience doing STEM work in an authentic and exciting way. These experiences should build in opportunities for Latin@ recognition, giving multiple audiences a chance to see these students as part of the STEM community. One great example of this is the Freshman Research Initiative (FRI) at The University of Texas at Austin, which gives first-year students the opportunity to initiate and engage in real-world research experience with faculty and graduate students. Students get to participate in one of several research streams; for example, in the Autonomous Robots research stream, freshmen program intelligent machines to interact on their own with visitors to the UT Austin campus. In the Biofuels research stream, undergraduates contribute to a major National Science Foundation-funded project to examine whether plants like switchgrass can be used for energy in place of oil. Programs like FRI provide a means for students to connect their classwork with authentic work experiences. These authentic experiences provide an opportunity, particularly for Latin@s, to positively engage with communities that are often unwelcoming to women and people of color. In creating explicit communities of practice, educators have the opportunity to integrate multiple STEM perspectives in order to demonstrate to Latin@ students that there are varying career possibilities for STEM careers (e.g., societal impact, humanitarian purposes, and discovery). Such experiences may facilitate STEM identity development and grow a community of practice for Latin@s in STEM.

Finally, educators can consider students' development from an intersectional, holistic approach when structuring collegiate STEM experiences. Policymakers at multiple levels must engage with multiple stakeholders regarding the institutionalized racism and sexism which are present within the STEM environment as well as offer solutions which address these issues. Supporting such an environment might involve training faculty and peers regarding intersectional identities and how those identities influence STEM success. It might also mean greater institutional support for identity-based STEM organizations in order to promote their efforts and sustainability. In order to holistically address student needs, institutions, particularly disciplinary units, must embrace the understanding of Latin@ students, as well as other groups, as complex individuals with a myriad of background experiences and desires that they bring with them to college.

References

American College Board. (2014). *The condition of college & career readiness 2014.* Retrieved from http://www.act.org/research/policy-makers/cccr14/index.html

Aschbacher, P. R., Li, E., & Roth, E. J. (2009). Is science me? High school students' identities, participation, and aspirations in science, engineering, and medicine. *Journal of Research in Science Teaching, 47*(5), 564–582.

Brickhouse, N. W., Lowery, P., & Schultz, K. (2000). What kind of a girl does science? The construction of school science identities. *Journal of Research in Science Teaching, 37*(5), 441–458.

Brickhouse, N. W., & Potter, J. T. (2001) Young women's scientific identity formation in an urban context. *Journal of Research in Science Teaching, 38*(8), 965–980.

Brown, B. (2004). Discursive identity: Assimilation into the culture of science and its implications for minority children. *Journal of Research in Science Teaching, 41,* 810–834.

Carlone, H. B. (2004). The cultural production of science in reform-based physics: Girls' access, participation, and resistance. *Journal of Research in Science Teaching, 41*(4), 392–414.

Carlone, H. B., & Johnson, A. (2007). Understanding the science experiences of successful women of color: Science identity as an analytic lens. *Journal of Research in Science Teaching, 44*(8), 1187–1218.

Cobb, P. (2004). Mathematics, literacies, and identity. *Reading Research Quarterly, 39*, 333–337.

Collins, P. H. (2008). *Black feminist thought: Knowledge, consciousness, and the politics of empowerment.* New York, NY: Routledge.

Crenshaw, K. (1991). Mapping the margins: Intersectionality, identity politics, and violence against women of color. *Stanford Law Review, 43*, 1241–1299.

Gee, J. P. (2000). Identity as an analytic lens for research in education. *Review of Research in Education, 25*, 99–125.

Gilbert, A., & Yerrick, R. (2000). Same school, separate worlds: A sociocultural study of identity, resistance, and negotiation in a rural, lower track science classroom. *Journal of Research in Science Teaching, 38*, 574–598.

Higher Education Research Institute. (2010). *Degrees of success: Bachelor's degree completion rates among initial STEM majors.* Los Angeles, CA: Higher Education Research Institute.

hooks, b. (1992). *Black looks: Race and representation.* Boston, MA: South End.

Kelly, G. J. (2007). Discourse in science classrooms. In S. K. Abell & N. G. Lederman (Eds.), *Handbook of Research on Science Education* (pp. 443–470). Mahwah, NJ: Lawrence Erlbaum.

Lemke, J. L. (2001). Articulating communities: Sociocultural perspectives on science education. *Journal of Research in Science Teaching, 38*, 296–316.

Lu, C. (2013). *STEM(ming) up from niños to científicos: Latino male science identity development in the First Semester* (Doctoral dissertation).

Lu, C. (2016). Finding Los Científicos Within: Latino Male Science Identity Development in the First College Semester. Journal of College Student Development, 56(7), 740–745.

National Science Foundation. (2017). *Women, minorities, and persons with disabilities in science and engineering—2017* (NSF 09–310). Arlington, VA: National Science Foundation. Retrieved April 14, 2017 from https://www.nsf.gov/statistics/2017/nsf17310/static/downloads/nsf17310-digest.pdf

Noddings, N. (1992). *The challenge to care in schools: An alternative approach to education.* New York, NY: Teacher's College Press.

O'Neil, J. M. (1981). Patterns of gender role conflict and strain: Sexism and fear of femininity in men's lives. *Personnel & Guidance Journal, 60*(4), 203.

O'Neill, D. K., & Polman, J. L. (2004). Why educate "little scientists"? Examining the potential of practice-based scientific literacy. *Journal of Research in Science Education, 41*(3), 234–266.

Rodriguez, S. L. (2015). *Las mujeres in the STEM pipeline: How Latina college students who persist in STEM majors develop and sustain their STEM identities* (Doctoral dissertation).

Saenz, V. B., Bukoski, B. E., Lu, C., & Rodriguez, S. L. (2013). Latino males in Texas community colleges: A phenomenological study of masculinity constructs and their effect on college experiences. *Journal of African American Males in Education, 4*(2), 82–99.

Strauss, A., & Corbin, J. (1998). Basics of qualitative research: Techniques and procedures for developing grounded theory (2nd ed.). Thousand Oaks, CA: Sage.

Toldson, I. A., & Esters, L. L. (2012). *The quest for excellence: Supporting the academic success of minority males in science, technology, engineering, and mathematics (STEM) disciplines.* Washington, DC: Association of Public and Land-grant Universities.

Tonso, K. L. (1999). Engineering gender – gender engineering: A cultural model for belonging. *Journal of Women and Minorities in Science and Engineering, 5,* 365–404.

Tonso, K. L. (2006). Student engineers and engineer identity: Campus engineer identities as figured world. *Cultural Studies of Science Education, 1,* 237–307.

Torres, J. B., Solberg, V. S., & Carlstrom, A. H. (2002). The myth of sameness among Latino men and their machismo. *The American Journal of Orthopsychiatry, 72*(2), 163–181.

U.S. Census Bureau. (2010). *The Hispanic Population: 2010.* Washington, DC: U.S. Government Printing Office.

U.S. Department of Commerce. (2010). *STEM: Good jobs now and for the future* (ESA Issue Brief #03–11). Washington, DC: U.S. Government Printing Office.

Varelas, M., House, R., & Wenzel, S. (2005). Beginning teachers immersed into science: Scientist and science teacher identities. *Science Education, 89,* 492–516.

3. Navigating Hurdles into and through Undergraduate Engineering and Computer Science Studies

ELSA Q. VILLA, ELAINE HAMPTON, AND PEI-LING HSU

This chapter focuses on three case studies to highlight the historical, cultural, and structural factors posing opportunities and hurdles for Latinas who chose majors in engineering and computer science (CS), hereafter referred to as engineering. The motivation for this research investigation was to address historically low numbers of women in engineering undergraduate studies, particularly those in the intersection of being female and Latina. The overarching research question driving the study was: What is the relationship among identity, resilience, and persistence of Latinas in engineering?

Relevant Scholarship

Numerous studies describe the world of engineering as male dominated (see, for example, Camacho & Lord, 2013; Godfrey & Parker, 2010); and Latinas receiving undergraduate degrees in engineering represent a mere 2% of all degrees awarded (National Science Foundation [NSF], National Center for Science and Engineering Statistics, 2017). In science, technology, engineering and mathematics (STEM) fields, women, who are in the intersection of gender and race, tend to have the lowest persistence rates (Smyth & McArdle, 2004), which is a phenomenon more pervasive in highly selective, predominantly White universities (Johnson, 2011; Ong, Wright, Espinosa, & Orfield, 2011). This historical underrepresentation of those who do not fit the norm is prevalent across many, if not most, institutions of higher education (Hill,

Corbett, & St Rose, 2010; Moss-Racusin, Dovidio, Brescoll, Graham, & Handelsman, 2012; Seymour & Hewitt, 1997).

The climate of STEM undergraduate studies has been described as "chilly," particularly in traditional gateway courses offered in the first two years of study (Crisp, Nora, & Taggart, 2009; Gainen, 1995; Mervis, 2011). Nonetheless, underrepresented students in STEM *do* persist to graduation (Graham & Caso, 2001), and our study corroborates that notion.

Theoretical Framework

Our research team drew on a sociocultural theoretical framework to analyze dense narratives derived from an ethnographic interview method to understand how learning and identity are co-constructed in social practice (Holland, Lachicotte, Skinner, & Cain, 1998; Holland & Lave, 2001, 2009). An aspect of sociocultural theory is social practice theory that further argues learning and identity are constructed in tandem as actors engage in everyday social practice with others and artifacts. As such, identity is in continuous flux, dynamic, and dependent on particular social configurations. Holland *et al.* (1998) refer to these configurations as "figured worlds"—an environment in which "particular characters and actors are recognized, significance is assigned to certain acts, and particular outcomes are valued over others" (p. 52).

Social actors shape and are shaped by figured worlds as they author themselves as a particular kind of person (Holland *et al.*, 1998; Holland & Lave, 2009). For example, a student may author herself as "good at math" if she performs well on tests and is recognized by her teacher as such. Or, she might not perform well on a test and author herself as "not good at math" and, thus, not someone who could pursue a STEM degree. Thus, the figured world is a space where an actor may be welcomed as an insider or alienated as an outsider by others.

Social practice theory, as articulated by Holland and Lave (2009), further posits particular figured worlds are institutional structures historically constituted, such as a family, student organization, study group, or engineering school. Local practice in these institutional structures comes into play as people "address and respond to each other while enacting cultural activities under conditions of political-economic and cultural-historical conjuncture" (p. 3). These encounters alter identities as individuals adapt "to author himself or herself in the moment" (p. 4).

The three case studies in this chapter each highlight the various figured worlds each Latina encountered in her trajectory toward and through engineering undergraduate studies, as each authored herself as an engineer, despite the various hurdles she encountered.

Research Design

Study Context

The study context was a public, four-year Minority Institution, a U.S. Department of Education designation given the majority minority population of primarily Latin@s of Mexican descent. The institution resides on the U.S. border with Mexico in a bilingual, bicultural community. A mere 20% of the enrollment in undergraduate engineering, Latinas were the population from which study participants were drawn, which is the bounded system for our case studies, or the "instance of concern" (Merriam, 1998, p. 28), in deriving a deeper understanding of Latinas' experiences.

Twenty-six undergraduate students self-identified as Latina and self-selected to participate in this research study. In this chapter, we focus on three specific participants whose case studies provided insights into the hurdles that these women navigated in the varying figured worlds they encountered, as their engineering identities were formed and reformulated while negotiating these hurdles and authoring themselves as engineers.

Data Collection and Analysis Method

Data were collected through a process of focused, in-depth interviewing (Seidman, 2006) in which each participant shared stories of their trajectories into and through engineering in a series of three different interviews. These data were analyzed across and within each rich narrative (Chase, 2005), highlighting unique contexts associated with particular social practices. The following dominant themes emerged across all 26 narratives: Latinas (1) negotiated adversity in their nonacademic and academic lives; (2) were aware of their intersectional gendered status; and (3) developed engineering identities with supportive others.

Case Study 1: Elena's Journey to Environmental Engineering

Choosing Engineering

When invited to reflect on her reasons for choosing engineering as her major, Elena identified her love for science and mathematics and the support she received from family, teachers, and friends. Elena described several teachers as "energetic," "hands-on," "knowledgeable," and "funny"; and recalled being influenced by a teacher to take prealgebra while in 6th grade. Elena further elaborated on the interpersonal support her family and friends provided. At age six, she and her dad solved problems together, as they shared an interest in science and mathematics. Elena's mother worked in a career center where employers sought graduates in STEM fields. This recognition of the shortage of STEM workers supported Elena's choice in studying engineering. Further, Elena interacted with friends who shared her interest and discussed "different theories in engineering." These early interactions contributed to Elena's learning of different engineering perspectives and practices that contributed to her engineering identity development.

Undergraduate Engineering Studies

When Elena became an environmental engineering undergraduate, she encountered challenges in coursework yet was able to overcome these struggles with support from friends and family.

Questioning Engineering Identity. Having been a straight-A student in high school, Elena passed half of her courses in her first two years of college and expressed frustration in describing these failures as "really hard."

> I never wanted to quit college, and I still don't. I still plan on pursuing it. But, I definitely considered changing majors because I thought, "Well maybe I'm just not—maybe I'm not as smart as I thought I was. Maybe math and science really aren't my strong points. Maybe something else is." So, I considered changing majors because I felt—I felt squashed.

This passage illustrates Elena's shifting identity in the figured world of engineering. She is situated in contentious local practice (Holland & Lave, 2009) where her identity as a high-achieving student was interrupted by her academic struggles.

Support of Family and Affinity Groups. While experiencing challenges in her coursework, Elena shared her frustration with her family. Her parents provided the support she needed to keep going. Elena also reached out to upper division students who had successfully passed all the challenging courses. "Everyone kept telling me, 'Just get to your upper division. Get to your upper division. After you pass these lower division courses, you're going to do fine.'" They recommended strategies, and Elena followed those recommendations: She borrowed useful slide shows from a peer, practiced solving problems, reviewed old homework, and joined a study group that met regularly.

Elena's understanding about the challenges of lower and upper division courses in engineering served as motivation for her to persist. Elena further articulated. "Quitting was not an option. I did not want to let my parents down, and I hate to disappoint them!" Thus, with support from her family and friends, an understanding of the engineering coursework, and a series of trial-and-error study strategies, Elena finally completed all of her lower division coursework.

Strengthening Engineering Identity. Elena served as president of the Society of Women Engineers (SWE), a student organization that aims to address gender inequity in engineering. As president, Elena had many opportunities to network with engineering practitioners, attend conferences, and meet successful female engineers.

> I like it because I'm always getting to meet new people. It's a great networking and career tool for the future. I like getting to know these different women because they all have different stories and I get to learn from them.

Elena credits her participation in SWE for contributing to her understanding of the gender inequities in engineering; and, through the stories of successful female engineers, was inspired to complete her degree, further strengthening her identity as a female environmental engineer. She attributed her persistence to support from her family, her peer study group, and her interaction with successful women in engineering.

Case Study 2: Juliet's Journey to Computer Science

Choosing Computer Science

Juliet identified several support structures for choosing CS: her two years in a high school computer maintenance class, peer support for learning computing skills, and her family's acknowledgment of her as a problem solver.

High School Computer Maintenance Class. While a junior in high school, Juliet selected computer maintenance as an elective because "my interest in computers for some reason just overtopped" other choices, such as her love for being a mariachi. She attributed her career decision to "the need of technology now." Juliet ultimately enrolled in the yearlong introductory class to computer maintenance as a high school junior and continued into the advanced computer maintenance class during her senior year. Describing her first day in computer maintenance, Juliet stated:

> Now the first day of classes, I was really nervous actually because I was actually the only girl in computer maintenance. I felt intimidated by the other guys [except for] the teacher [who] was a female. I also was excited about it [being the only female student], and also had this feeling of like, "I'm a girl. I can beat all these guys. I can be just as good as them."

When Juliet first entered this particular figured world of a high school computer maintenance classroom, she recognized herself as an "outsider"—a female in a male-dominant space. She felt more comfortable knowing that the other female was the teacher, which supported her subordinate positionality in that classroom. Soon after, Juliet joined a community of "guys" through her love of playing video games. She described her "ticket" into this figured world:

> Before the class would actually begin, we'd start playing a little bit of some of the video games that were on the computers. And so [the guys] found out that I had an interest in video games. I would just start playing with them, and they would make me feel like a lot more comfortable in the environment, and we actually had a lot of like good times.

Peer Support for Learning Computing Skills. Unlike Elena who found precollege work "easy," Juliet described her struggle with the technical material and "felt like a lot slower, like, I guess, not so much dumber, but just kind of put myself down knowing that I was the last one done, and so it was kind of like a little bit frustrating." She found working in a group helped her to better understand, and decided to take the second computer maintenance course during her senior year. Juliet once again made friends with a group of males.

> They were actually a lot more talkative and interactive, and I would always be the one listening because they would talk mostly about computers, or video games, and I had no idea what they would be talking about. A lot of like the technical terms they would use, and so I would try to just listen and pick it up.

Family Contribution to Juliet's Identity Development as Problem-Solver. In one of her high school projects, Juliet was allowed to take a project home, which she shared with her family.

> [My family was] actually really like excited for me, and like now they were always asking me questions if there's something wrong with their laptop. So, it's always nice having their support. If I come home, and I show them my project, they would always really support me and be amazed like "Wow, she's smart. She can do that?"

This passage illustrates the role of supportive people (her family) and engineering-related artifacts (the computer maintenance project) in positively influencing her identity development as a computer scientist/engineer who was capable of fixing computers and solving technical problems. This interaction with her family continued throughout her university CS classes.

And it's actually the same thing now with my computer science classes that I'm taking. Every time I finish a lab, I show [my family] the results. They're really supportive, like "Wow, that's really cool."

Juliet's ability to problem solve with support from her family contributed to her computer scientist identity development.

Juliet's Struggles as an Undergraduate Student

After taking some of her required mathematics courses at the community college, Juliet entered the university as a CS major where she found her struggles continued much as they did when she was in high school. She felt that others in the introductory class were much more knowledgeable than she, and this contributed to her perception as someone who maybe did not belong in this particular figured world.

I was getting frustrated with it, because this was my very first time learning Java. That was really actually frustrating. And I actually found that all the guys, or almost all of them, were actually the ones who already had experience. And I wondered, "Where did they gain this experience from? How come I didn't go through it?"

Once again, Juliet found a peer who worked with her to understand the material. In the second CS course, Juliet failed the course and retook it in the following summer. At that time, she met another Latina who had previously dropped the CS course, and was retaking it in the summer. This relationship grew into a strong friendship, and they continued to take courses together after being successful in their second CS course. Juliet's frustrations diminished, and she reflected on her coursework at a point closer to graduation:

I go back and I think of like of some of the labs that we had to do, and I think I could have been done with that so much faster if I had known what I know now. I could have finished it. I wouldn't have had to go through so much of that frustration.

And now in her advanced coursework, Juliet felt more confident about her ability to problem solve.

There's one guy who, I think he's struggling even more than I am. So, he's the one always constantly asking everyone for help, and so there's been times where I've actually helped him, and I think it's kind of nice because it kind of reinforces that I know, that I'm getting a little bit more in practice explaining. For once, I'm the one who actually knows what they're doing. So, I love those moments, I really enjoy those moments when I feel like I'm actually the one giving the help.

With persistence and perseverance Juliet sought out support mechanisms and found the figured world of CS to be challenging and rewarding as her identity shifted from "learner" to "explainer," affirming her identity as a computer scientist.

Case Study 3: Gina's Journey to Mechanical Engineering

Born in central Mexico, Gina was one of eight children, all of whom helped their father earn a small income making fireworks to sell for religious and cultural festivals. Gina described a time when a heavy rain ruined the family home. As a result, her mother rebuilt the kitchen and bathroom with help from the children to also make *adobe* bricks. "My mom was the one who had the ideas and the motivation. She taught us to be independent. She taught us strength."

Gina attributed her success in accomplishing the demanding engineering degree to the love of her parents, the hope for her children's future, her religious beliefs in mediating difficult situations, her love of learning, and the power that knowledge would bring to her life. With emphasis and tears, Gina stated: "It was horrible living in poverty, horrible! And I did not want that!"

Gina's journey across vast cultural transitions was contentious and filled with hurdles for this nontraditional actor—a Latina mother negotiating poverty and new cultures in order to complete a degree. Gina was challenged by marital problems, being a single mother with minimal financial resources to care for her children, and minimal English language skills and understanding of U.S. and university cultures. Her confidence in her mathematics skills ("I chose engineering because I like numbers, and I like to apply scientific concepts") and her drive to escape poverty led her through these foreign, figured worlds.

Negotiating Identity: Traditional Roles and Education

As a daughter in a rural, Mexican home, Gina was expected to take up the traditional roles as a mother and housekeeper.

> I had to get water from the river and serve my brother, prepare everything… Even though I knew it would be hard, I decided to study engineering because I no longer wanted to do the expected roles of women. I wanted to know that I could be at the same level as a man.

At age 12, she was expected to help the family financially, and her family found a job for her working as a maid in a home nearby. Gina did not give up on her education and convinced her mother to allow her to go to middle school while she worked as a maid.

> My mother had to beg my dad to let me go to school. I was the only one in the family to finish middle school. I felt bad because it was if my mom was covering up for me, so I could go to school. My dad always believed in me even though he was *machista* [a term denoting a man who treats women as lower status than men] with his daughters.

After her middle school years, her parents separated; and Gina, her mother, and siblings relocated to Ciudad Juárez where four of them found jobs in a *maquiladora*, one of the 200 foreign factories located in this Mexican border city to take advantage of the low-income laborers in the city. Her mother told her that, if she wanted to continue school, she had to pay all the expenses. At age 14, she forged a birth certificate showing that she was 16 in order to work in the factory where she and her siblings would bring in less than $100 per week. They relied on bus transportation that the factories provided. She described her daily schedule during these years of high school:

1. Wake up at 3:15 to catch the bus at 3:50 a.m.
2. Arrive at maquiladora at 6:00 a.m. with 30 minutes for breakfast.
3. Leave work at 4:00 p.m.
4. Arrive at her high school at 5:15 p.m. and stay until after 9:00 p.m.
5. Take bus home and arrive at 9:30 or 10:00 p.m.
6. Dinner and homework until 11:00 p.m.

Gina described how the day began:

> I slept on the way to work. I will never forget that my mom combed my hair when we were in the bus. We were one of the first to get on the bus so we always had seats. I would lay down my head on my mom's lap, and she would braid my hair.

The family of six lived in a small house sharing a bedroom with no heating other than a cook stove.

> Mom would always say "turn off the lights, turn off the lights;" and, now that I am a mom, I understand why she would tell us that. It was because she was so tired. In Juárez, we were very poor. There is a lot of trash over there because the city landfill is located close by. That was the only place where the rent was affordable. There were cockroaches everywhere. It was horrible, horrible; the worst thing you can imagine…but I never felt ashamed of my family or my life story.

Gina recalled being in high-school when her father begged in the streets and saved up $15 to buy her school uniform. At age 17, she got pregnant even though she did not want a child. "I had to manage studying and taking care of my baby." Her boyfriend left, and she worked in the maquiladoras for 10 years.

Negotiating Identity: Mother and Engineering Major

Gina advanced to an administrative position at the *maquiladora*, and eventually fell in love with a man who also worked at the factory. He was a U.S. citizen; and, with her older daughter and the couple's baby, moved to El Paso. Gina received financial support and enrolled at UTEP. However, the baby's father became physically abusive and provided no support for her education. She described some of the difficult situations she had to negotiate in order to get to her classes.

> I had to go everywhere with my baby and some people would help me out, like going up stairs. At the end of the day I was feeling so tired because it had been very difficult carrying the baby around. I was still breastfeeding. At the end of orientation [to college] day, I called my friends and my husband to see who could give me a ride, but nobody answered my call. I thought, "If it is going to be like this, I can't do it." I had to bring my baby to school many times. We could hear my baby crying. He was downstairs with the babysitter. I was so embarrassed that I was sweating. I had to go downstairs to feed him. The baby started to cry again, and I had to leave the classroom for the second time. When I got back to the classroom, they were taking a quiz. I grabbed my notebooks and left.

The abuse at home became severe, and Gina and her children escaped to the Women's Shelter where they lived for a time. She was not a legal resident at this time, but officials at the shelter helped her and her children with the legal papers to get out of the abusive relationship and acquire documentation for legal residence. She worked to get student loans, Medicaid, and food assistance for her children.

Gina authored and reauthored herself as an engineering student, as she encountered and navigated hurdles, which were higher than those of a traditional student with resources and minimal family responsibilities. She stayed in school despite knowing very little English, and teamed with friends who spoke English: They tutored her in the language arts classes, and she tutored them in the math classes. Like all of the women in our study, Gina drew strength from her study groups to navigate the difficult engineering problems. She had to retake several classes as she was continually negotiating family responsibilities and poverty, yet accomplished the degree in eight years.

In her last semesters, Gina could not pay the rent. She and her three children stayed off and on with friends, tried living in Ciudad Juárez, and finally moved into the Salvation Army's shelter for homeless families. They stayed there 11 months. Although her situation was difficult, the shelter provided day care for the children and transportation to their school. She was able to focus more on her engineering studies. Eventually, Gina moved her family into an apartment subsidized by the city's housing authority; and, in the last semester of her undergraduate studies, worked part time for an externally funded program at the community college.

Discussion and Conclusion

These case studies illustrate how each Latina was intertwined in conflict, particularly at the outset of their engineering studies, as each negotiated the various hurdles they encountered in their particular figured worlds while at the same time mediating their learning through sociocultural practice in those figured worlds. As the theoretical framework suggests, the historical institution of engineering was structured as one posing challenges for these learners, especially in their first two years where gateway courses, in some cases, tend to be "filters." Each of these case studies exemplified Latinas positioned as subordinate, or at least perceived as such. Each "learned" to navigate hurdles to continue their trajectories toward completing their degrees.

In their study of women in science, Carlone and Johnson (2007) found women, who were in the intersection of gender and race, more likely to have "disrupted scientist identities" (p. 1202) where they felt their experiences in the figured world of science were "overlooked, neglected, or discriminated against by meaningful others within science" (p. 1202). The authors further suggested these disrupted identities might have been attributed to subtle racism, a notion aligning with our theoretical framework. Our case studies, and indeed the other 23 cases in the larger study, similarly had stories of conflict with academic courses and feelings as an outsider in the figured world of engineering. As did the women in the Carlone and Johnson (2007) study, the Latinas in our study nonetheless exerted their agency and found resources and support among peers and family while becoming knowledgeable of ways to "jump hurdles" and persist in their studies.

Affordances and constraints emerged as each Latina mediated her learning, negotiated hurdles, and developed her engineering identity. Elena was a straight-A student during her K-12 education, yet struggled when she entered her university studies in engineering. Juliet described her early courses in CS as highly contentious, as she envisioned others more knowledgeable than she; yet she found the means to negotiate her learning, resulting in her identity development as a computer scientist. Gina struggled on a daily basis with her family responsibilities while negotiating her pathway in an institution of higher education ill-designed for single mothers.

In these case studies, each Latina entered and participated in figured worlds that were both contentious and inviting. While their engineering identities were in flux, each was nourished by a combination of family, friends, and other supporting structures, as they participated in these figured worlds and developed the agency to successfully earn their engineering degrees. In particular, these supporting others and structures contributed to these Latinas' perseverance and persistence in engineering.

This study affirms the need for creating more inclusive environments in engineering. The National Science Foundation (NSF) recognizes this need for more inclusiveness if the nation is to broaden participation of underrepresented minorities in engineering, as evidenced by their release in 2014 of a solicitation under their Improving Undergraduate STEM Education (IUSE)/ Professional Formation of Engineers: REvolutionizing engineering and computer science Departments (RED). This solicitation was designed to "revolutionize" engineering departments through "successfully achieving significant sustainable changes necessary to overcome longstanding issues in their undergraduate programs and educate inclusive communities of engineering and computer science students" (NSF, 2016, p. 1). It is possible then that a shift in engineering culture might occur and break down existing barriers for those not currently fitting the traditional image of engineer.

Acknowledgements

This material is based upon work supported by the NSF under NSF HRD-1232447. Any opinions, findings, and conclusions or recommendations expressed in this material are those of the authors and do not necessarily reflect the views of the NSF.

We especially want to thank UTEP Associate Professors Alberto Esquinca, College of Education; Martine Ceberio, Department of Computer Science; Guillermina Nuñez-Mchiri, Department of Sociology and Anthropology, and former doctoral candidate Luciene Wandermurem, Ph.D., for their contributions to the research that made this chapter possible.

References

Camacho, M. M., & Lord, S. (2013). *The borderlands of education: Latinas in engineering.* Lantham, MA: Lexington Books.

Carlone, H. B., & Johnson, A. (2007). Understanding the science experiences of successful women of color: Science identity as an analytic lens. *Journal of Research in Science Teaching, 44*(8), 1187–1218.

Chase, S. E. (2005). Narrative inquiry: Multiple lenses, approaches, voices. In N. K. Denzin & Y. S. Lincoln (Eds.), *The Sage handbook of qualitative research* (3rd ed., pp. 651–679). Thousand Oaks, CA: Sage Publications.

Crisp, G., Nora, A., & Taggart, A. (2009). Student characteristics, pre-college, college, and environmental factors as predictors of majoring in and earning a STEM degree: An analysis of students attending a Hispanic serving institution. *The American Educational Research Journal, 46*(4), 924–942.

Gainen, J. (1995). Barriers to success in quantitative gatekeeper courses. In J. Gainen & E. W. Willemsen (Eds.), *Fostering student success in quantitative gateway courses (New Directions for Teaching and Learning)* (pp. 5–14). San Francisco, CA: Jossey-Bass Publishers.

Godfrey, E., & Parker, L. (2010). Mapping the cultural landscape in engineering education. *Journal of Engineering Education, 99*(1), 5–22.

Graham, J. M., & Caso, R. (2001). *Retention of women in undergraduate engineering programs: An empirical investigation of the role of educational resilience.* Paper presented at the meeting of the Women in Engineering Programs and Advocates Network, Alexandria, VA.

Hill, C., Corbett, C., & St Rose, A. (2010). *Why so few? Women in science, technology, engineering, and mathematics.* Washington, DC: American Association of University Women.

Holland, D., Lachicotte, W., Jr., Skinner, D., & Cain, C. (1998). *Identity and agency in cultural worlds.* Cambridge, MA: Harvard University Press.

Holland, D., & Lave, J. (2001). History in person: An introduction. In D. Holland & J. Lave (Eds.), *History in person: Enduring struggles, contentious practice, intimate identities* (pp. 3–35). Santa Fe, NM: School of American Research.

Holland, D., & Lave, J. (2009). Social practice theory and the historical production of persons. *International Journal of Human Activity Theory, 2,* 1–15.

Johnson, D. R. (2011). Women of color in science, technology, engineering and mathematics (STEM). *New Directions of Institutional Research, 152,* 75–85.

Merriam, S. B. (1998). *Qualitative research and case study applications in education.* San Francisco, CA: Jossey-Bass Publishers.

Mervis, J. (2011). Undergraduate science. Weed-out courses hamper diversity. *Science, 334,* 1333. Retrieved from http://www.sciencemag.org/content/334/6061/

Moss-Racusin, C. A., Dovidio, J. F., Brescoll, V. L., Graham, M. J., & Handelsman, J. (2012). Science faculty's subtle gender biases favor male students. *Proceedings of the National Academy of Sciences, 109*(41), 16474–16479.

National Science Foundation (NSF). (2016). *IUSE/professional formation of engineers: REvolutionizing engineering and computer science departments,* 17–501. Retrieved from https://www.nsf.gov/funding/pgm_summ.jsp?pims_id=505105

National Science Foundation (NSF), National Center for Science and Engineering Statistics. (2017). *Women, minorities, and persons with disabilities in science and engineering: Special report NSF17–310.* Washington, DC.

Ong, M., Wright, C., Espinosa, L. L., & Orfield, G. (2011). Inside the double bind: A synthesis of empirical research on undergraduate and graduate women of color in science, technology, engineering, and mathematics. *Harvard Educational Review, 81*(2), 172–390.

Seidman, I. (2006). *Interviewing as qualitative research: A guide for researchers in education and the social sciences.* New York, NY: Teachers College Press.

Seymour, E., & Hewitt, N. M. (1997). *Talking about leaving: Why undergraduates leave the sciences.* Boulder, CO: Westview.

Smyth, F. L., & McArdle, J. J. (2004). Ethnic and gender differences in science graduation at selective colleges with implications for admission policy and college choice. *Research in Higher Education, 45,* 353–381.

Part 2: Teacher Preparation and Professional Development

4. Making a Way for Latin@ ELLs to Engage in STEM: Transforming Teacher Preparation through a Simulated Language Learning Experience

Estanislado S. Barrera, IV and Angela Wall Webb

Historically, the educational needs of Latin@s have been deserving of significant attention (Berger & Wilborn, 2012; MacDonald, 2001) and continue to be critical, yet these students consistently receive inadequate schooling and language instruction across grade levels, in the content areas, and throughout the nation. All the while, Latin@s are the fastest growing demographic in schools today. At the national level, the number of Latin@ students enrolled in public schools has increased from 9 million in 2003 to more than 12.5 million in just over ten years (National Center of Education Statistics [NCES], 2016a). Of those 12.5 million Latin@ students, approximately 3.7 million of them are English language learners (ELLs) and make up 80% of those who are working toward acquiring a second language (NCES, 2016b). And, if we accept that the predicted enrollment of Latin@ students will be 14.7 million in 2025 (NCES, 2016a), then there is the potential for approximately 4.4 million of them being Latin@ ELLs nine years from now. However, despite this student group being a large demographic based on both ethnicity and language needs, Latin@s and more specifically, Latin@ ELLs, are two populations that have been consistently underserved. The denial of quality educational opportunities has resulted in significant achievement gaps and high dropout rates for these students when compared to their White counterparts (Balfanz *et al.*, 2014; Howard, 2015; Umansky & Reardon, 2014). Even more critical, these inadequacies have resulted in an underrepresentation of Latin@s in areas such as science, technology, engineering, and mathematics (STEM). In fact, it is reported that only 15% of those in STEM fields are Latin@, up only 12 percentage points from 3% in 1970 (Landivar, 2013).

In order to address this dearth in STEM fields, this chapter presents significant aspects relevant to teacher preparation programs and discusses transformative ways to develop responsive teacher candidates who can better meet the needs of those Latin@s who are also ELLs in order to improve science instruction and increase STEM engagement. Given that 67% of the nation's ELL population can be found in grades Kindergarten through five (Barrera, 2016; NCES, 2016b), the discussion will primarily focus on those issues relevant to elementary education. In response, this chapter discusses the context in which Latin@ ELLs are currently being educated and offers the transformative practice of using simulated language learning experience as a means of improving their educational responsiveness and understanding of emotions and effective instruction.

The Educational Context of Latin@ ELLs

Recalling that approximately 80% of all ELLs are Latin@, it can be argued that concentrating efforts toward improving "their academic success in both content and language is critical for their participation in college, careers, and citizenship in U.S. society and the global community" (Llosa *et al.*, 2016, p. 420). However, when looking specifically at Latin@ ELLs and their performance on NAEP science assessments, it can be surmised that although both Latin@s and Latin@ ELLs have experienced slight gains from 2009 to 2015, both groups are still scoring lower than the White students in their respective grade levels.

These national statistics on Latin@ ELLs' performance on science assessments should not be surprising when you consider that many of the teachers who are currently in the field have not been prepared to appropriately teach science across the grade levels. More concerning is the fact that, nationally, only 17% of elementary teachers reported feeling capable in their ability to teach science to ELLs (Banilower, Trygstad, & Smith, 2015). In fact, according to a meta-analysis by Samson and Lesaux (2015), ELLs are most often taught by teachers with temporary or alternative certifications. These teachers also have the fewest years of experience compared to those not teaching ELLs. Despite these efforts, this lack of content and pedagogical knowledge required to support Latin@ ELLs is not entirely the fault of teachers. Instead, we need to look at teacher preparation programs and call on them to acknowledge this disservice and address the underrepresentation of Latin@s in STEM fields.

(Under)Prepared Preservice Teachers

For the most part, teacher preparation programs attempt to address working with the general ELL population in some way or another. Many programs require coursework specific to working with ELL students and concentrate on knowledge, skills, and dispositions as they relate to language and culture (de Jong & Harper, 2011). However, these additional courses and their content often supplant discipline-specific courses, resulting in shallow understandings of topics relevant to literacy, science, and math. And even with these attempts at a programmatic level, many preservice elementary teachers (PSETs) reported that they still experienced difficulties when it came to connecting with their students on a cultural level (de Jong & Harper, 2011).

This lack of confidence in ability to teach combined with culture shock or a cultural disconnection is yet another obstacle preventing Latin@ ELLs from being better prepared to not only engage, but even consider a future in a STEM field. Instead, teacher preparation programs need to implement ways that develop and foster "educational responsiveness and an awareness of social and linguistic diversity" (Webb, Barrera, & Calderon, 2014). One way that this can be accomplished is through the use of a simulated language learning experience.

Transformation through a Simulated Language Learning Experience

With a long history in fields such as military science and healthcare, "simulation is a technique that enables the learning and training of individuals and teams through the re-creation of some aspect of the real clinical situation" (Bradley, 2006, p. 261). In healthcare, for example, utilizing simulation has been shown to increase students' clinical skills along with their self-confidence and perceived competence (Harder, 2010). These benefits of simulation emanate from its use *prior* to students applying the target knowledge, skills, and dispositions in practice (Bradley, 2006; Harder, 2010); and inasmuch, this approach has value in teacher education, too (Cruickshank, 1969; Grossman, 2005).

Notably, in the context of teacher education, computer simulations have been utilized to develop teachers' pedagogical knowledge, skills, and dispositions; and increase content knowledge (Girod & Girod, 2008; Grossman, 2005). Often, simulations tend to have a technological component (e.g., computer simulation/demonstration, serious digital game, etc.); however, this is not a requirement. As Gaba (2004) delineates, "Simulation is a technique—not a technology—to replace or amplify real experiences with guided experiences that evoke or replicate substantial aspects of the real world in a fully interactive manner" (p. i2). Given this, simulations used in teacher preparation and professional development need not be technology based; rather, these must provide specific, guided experiences to complement candidates' and teachers' actual work with students. The simulation discussed in this chapter is a precursor to even actual work with students, designed instead to direct attention to the importance of supporting ELLs in the science classroom (as opposed to simulating the teaching of ELLs in the science classroom).

We developed the simulated language learner experience to give PSETs a glimpse, albeit brief, into the science learning experiences of ELLs. Our simulated language learner experience consisted of two brief, back-to-back lessons, described below, and took place in the elementary science methods course during a study of diverse learners in science. To position the PSETs in the role of language learners in science, both lessons were taught in French. Lesson One mimicked a traditional, average-paced elementary science lesson and lacked supports for language learners; Lesson Two addressed the same science concepts (series and parallel circuits), but included research-based supports for teaching science to ELLs (see Lee & Buxton, 2013).

Prior to the start of Lesson One, the teacher (a foreign language educator fluent in French) asked two or three students (PSETs) to respond *oui* (yes) each time she asked, *Vous comprenez, oui?* (You understand, yes?), regardless of whether they understood the question itself or knew the answer. Once the preselected students understood these directions, Lesson One started with the teacher speaking quickly in French about series and parallel circuits. She followed an average pace despite the students having little to no experience with French. When she paused to ask, *Vous comprenez, oui?*, at first only the preselected students responded, *oui*. Responses of *oui* spread throughout the class with each subsequent question, however. To accompany the oral presentation of the science content, the teacher sketched rough diagrams of series and parallel circuits on the board. She maintained a typical pace of instruction, never adjusting the rate of delivery to ensure students understood the diagrams or the science concepts they represented. Following Lesson One, the teacher gave a formative assessment with high academic language demands. Students were asked to draw a series and parallel circuit and write a paragraph to describe each. After a few minutes—sufficient time for native French speakers to complete the assessment—the teacher walked around and scored students' papers with a smiley face (acceptable) or frowny face (unacceptable). Unsurprisingly, nearly all students received a frowny face at the top of their papers (Webb, 2016; Webb *et al.*, 2014).

Although the science concepts taught were the same, unlike the first lesson, Lesson Two incorporated research-based supports for language learners (Lee & Buxton, 2013). Specifically, the pace of Lesson Two was slowed; and the teacher used realia (objects to relate teaching to everyday life), demonstrations, an interactive word wall, and a hands-on activity to introduce and reinforce the science concepts. For realia, the teacher directed the students' attention to an actual C-cell battery and then a visual representation of a battery on an interactive word wall to introduce the term *pile* (battery). For an example of a demonstration, the teacher turned the lights in the classroom off and on with the switch while reciting the term *allumer* (to light) multiple times. The students' attention was again directed to the interactive word wall in order for them to engage in matching pictures to corresponding terms for battery, wire, light bulb, danger and to light. These steps prepared the students for a hands-on activity that required the students to work in small groups and utilize actual light bulbs, wire, and a C-cell battery in order to assemble functioning series and parallel circuits. Following the hands-on activity, the teacher administered a formative assessment. Consistent with scaffolding the academic language demands of Lesson Two, this assessment facilitated the students' communication of their content understanding. Specifically, images of a battery and two light bulbs were already provided; students were asked to draw the wires, indicating appropriate configurations for series and parallel circuits (Webb, 2016; Webb *et al.*, 2014).

Through a supportive context for learning, the PSETs briefly assumed the roles of language learners while engaged in this simulated language learner experience, resulting in the acquisition of new knowledge and strategies that can be applied when they are teaching ELLs. The simulated language experience also allowed for reflection of how these strategies could be applied in the future (Bradley, 2006; Hill, Davidson, McAllister, Wright, & Theodoros, 2014). Through the simulation, PSETs experienced the science learning that can be enabled if and when language learners are provided appropriate supports. This has implications for PSETs' empathy toward ELLs, including the emotional responses they may have to learning in a nonnative language, as well as their science planning and instruction.

Method of the Study

These sections that follow discuss tangible takeaways from the more than 215 PSETs who have participated in the simulated language learner experience. As discussed previously, we designed the simulated language experience to teach PSETs about instruction and assessment strategies for working with ELLs in science by positioning the PSETs, although unbeknownst to them at the onset of the simulation, in the role of language learners. When we first started exploring participants' impressions of the simulated lessons, 180 PSETs assumed the role of students during five consecutive semesters, from Spring 2012 to Spring 2014. During this time, our data were class-level (rather than individual student) responses to the pre- and postquestions detailed below, and researcher observations. We then decided to collect individual participant responses during two subsequent semesters, Fall 2014 (n=24 PSETs) and Fall 2015 (n=13 PSETs). Our most recent phase of data collection involved a small longitudinal sample of participants (n=4 PSETs) who student taught during Spring 2016. We administered an online survey that included questions on participants' attitudes and dispositions toward culturally and linguistically diverse students as well as what they learned from various aspects of the elementary teacher education program (e.g., coursework, practicum experiences, student teacher, mentor teachers, etc.) that influenced their perspectives of diversity and teaching ELLs.

Before the simulation, participants were asked to anticipate the obstacles ELLs might face in the science classroom as well as identify instructional strategies that may be effective for teaching science to ELLs. Following the whole simulation (Lesson One and Lesson Two), participants were then asked about their impressions of Lesson One and Lesson Two, the supports provided in Lesson Two that facilitated their learning, and what they gained from the simulation with regard to teaching ELLs. Notably, participants experienced an emotional reaction, mostly frustration, to Lesson One. Before the simulation, they had not predicted that ELLs might have emotional reactions or experience emotional barriers to learning. The simulation brought this reality for ELLs of learning content and developing language proficiency concurrently to the fore for participants. This, then, fostered empathy for ELLs and their science-learning experiences. Likewise, participants experienced responsive and effective instruction to support ELLs' language development and science learning. These main points on the transformative practices of simulation to develop PSETs' emotional awareness and instructional effectiveness to support STEM learning for ELLs are discussed in the following sections.

Emotional Awareness Transformed to Support Language Acquisition

Through the use of a simulated language learning experience, the PSETs momentarily took on the roles of ELLs engaged in science lessons and experienced a transformation of their own emotions. In their responses to post-experience questions, over one-third of participants (35%) cited emotional experiences regarding their own impressions of being positioned as language learners during Lesson One, which lacked supports for language learners. Some PSETs offered that they felt "*amused at first*" and "*more intrigued by the language than the lesson.*" However, the most common emotions evoked were feelings of being lost and confused. One PSET went as far as to describe the experience as "*scary*" due to her feelings of being overwhelmed and lost. This is similar to what Darling-Hammond (1997) spoke of in her research— reporting that ELLs' emotional states are triggered when they are in an unfamiliar school environment and/or receive instruction in a foreign language.

Other PSETs (16%) not only experienced frustration, but also spoke of ways of coping during Lesson One. Some reported that they attempted to identify cognates or decipher drawings. Yet, others coped by giving up or mentally checking out of the lesson when their attentional resources were being utilized to manage emotions instead of managing the academic tasks expected of them (Blankstein, Toner, & Flett, 1989; Garner, 2010). As one participant commented, "*At first I tried to understand by listening for cognates and looking at the pictures, [but I] eventually gave up.*"

In contrast, the language supports used during Lesson Two resulted in the PSETs experiencing emotional reactions less often (16%). Not only were there less emotional reactions, the reactions that were reported during Lesson Two were more positive. Specifically, the PSET's shared that they felt better about their learning during Lesson Two and were surprised at their own abilities to comprehend the lesson despite it being taught in a foreign language. As one PSET explained, "*I don't know French at all, but I was still able to follow the lesson.*" Another went a little further, explaining that "*[She] understood everything, even when the whole lesson was taught in French, and was able to complete the exam and understand how electricity travels through circuits.*"

Strategy Knowledge Transformed to Support Effective Science Instruction

In addition to changing PSETs' emotional awareness of the science-learning experiences of ELLs, the simulation transformed the PSETs' understanding of effective science instruction by demonstrating that science learning can be possible if and when language learners are provided appropriate supports. This transformation is noteworthy since oftentimes teachers "may not consider the significance of" addressing "both science content and students' linguistic and cultural backgrounds" (Buxton, Lee, & Santau, 2008, p. 496). Responding to the needs of ELLs entails providing several types of scaffolds (e.g., linguistic, conceptual, sociocultural) within the content-area classroom (Pawan, 2008), and this simulation enabled participants to see and experience such scaffolds and strategies in practice. For instance, Lee and Buxton (2013) discuss strategies that scaffold science learning for ELLs in five principal categories: content area literacy strategies, English to Speakers of Other Languages (ESOL) strategies, strategies that facilitate ELLs' participation in classroom discourse practices, strategies that focus on home language, and strategies that build on funds of knowledge. It was this categorization of strategies around which we designed the simulated lessons.

Before the simulation, PSETs were asked to identify instructional strategies that would support the science learning of ELLs. Their ideas were coded based on the categories from Lee and Buxton (2013), with 44.30% of the strategies named by PSETs being typically identified as ESOL strategies, 30.38% of strategies intentionally orchestrating ELLs' participation in classroom discourse, 16.45% of strategies focused on students' home language, and 8.86% of strategies developing content area literacy skills. PSETs did not name any strategies to identify and build upon students' funds of knowledge.

As previously mentioned, we designed the simulation to purposefully include strategies to support ELLs in the science classroom. Specifically, the simulated language learner experience in which PSETs participated included the following strategies to scaffold science learning for ELLs: content area literacy strategies, ESOL strategies, strategies to facilitate ELLs' participation in discourse, and strategies that build on funds of knowledge (Lee & Buxton, 2013). When asked to identify aspects of Lesson Two that facilitated their science learning, nearly all PSETs mentioned pedagogical strategies typically identified as ESOL strategies as most supportive. Specifically, these included the use of realia, demonstrations, and the hands-on activity; multiple modes of representation; and repetition. Similarly, when reflecting on the simulation and what they gained to draw from in the future when teaching ELLs, a majority of participants reported learning strategies that are typically identified as ESOL strategies (i.e., pictures, demonstrations, visual aids, hands-on activities, multiple modes of representation, repetition, Lee & Buxton, 2013). Additionally, strategies to identify and build on students' funds on knowledge were also mentioned, though less frequently than ESOL strategies. Namely, participants cited the teacher's discussion of Christmas tree lights as an example of how they intend to support ELLs by *"incorporating everyday [familiar] ideas (ex—Christmas trees) is helpful."* Further, *"it is important to use objects that students from all over the world can recognize to connect the learning."* Drawing on students' funds of knowledge reflects one way *"to relate even if we are teaching [in] a completely different language."*

Preservice Teachers' Dispositions Transformed and Diversified

It can be challenging to alter teachers' beliefs and practices as to teaching culturally and linguistically diverse students (Lee, Luykx, Buxton, & Shakter, 2007). However, as populations of ELLs, including Latin@ ELLs, continue to increase in our nation's public schools (NCES, 2016a, 2016b), it is imperative that teachers attain "the dual goals of promoting high academic achievement while simultaneously pursuing educational equity for diverse student groups" (Lee *et al.*, 2007, p. 1269). This requires today's teachers to have "a broader array of knowledge, skills, and dispositions to provide equitable learning opportunities for all students" (Buxton *et al.*, 2008, p. 509).

Awareness of the emotional responses of ELLs to learning science content and developing language proficiency concurrently as well as strategies to support this learning were, admittedly, short-term gains of participating in the simulated language learner experience. Based on our emerging research with a small subset of recent participants, it seems the elementary teacher education program, of which the simulated language learner experience was a small part during the science methods course, had a positive influence on shaping participants' attitudes and dispositions toward teaching culturally and linguistically diverse students. For instance, when asked about their attitudes toward culturally and linguistically diverse students, one participant in our small longitudinal sample commented, "*I love when students are able to bring their different cultures and backgrounds into the classroom. It can help students see from a different perspective and it can help them develop empathy.*" Such inherent learning opportunities were echoed by another participant:

> Rather than view culturally and linguistically diverse students as challenges or "burdens," I like to think of the learning opportunities this diverse presence brings to the classroom. Having a student that is culturally and linguistically diverse gives me as the teacher as well as my students the opportunity to learn more about cultures that differ from my own.

When asked specifically about what they learned from education courses about teaching ELLs, participants, unsurprisingly, wished they had learned more. One of them cited the simulated language learner experience discussed in this chapter as a rich opportunity for learning to teach ELLs:

> The example we had about teaching ELLs science was an awesome experience because it helped me see what those students go through in the classroom each day and what I can do to help them learn and to be welcomed in the classroom.

Other participants also discussed inclusion and success as well. For instance,

> The biggest thing I've learned about teaching English language learners doesn't differ much from what I've learned about teaching every other student: give the student the tools he or she needs to be most successful. While these tools and resources may require more differentiation and specialization, it is my job as the teacher to identify what my ELL students need to be most successful and [to] provide nothing less.

Although these points showcase the potential of the simulated language learning experience to affect PSETs' attitudes and dispositions toward teaching culturally and linguistically diverse students, this simulation is but one set of lessons within the whole elementary teacher education program. A focus on diverse student populations, including ELLs, should be more programmatic, integrated into each course and woven purposefully throughout the program of study.

Conclusion and Implications

Having PSETs temporarily take on the role of language learners by participating in a simulated language learner experience transformed their perceptions of what constitutes effective science instruction for ELLs. The contrasting nature of Lesson One to Lesson Two also served in making this experience more impactful. With respect to transforming emotional awareness, the PSETs realized and better understood the gatekeeping role that emotions and the affective filter (Krashen, 2003) play in comprehending new content and in developing a second language. The simulated language learning engagement also afforded the PSETs an opportunity to transform their understanding of effective instructional practice by experiencing firsthand how the absence of and use of language scaffolds can either impede or facilitate an ELLs' learning—especially in a demanding content area such as science. Overall, these PSETs will be better prepared to work with ELLs in science because they have developed an empathetic lens and are better informed about second language acquisition with respect to elementary science instruction.

The transformative experiences of the PSETs can also prove beneficial to those who are already working with Latin@ ELLs. The use of simulated language learner experience could also be adapted to become part of professional development for inservice teachers. The incorporation of this approach could broaden the perspectives of many current teachers who may feel ill prepared to teach science to ELLs responsively and effectively. Engaging in such opportunities may even help teachers to identify specific language supports that could be incorporated into their daily teaching practices. The use of simulated language learning could also be carried over into other STEM fields, such as math and technology.

References

Balfanz, R., Bridgeland, J. M., Fox, J. H., DePaoli, J. L., Ingrim, E. S., & Maushard, M. (2014). *Building a grad nation: Progress and challenge in ending the high school dropout epidemic.* Washington, DC: Civic Enterprises. Retrieved from http://files.eric.ed.gov/fulltext/ED556758.pdf

Banilower, E. R., Trygstad, P. J., & Smith, P. S. (2015). The first five years: What the 2012 National Survey of Science and Mathematics Education reveals about novice science teachers and their teaching. In J. A. Luft & S. L. Dubois (Eds.), *A better beginning: Supporting our newly hired science teachers* (pp. 3–29). Boston, MA: Sense.

Barrera, E. S., IV. (2016). Not hot enough for English language learners: Instructional challenges at the state, national, and international level. In E. Martinez & J. Pilgrim (Eds.), *Texas Association of Literacy Education yearbook: Literacy, research, and practice* (Vol. 2, pp. 1–4). San Antonio, TX: Specialized Literacy Professionals & Texas Association of Literacy Educators.

Berger, M., & Wilborn, L. (2012). Education. In *Handbook of Texas online*. Texas State Historical Association. Retrieved from https://tshaonline.org/handbook/online/articles/khe01

Blankstein, B., Toner, B. B., & Flett, G. L. (1989). Test anxiety and the contents of consciousness: Thought listening and endorsement measures. *Journal of Research in Personality, 23,* 269–286. doi:10.1016/0092–6566(89)90001–9

Bradley, P. (2006). The history of simulation in medical education and possible future directions. *Medical Education, 40,* 254–262.

Buxton, C., Lee, O., & Santau, A. (2008). Promoting science among English language learners: Professional development for today's culturally and linguistically diverse classrooms. *Journal of Science Teacher Education, 19,* 495–511. doi:10.1007/s10972-008-9103-x

Darling-Hammond, L. (1997). *The right to learn: A blueprint for creating schools that work.* San Francisco, CA: Jossey-Bass.

de Jong, E. J., & Harper, C. A. (2011). Accommodating diversity: Preservice teachers' views on effective practices for English language learners. In T. Lucas (Ed.), *Teacher preparation for linguistically diverse classrooms: A resource for teacher educators* (pp. 73–90). New York, NY: Routledge.

Cruickshank, D. R. (1969). The use of simulation in teacher education: A developing phenomenon. *Journal of Teacher Education, 20*(1), 23–26.

Gaba, D. (2004). The future vision of simulation in health care. *Quality & Safety in Health Care, 13*(Suppl. 1), i2–i10.

Garner, P. W. (2010). Emotional competence and its influences on teaching and learning. *Educational Psychological Review, 22,* 297–321. doi:10.1007/s10648-010-9129-4

Girod, M., & Girod, G. R. (2008). Simulation and the need for practice in teacher preparation. *Journal of Technology and Teacher Education, 16,* 307–337.

Grossman, P. (2005). Pedagogical approaches to teacher education. In M. Cochran-Smith & K. M. Zeichner (Eds.), *Studying teacher education: The report of the AERA panel on research and teacher education* (pp. 425–476). Mahwah, NJ: Lawrence Erlbaum.

Harder, B. (2010). Use of simulation in teaching and learning in health sciences: A systematic review. *Journal of Nursing Education, 49,* 23–28.

Hill, A. E., Davidson, B. J., McAllister, S., Wright, J., & Theodoros, D. G. (2014). Assessment of student competency in a simulated speech-language pathology clinical placement. *International Journal of Speech-Language Pathology, 16,* 464–475.

Howard, T. (2015). *Why race and culture matter in schools: Closing the achievement gap in America's classrooms.* New York, NY: Teachers College Press.

Krashen, S. D. (2003). *Explorations in language acquisition and use.* Portsmouth, NH: Heinemann.

Landivar, C. L. (2013). *Disparities in STEM employment by sex, race, and Hispanic origin* (ACS-24). Washington, DC: U.S. Census Bureau. Retrieved from http:// s3.document cloud.org.s3.amazonaws.com/documents/2095451/census-stem.pdf

Lee, O., & Buxton, C. A. (2013). Teacher professional development to improve science and literacy achievement of English language learners. *Theory into Practice, 52,* 110–117.

Lee, O., Luykx, A., Buxton, C., & Shaver, A. (2007). The challenge of altering elementary school teachers' beliefs and practices regarding linguistic and cultural diversity in science instruction. *Journal of Research in Science Teaching, 44,* 1269–1291. doi:10.1002/tea.20198

Llosa, L., Lee, O., Jiang, F., Haas, A., O'Connor, C., Van Booven, C. D., & Kieffer, M. J. (2016). Impact of a large-scale science intervention focused on English language learners. *American Educational Research Journal, 53*(2), 395–424.

MacDonald, V.-M. (2001). Hispanic, Latino, Chicano, or other: Deconstructing the relationship between historians and Hispanic-American educational history. *History of Education Quarterly, 41,* 365–413.

National Center of Education Statistics. (2016a). Indicator: English language learners in public schools. In U.S. Department of Education, National Center for Educational Statistics (Ed.), *The condition of education* (2016 ed.). Retrieved from https://nces.ed.gov/programs/coe/indicator_cgf.asp

National Center of Education Statistics. (2016b). Table 204.27: English language learner (ELL) students enrolled in public elementary and secondary schools, by grade and home language: Selected years, 2008–2009 through 2013–2014. In U.S. Department of Education, National Center for Educational Statistics (Ed.), *Digest of education statistics* (2016 ed.). Retrieved from https://nces.ed.gov/programs/digest/d15/tables/dt15_204.27.asp

Pawan, F. (2008). Content-area teachers and scaffolded instruction for English language learners. *Teaching and Teacher Education, 24,* 1450–1462. doi:10.1016/j.tate.2008.02.003

Samson, J., & Lesaux, N. (2015). Disadvantaged language minority students and their teachers: A national picture. *Teachers College Record, 117,* 1–26.

Umansky, I., & Reardon, S. F. (2014). Reclassification patterns among Latino English learner students in bilingual, dual immersion, and English immersion classrooms. *American Educational Research Journal, 51,* 879–912.

Webb, A. W. (2016, March). Simulated language learner experiences: An innovation for preparing teachers to teach English language learners. *Professionalism to Practice.* Retrieved from http://nebula.wsimg.com/ee7dd2307b39fa06ded8dbf68e5f390d?AccessKeyId=DC47318370B1BD529AA6&disposition=0&alloworigin=1

Webb, A. W., Barrera, E. S., IV., & Calderon, P. (2014). Teaching responsively: Developing an awareness of responsibility to English language learners in pre-service elementary science teachers. *Literacy and Social Responsibility, 7*(1), 20–38.

5. Preparing Bilingual Preservice Teachers to Support Latin@ Student Participation in Scientific Practices

JORGE L. SOLÍS, MARCO A. BRAVO, KARMIN SAN MARTIN, AND EDUARDO MOSQUEDA

Purpose

Recent analysis of statewide bilingual programs in the U.S. demonstrate that K–5 English learners (ELs) fare better in science achievement tests if they are part of additive bilingual programs compared to transitional bilingual programs or English immersion programs (McEneaney, López, & Nieswandt, 2014). However, science instruction in an English langue medium tends to dominate even within additive bilingual programs in elementary school grade levels, which results in limited opportunities for bilingual teacher candidates to teach science in students' native language. Over the past two decades, Latin@ student enrollment has increased dramatically in U.S. public schools from 4.8 to 11.4 million students, a shift from 11 to 22% (National Center for Education Statistics [NCES], 2011). Latin@ students are linguistically heterogeneous, and the subpopulation of linguistic minority (LM) Latin@s, those who speak a language other than English at home, has also grown. Given the rapid growth of Latin@ students, the issue of access and participation in STEM has gained the attention of educators concerned with closing achievement disparities that exist between Latin@s and their White peers. Redressing the pervasive disparities in math and science achievement in the early grades is of critical importance for Latin@ students given the contextual challenges such students face. Latin@ students, and ELs are more likely to live below the poverty line, attend schools that are underperforming, have little knowledge of U.S. schools and, as a result, many begin school behind in the math and science content knowledge their language majority counterparts possess (Abedi & Gándara, 2006; Ruiz de Velasco and Fix, 2000).

The persistent achievement disparities in Latin@ student outcomes on the National Assessment of Education Progress (NAEP) in science has showed little improvement, relative to White students. In 2011, Latin@ students had an average score that was 31 points lower than White students, and the gap in performance was not significantly different from that in 2009 (35 points). NAEP and other standardized assessments of science performance show that the subpopulation of Latin@ students who are also ELs score considerably lower compared to the scores of their native English speaking peers (Gándara & Contreras, 2009; Mosqueda & Maldonado, 2013). While on average, 66% of English proficient students scored at the "basic" level or better on the NAEP, 20% of ELs scored at "basic" level of better, nationally.

The data analyzed in this chapter draws from a broader longitudinal quasi-experimental four-year study testing the impact of a new science teacher model (Bravo, Mosqueda, Solís, & Stoddart, 2014; Solís, 2017). The Integrating Science and Diversity Education (ISDE) project involved 110 teacher candidates including 65 participants who were part of the intervention group. The demographic characteristics of the participants involved approximately 10% Asian/Asian-American, 33% Hispanic/Latino, and 52% White/Non-Hispanic teacher candidates. Participants for the study are recruited from two similar Northern California teacher education programs that prepare both mainstream and bilingual credential K–8 teachers. Teacher candidates were placed in culturally and linguistically diverse schools including rural, urban, and suburban settings. For example, the ethnic demographics of one school district included 33% Chinese; 10% African-American; 11% White; 23% Latino; 6% Filipino with 27% of students designated as ELs and 61% of students on free and reduced lunch. Another large school district included students who were 61.7% Hispanic; 29.9% White; 2.2% African-American; 3.1% Asian. In this second district, 36% of students were designated ELs and 72% of students qualified for free or reduced lunch.

This chapter focuses on the study of a set of pedagogical practices that make science more accessible to students from diverse cultural and linguistic backgrounds, including Latin@ children. In this study, preservice teachers pursuing a bilingual authorization were provided with professional learning opportunities that allowed them to leverage the language and cultural experiences of Latin@ students to make sense of science concepts and practices. Teacher candidates completed a required science methods course that was restructured to model and support sociocultural practices in science teaching through micro-teaching activities and course assignments. Moreover, mentor teachers hosting teacher candidates were exposed to the intervention framework and were coached on providing feedback to teacher candidates in their classrooms focused on the reform pedagogy. A full discussion of the ISDE professional development activities is beyond the scope of this chapter, but a more detailed discussion is available in other publications (see Bravo *et al.*, 2014; Solís, Bravo, & Mosqueda, 2017; Stoddart, Solís, Tolbert, & Bravo, 2010).

Theoretical Framework

The ISDE framework used in this study combines theoretical approaches from sociocultural theory, language and literacy integration in science education, and responsive teacher education approaches to advance a model for preparing teachers to teach science in linguistically diverse elementary school classroom contexts (Bruna, Vann, & Escudero, 2007; Flores & Smith, 2009; Hornberger & Link, 2012; Lucas, Villegas, & Freedson-Gonzalez, 2008; Martínez-Álvarez, Cuevas, & Torres-Guzmán, 2017; Reyes, 2009; Stoddart *et al.*, 2010). The collaborators in this study adapted the Five Standards for Effective Pedagogy framework (Tharp & Dalton, 2007) to elementary level science content area teaching and learning with the goal of preparing future teachers to utilize culturally and linguistically responsive pedagogies, including native language development support, in their delivery of science instruction. The adapted framework infuses language and literacy development in science for Spanish-speaking Latin@ students through six related pedagogical practices including: (1) Collaborative inquiry in science activity, (2) Integrating literacy in science, (3) Scaffolding and development of language in science, (4) Contextualizing science instruction, (5) Developing scientific understanding, and (6) Engaging students in scientific discourse.

Methodology and Data Sources

The sample used in this analysis involved six Latin@ bilingual credential participants. These participants were selected because they taught science in Spanish during their clinical practicum. Teacher candidates were observed three times during their 15-week clinical practicum following the completion of the restructured science methods course and each observation was audio-recorded. While all bilingual teacher candidates were expected to teach science in Spanish during their clinical practicum, there were several instances where science lessons could only be completed in English. An initial observation took place during the first two weeks of their placement followed by a second observation after 6–12 weeks and finally a third observation during the final two weeks. Observations averaged 45 minutes. A validated observation protocol was used to gauge the effectiveness of the science instruction implemented by each participant (Bravo *et al.*, 2014).

The bilingual preservice teachers were mentored in the six pedagogical practices through a restructured science methods course that was part of their teacher credential program. The 15-week course provided candidates with readings, hands-on examples, discussions and assignments that allowed them to learn and produce instructional activities that leveraged the six pedagogical practices identified by previous research (Tharp & Dalton, 2007) as effective practices in culturally and linguistically diverse classrooms. Science lessons that candidates completed for the course, for example, addressed how they would tap into students' previously learned knowledge, whether it originated at school or in out-of-school settings.

A second pathway through which candidates learned about the reform pedagogy was through their mentor teacher. Each candidate was placed in a classroom for their practicum experience in the following semester from when they enrolled in the restructured science methods course. In this field placement, candidates were mentored by a master teacher with at least 10 years of teaching experience that received professional development that paralleled what they preservice teachers experienced in the restructured science methods course. The mentor teachers learned to provide feedback to candidates as the candidates taught lessons with the integrated reform pedagogy. Bringing into alignment what preservice teachers experienced in the teacher education program and what they experienced in their field placement allowed for a common voice that ensured the reform pedagogy was learned, applied to instruction and feedback was also provided about the reform pedagogy.

Oral language in each lesson was first coded using computer assisted qualitative data analysis software (i.e., Dedoose). The coding tool allowed the researchers to systematically identify discourse features associated with particular pedagogical approaches used by each participant. A coding scheme was developed over two rounds of analysis including an initial review of sample transcripts focused on the reform practices and followed by a grounded analysis of codes emerging from the data (i.e., questions types, cognates, translanguaging, student-initiated questions, figurative language, science vocabulary). Selected transcripts were then analyzed to capture the epistemic and pragmatic functions of classroom interactions.

Results

In our findings, we address two themes that emerged in bilingual science lessons related to scientific discourse practices including (1) contextualizing science activity and (2) language play. For the purposes of this chapter, we include in our discussion examples of science language related to these two themes. In each section, we provide an overview of each theme by connecting relevant sources and theoretical perspectives, providing general patterns found in the data, and examples related to these patterns or sub-themes.

Contextualizing Bilingual Science Knowledge

Overview. Prior science-related experiences in school and outside of school are productive sources for making-sense of new scientific practices and concepts. All students bring experience from the natural world to the classroom that can be used to connect and sometimes transform academic knowledge (Baquedano-López, Solís, & Kattan, 2005; Kamberelis & Wehunt, 2012; Tharp & Dalton, 2007). Moreover, students possess a range of experiences and resources including familiarity with specific language and cultural practices that are sometimes directly related to classroom topics, scientific ideas, and practices; on most other occasions, these links may be potentially available but usually not leveraged by the teacher or students (Perin, 2011). These "funds of knowledge" (Moll, Amanti, Neff, & González, 1992) seem to be more easily accessed through the use of the students' native language. Contextualizing scientific knowledge by eliciting and elaborating on bilingual Latin@ students' prior experiences in the community, at home, in school, and in the natural environment are especially important ways to make science learning relevant to student lives and to promote comprehension and appropriation of science knowledge (Civil, 2016).

Analysis. In our analysis of contextualizing bilingual science knowledge by Latin@ preservice bilingual teachers, we coded recurring sub-themes found in the observations related to four types of contextualizing activities including:

1. contextualizing nonscience-related knowledge
2. contextualizing prior science knowledge related to classroom activities
3. contextualizing science knowledge connected to the natural environment or local surroundings
4. contextualizing science knowledge related to home/family and community activities/experiences

Patterns. Our analysis identified several patterns related to contextualizing activities by Latin@ preservice bilingual teachers in science. First, our analysis of the bilingual science lessons indicates that there were several examples of teachers contextualizing science knowledge yet most of this work focused on connecting science lessons to previous class learning. Bilingual teachers spent the most amount of time (56% of Contextualizations) attending to previous and ongoing classroom activities during our observations. A second common theme that emerged related to connections to the natural or local environment. These examples (27% of Contextualizations) included identifying or relating familiar examples to the local environment. Of note here, bilingual teachers rarely made a reference to prior experiences that were *not* related to science topics when teaching a science lesson (17% of Contextualizations). That is, bilingual teachers keenly focused on closely related topics to focal science lessons. Moreover, connections to home/family and community-related connections were the least common science-related Contextualizations (20%). Table 5.1 summarizes the coding distribution for Contextualizations of science knowledge. Of note here also is that instances of Contextualization sometimes overlapped across the four types of Contextualizing activities. Several themes work together in creating coherent bilingual science lesson for Latin@ students in these classrooms.

Table 5.1. Distribution for contextualizing science knowledge

	1. Nonscience-related knowledge	2. Prior science classroom knowledge	3. Natural environment	4. Home/family and community
Instances	17	99	47	35
Percentage (%)	10	56	27	20

Source: Authors

Examples of Contextualization. The following example in Excerpt 1.1 describes how bilingual teachers elicited prior science knowledge related to classroom experiences. Preservice teachers often framed the initiation of an observation as an extension of an ongoing lesson or the continuation of a previous lesson or set of science activities. Excerpt 1.1 begins with the teacher (Mr. Juan) probing students to remind him of what the class talked about the previous week (Line 1) with the construction "*Okay niños, recuérdame*" (Ok children remind me) and "*¿De qué hablamos?*" (What did we talk about?).

This line of questioning leads to a series of exchanges where students provide their own recollections of seeds, plants, water, sunlight, and plan growth.

Excerpt 1.1. Connecting science lessons to previous class activities

Ln	S	Talk	Theme
1	T	Okay niños, recuérdame lo que empezamos a hablar la semana pasada en los centros. ¿De qué hablamos? *Okay children, remind me what we started to talk about last week in centers. What did we talk about?*	Collective remembering
2	Ss	Uhh de plantas *Uhh of plants*	
3	T	De plantas. *Of plants*	
4	Ss	De semillas. *Of seeds.*	
5	T	Sí, semillas. ¿Y qué aprendiste de las semillas? *Yes, seeds. And what did you learn of seeds?*	Repeats student talk
6	Ss	Que cuando, que cuando… *That when, that when…*	
7	T	Uno primero, sí diga. *Somebody first, yes tell me.*	
8	S	Cuando las plantas y y y ta no pueden crecer necesitan se echa agua y dejarlos en el sol. Déjalos que umm la lluvia como… *When plants and and and can't grow they need water and leave them in the sun. Leave them umm rain like…*	
9	S	Necesitan aire. *They need air.*	
10	S	Lo uno necesita esperarte para que crece. *What we need to wait for it to grow.*	
11	T	Ummm. Ummm.	
12	S	Cuando se mueren las semillas se caen y luego crecen otra. *The seeds fall off when it dies and then more grow.*	

(Continued)

Excerpt 1.1—Continued

Ln	S	Talk	Theme
13	T	Otra planta vuelve a crecer. Muy bien, sabes mucho sobre la planta.	Revoices student talk
		Another plan grows again. Good, you know a lot about the plant.	

[#10061.2]

There are several practices of repetition used in Excerpt 1.1 including the rephrasing and extending (line 5) and revoicing of student previous science learning (Line 13) that enables student engagement of science knowledge through contextualizing current learning in previous instructional activities (Moore, 2014).

In this second Contextualization example in Excerpt 1.2, the teacher began a lesson on magnetism by asking students the following question, "*A ver me pueden decir ustedes, ¿en dónde en SU casa pueden ustedes encontrar imanes?*" (Ok can you tell me, where can you find a magnet in YOUR house?). This question leads to a series of exchanges where students are remembering about "sticky" and metal objects found at home including irons and door handles. Excerpt 1.2 continues where a student (Julia) offers her own home-related connection to magnets. She shares an example of a toy that contains a magnet attached to a toy dog and bone.

Excerpt 1.2. Connections to home/family and community-related connections

Ln	S	Talk	Theme
1	T	Muy bien Josué. ¿Entonces tu sí has visto imanes en tu casa? ¿Verdad? Okay muy bien. Julia.	
		Very good Josué. And then you have seen magnets in your house? True? Ok very good. Julia.	
2	Julia	Umm yo tengo un juguete que umm que tiene un imán en and it's kind of like a bone.	Translanguaging
		Umm I have a toy that has a magnet in- and it's kind of like a bone.	
3	T	Como un hueso.	Repeats student talk
		Like a bone.	
4	Julia	Like a bone.	

Ln	S	Talk	Theme
5	T	Hueso tiene un imán adentro	Connection to magnets
		Bone has a magnet inside	
6	Julia	Kind of like, it's like a, it's like something. It came with a dog and you can move like its head because it has like a.	
7	T	O porque tiene porque tiene el imán. Y el imán deja que se mueva la cabeza del perr. Del animalito. También la colita, oh okay muy bien. Jennifer muy bien. Julia.	
		Or because it has a magnet inside. And the magnet allows it move the head if the do- of the little animal. Also the tail, oh okay very good. Jennifer very good. Julia.	

[10075.1]

The teacher brackets the previous student contribution (Line 1) by affirming that Josué has seen magnets in his house and then moves on to Julia. Julia then shares an example from home related to magnets (Line 2: tengo un juguete que umm que tiene un imán en and it's kind of like a bone) while translanguaging. The teacher manages this occurrence by again affirming Julia's contribution through the repetition of "*Como un hueso*" (Like a bone) (Line 3) description offered by Julia yet also reinforcing the Spanish meaning for Julia's observation and contribution. Julia continues in English and again the teacher affirms her contribution while again pivoting to Spanish (Line 5). This mediation of both languages by the teacher and students occurs often across preservice teacher participants in the study. These are also instances where student contributions are unexpected yet rich learning episodes arise as Latin@ students make sense of science topics related to familiar home/ community contexts and experiences.

Language Play

Overview. We examine language play in the classroom as a way to examine language development, biliteracy, and emerging scientific identities. Our observations of bilingual classrooms noted the occurrence of language play during bilingual science lessons. Language play is a particularly productive theme to understand how classrooms become contexts for socialization and language learning related to scientific practices. Moore (2014) refers to language play along with other language socialization practices of repetition in her review of research on language socialization and repetition. Practices of repetition, when properly used in the classroom, can provide bilinguals strategic opportunities for augmenting language use in both languages while also promoting collective knowledge-making and community. Moore (2014) describes language play as "the use of rhyme, rhythm, alliteration, and other repeating patterns in language to amuse, delight, dispute, and confound" that connects to children's exploration of verbal play across communities (p. 215). For the purposes of our analysis, we focused on two recurring forms of language play in the classroom: (1) figurative language and (2) translanguaging. We acknowledge that both these sub-themes represent much larger social, cultural and linguistic processes that are not solely related to language play but rather that language play occurred through these two mechanisms in bilingual science lessons led by bilingual preservice teachers. In her analysis of classroom language practices and policies, Langman (2014) finds that breaks from official and routine interactions are bids for language play through the switching of registers and languages. She notes that these instances are tactics and strategies for engaging students "in ways that open up spaces in the classroom for students' lives and concerns to be valued" (p. 196). In the context of bilingual science lessons, language play creates intertextual links that tap into school and nonschool-related experiences as well as opportunities for negotiating student voices in constructing scientific knowledge. Figure 5.1 clarifies this distinction between and within language play.

Figurative language is part of the language of scientists inherent to creating productive epistemic spaces for imagining new or alternative scenarios and possibilities to understand and create scientific models (Duit, 1991; Lancor, 2014). Figurative language is commonly utilized in textbooks with the use of personification of animals or inanimate objects and also in oral language speech (Darian, 2000). One example found in our observations is the use of analogies and metaphors for making observations. For example, in one lesson a bilingual preservice teacher notes how reptile eggs are submerged in a gelatinous, sticky substance similar to one we use for eating or grooming our hair. A student responds similarly to this observation by comparing the color and shape of reptile eggs to marshmallows noting that they look *like* marshmallows ("Los huevos blancos parecen bombones") (Solís, 2017). These parallels of scientific sense-making by the teacher and student rely on figurative language and language play producing unique yet coherent descriptions through bilingual language strategies (Cuadrado Esclapez, 2009).

Figure 5.1. Bilingual science: Language play, figurative language, translanguaging.

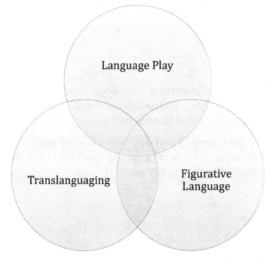

Source: Authors

Analysis. Our analysis of the language play noted the co-occurrence of these features more often with respect to attention to scientific discourse than to contextualizing science activity. In particular, there were more instances of translanguaging and language play (88%) in our observations of bilingual classrooms than of figurative language and language play (13%). We draw from García and Wei (2014) in our descriptions of translanguaging in the classroom as "purposeful pedagogical alternation of languages in spoken and written, receptive and productive modes (Baker, 2001, 2003; Williams, 1994)" (p. 262). In the context of classroom interactions we find it useful to consider translanguaging as ubiquitous language functions in learning contexts that help coconstruct meaning with another person, construct meaning for ourselves, include others, and demonstrate knowledge (García & Wei, 2014). The frequent occurrence of translanguaging and language play in bilingual science lessons supports the notion that translanguaging practices permeates in scientific sense-making as well.

Students and teachers used a range of observations about focal science topics to imagine new contexts for understanding scientific concepts as well as creating analogies to everyday examples, hyperboles, hypothetical scenarios, other unlikely examples or approximations to examine scientific ideas. Excerpt 2.1 describes one such example where the teacher reminds students about a lesson on seeds and plants. As the teacher reminds the students about what occurred before with seeds, the teacher asks about the purpose of the seed shells or coats (*tecatas*) and makes a comparison between the functions of jackets/sweaters to seed shells.

Excerpt 2.1. Seeds and jackets

Ln	S	Talk	Theme
1	T	¿Qué es? Cuidadosamente y lo abres. ¿Abriste tu semilla? Mmmm ¿Qué hay adentro de esta semilla? ¿Qué es lo que estás haciendo? ¿Qué le estás quitando?	
		What is it? Carefully and don't open it. Did you open your seed? Mmmm. What is it inside this seed? What is it that you are doing? What are you removing?	
2	S	Elllll	
		Theee	
3	T	¿Qué le quitaron a la semilla?	
		What did you remove to the seed?	
4	S	Tecatá.	
		Shells	
3	T	El tecatá. ¿Qué piensas tú que sirve la tecatá?	
		The shells. What do you think the shells are for?	
4	S	Para que esté buena. Para que te las puedas comer.	
		So it can be good. So you can eat it.	
5	T	Cuando cuando tú tienes frio, ¿Qué te pones? Cuando tú tienes frio, ¿Qué te pones? Brianna.	Analogy to clothes
		Like when you are cold, what do you wear? When you are cold, what do you wear? Brianna?	
6	S	Chaqueta.	
		Jacket.	
7	T	Un suéter te protege del frío. ¿Piensas que la tecatá protege a la semilla? Yo creo que sí protege la semilla. A ver fíjate bien a tu semilla, voltéate ¿Qué es lo que ves?	
		A sweater protects you from the cold. Do you think the shell protects the seed? I think it protects the seed. Look, look at your seed. Turn around, what do you see?	

[#10061.1]

There were other examples like this one where the teacher situates instruction for the children in relation to what they are studying; here the teacher relates children to the seeds needing protection from the outside elements to highlight particular observations about seeds shells.

In terms of examples of translanguaging (as in Excerpt 1.2), we found translanguaging occurring when engaging scientific terms that were also English-Spanish science non-cognates more than in exchanges where English-Spanish science cognates were the focus of the exchange. Examples of translanguaging occurred regularly involving scientific explanations and in others, it involved understanding scientific practices. Excerpt 2.2 offers an example where the teacher is describing the work of scientists. She extends the previous discussion of observations of wood materials that float by asking students about people who work doing science (Line 1: *las personas que trabajan en las ciencias. ¿Quiénes son estas personas?*).

Excerpt 2.2. Talking about scientists

Ln	S	Talk	Theme
1	T	De madera:: de madera:::y vamos hablar un poco de::- las personas que trabajan en las ciencias. ¿Quiénes son estas personas? ¿Quiénes son?	
		Of wood:: of wood:::and we are going to talk a little about:: the people that work in sciences. Who are these people? Who are they?	
2	S	Científicos	
		Scientist	
3	T	Si, los? Lo:::s cien- cie:::n	
		Yes, and? The::: scien::	
4	S	Dice cien-	
		Say scien-	
5	T	Cien, aquí esta. Los cie::n ti:: fi:::cos. ¿Quiénes son los científicos? ¿Qué hacien los científicos? Nelly? ¿Qué hacen los científicos?	
		Scien, here it is. The sci::en::tist. Who are the scientists? What does a scientist do?	
6	S	X	
7	T	¿Nayely? ¿Sabes- qué hacen los científicos?	Spanish
		Nayely? Do you know what scientists do?	

(Continued)

Table 2.2—Continued

Ln	S	Talk	Theme
8	S	They make like- they like- their brains like	English
9	T	¿Usan sus cerebros? ¿Sí? ¿Usan sus cerebros? *They use their brain? Yes? They use their brain?*	Spanish
10	S	Their brains to (X)	English
11	T	¿Usan sus cerebros a pensar, estudian? ¿Qué estudian los científicos? *They use their brain to think, study? What do scientists study?*	Spanish
12	S	They do experiments in five or six labs	English
13	T	Hacen experimentos a a contestar sus preguntas. SI. Hacen todas esas cosas. ¿Qué es una cosa que hacen los científicos? ¿Qué es esta palabra? *They do experiments to answer their questions. YES. They do all those things. What is one thing scientists do? What is that word?*	Spanish
14	S	OBSERVAR *OBSERVE*	Spanish
15	T	OBSERVAR. Los científicos- o::. Bb:: se::r: Observan. *OBSERVE. Scientists o::b:se::r:: Observe.*	Spanish

[#25141.3]

This example focuses on being and acting like scientists and scientific observations (Aikenhead, 2005; Archer *et al.*, 2010). While the lesson uses Spanish as the main language in science activities, there are multiple instances where both languages are used within one utterance or between exchanges. The teacher often models Spanish science talk with some exceptions (use of "so" frequently for explaining or transitional talk) (Bolden, 2009). There are common instances where student talk changes to English initiating a stretch of English and Spanish alternation as seen in lines 7–13 within Excerpt 2.2. Here each turn alternates between English and Spanish until line 14 where a student responds in Spanish departing from this pattern. García refers to the possibility that there are varied types of translanguaging related to advanced and emergent bilingual skills, which could be related to this kind of pattern. Nonetheless, this translanguaging pattern is a productive bilingual scientific sense-making practice that allows Latin@ emergent bilinguals to demonstrate their knowledge while also including other participants in the conversation with varied bilingual language skills and familiarity with a focal topic.

Limitations and Additional Analysis

The sample used in this new analysis does not allow us to make broader associations between varied classroom contexts (e.g., grade level, language program, mentor teacher support, curricular materials, student language skills, etc.), individual teacher development of pedagogical practices (pedagogical language knowledge), or the occurrence of scientific discourse within bilingual science lessons (availability and access to scientific discourse in Spanish and English lessons). Yet, we find some patterns in our analysis of classroom observations that point to need for more research on novice bilingual science practices while teaching science during "Spanish time" in bilingual programs.

For example, Table 5.2 shows that the majority of contextualizations related to *prior school experience and knowledge* also involved key science terms. Moreover, a majority of contextualizations of all types involved the use of *lower frequency Spanish-English cognates* (e.g., idea/idea; *movimiento*/movement) expressed in Spanish and not higher Spanish/lower English frequency cognates (*diagrama*/diagram; *anfibio*/amphibious) this occurrence counters the notion that bilingual teachers avoid more academic Spanish science terms in their teaching. However, it could also indicate that novice bilingual teachers are developing more general academic terms beyond the few technical terms associated with a lesson or concept or confidence switching science registers.

Table 5.2. Co-occurrence of contextualization and key science vocabulary

	Key Science Terms	Higher Frequency Spanish Cognates	Non-cognates	Lower Frequency Spanish Cognates
Contextualization Connections	162	55	81	97
Nonscience-Related Prior Knowledge	16	5	10	7
Recalling Prior Science Knowledge	102	35	42	74
Science Related to Environment/Personal Experiences	37	17	25	16
Science Related to Home Experiences/Personal Experiences	31	10	19	12

Source: Authors

Key Spanish science terms were frequently used in combination with each other. Non-cognates occurred less often than Spanish-English science cognates supporting earlier analysis about the salience of cognates in science (Bravo, Hiebert, & Pearson, 2007). The extent to which these types of cognates and non-cognates are part of scientific discourse practices also remains a question for further analysis. Nonetheless, we find that preservice bilingual teachers are able to leverage these language resources in teaching science if provided with support.

Finally, while we find some consistency in the use of higher frequency and lower-frequency Spanish-English cognates throughout our observations of preservice teachers. Additional analysis of preservice bilingual lessons over longer periods of time and into the first few years of full-time teaching may indicate a developmental trajectory associated with the use of Spanish-English science cognates. Methodologically sound analysis of different aspects of scientific discourse involving language play, contextualizing science knowledge, and scientific language requires attention to both describing the features of these interactions and how they are situated within larger sociocultural activities and practices.

Discussion and Conclusion

Results from this study highlight the potential for bilingual preservice teachers to support scientific practices while making science accessible to Latin@ students through contextualizing and translanguaging interactions. As illustrated in the examples above, Latin@ students can access scientific practices through a range sense-making strategies found in bilingual science contexts. Latin@ students have resources that are both cultural and linguistic-based that can support Latin@ students' acquisition of the type of science knowledge outlined by the Next Generation Science Standards. Four of the eight NGSS science and engineering practices are particularly language intensive: developing and using models; constructing explanations (science) and designing solutions (engineering); arguing from evidence; and obtaining, evaluating, and communicating information. Science content and language intersect as students, for example, construct oral and written explanations and engage in argument from evidence (Lee, Quinn, & Valdés, 2013).

To more fully engage Latin@ students in science learning, and subsequently prepare them for STEM careers, science instruction must leverage the language and cultural background of the students themselves. Such integration of science, language and culture can have a positive impact on student engagement and subsequent conceptual understanding of science concepts.

Data from the study presented in this chapter illustrates that Latin@ bilingual teachers can adopt appropriate linguistic supports and contextualized pedagogical practices, but require models and experiences that support flexible and strategic use of language and cultural knowledge in science teaching. Providing such instructional models can ensure that teaching science is made relevant to Latin@ students and simultaneously open the doors for them to enter STEM careers in the future.

Acknowledgments

The analysis reported here draws from a larger study funded by the Institute of Education Sciences (IES). We thank the collaborators and teachers who participated in the ISDE project in Northern California. We're indebted to Trish Stoddart, Roland Tharp, Maxine McKinney de Royston, Jennifer Collett, Viviana Limon, and all the other members of the ISDE team.

References

Abedi, J., & Gándara, P. (2006). Performance of English language learners as a subgroup in large-scale assessment: Interaction of research and policy. *Educational Measurement: Issues and Practice, 25*(4), 36–46.

Aikenhead, G. (2005). *Science education for everyday life: Evidence based practice.* New York, NY: Teachers College Press.

Archer, L., DeWitt, J., Osborne, J., Dillon, J., Willis, B., & Wong, B. (2010). "Doing" science versus "being" a scientist: Examining 10/11-year-old schoolchildren's constructions of science through the lens of identity. *Science Education, 94*(4), 617–639.

Baker, C. (2001). *Foundations of bilingual education and bilingualism.* Clevedon: Multilingual Matters Limited.

Baker, C. (2003). Biliteracy and transliteracy in Wales: Language planning and the Welsh national curriculum. In N.H. Hornberger (Ed.). *Continua of biliteracy: An ecological framework for educational policy, research, and practice in multilingual settings* (pp. 71–90). Clevedon, UK: Multilingual Matters.

Baquedano-López, P., Solís, J. L., & Kattan, S. (2005). Adaptation: The language of classroom learning. *Linguistics and Education, 16*(1), 1–26.

Bolden, G. B. (2009). Implementing incipient actions: The discourse marker "so" in English conversation. *Journal of Pragmatics, 41*(5), 974–998.

Bravo, M. A., Hiebert, E. H., & Pearson, P. D. (2007). Tapping the linguistic resources of Spanish–English bilinguals. In R. K. Wagner, A. Muse, & K. Tannenbaum (Eds.), *Vocabulary development and its implications for reading comprehension* (pp. 140–156). New York, NY: Guilford.

Bravo, M., Mosqueda, E., Solís, J. L., & Stoddart, T. (2014). Possibilities and limits of integrating science and diversity education in preservice elementary teacher preparation. *Journal of Science Teacher Education, 25*(5), 601–619.

Bruna, K. R., Vann, R., & Escudero, M. P. (2007). What's language got to do with it?: A case study of academic language instruction in a high school "English Learner Science" class. *Journal of English for Academic Purposes, 6*(1), 36–54.

Civil, M. (2016). STEM learning research through a funds of knowledge lens. *Cultural Studies of Science Education, 11*(1), 41–59.

Cuadrado Esclapez, G. (2009). La comprensión oral en el aula de inglés para fines específicos: Propuestas metodológicas [The oral comprehension in the English language classroom for specific purposes: Methodology Proposal] *Revista de investigación e innovación en la clase de idomas, 18*, 12–22.

Darian, S. (2000). The role of figurative language in introductory science texts. *International Journal of Applied Linguistics, 10*(2), 163–186.

Duit, R. (1991). On the role of analogies and metaphors in learning science. *Science Education, 75*(6), 649–672.

Flores, B. B., & Smith, H. L. (2009). Teachers' characteristics and attitudinal beliefs about linguistic and cultural diversity. *Bilingual Research Journal, 31*(1–2), 323–358.

Gándara, P., & Contreras, F. (2009). *The Latino education crisis: The consequences of failed social policies.* Cambridge, MA: Harvard University Press.

García, O., & Wei, L. (2014). *Translanguaging: Language, bilingualism and education.* London: Palgrave Macmillan.

Hornberger, N. H., & Link, H. (2012). Translanguaging and transnational literacies in multilingual classrooms: A biliteracy lens. *International Journal of Bilingual Education and Bilingualism, 15*(3), 261–278.

Kamberelis, G., & Wehunt, M. D. (2012). Hybrid discourse practice and science learning. *Cultural Studies of Science Education, 7*(3), 505–534.

Lancor, R. (2014). Using metaphor theory to examine conceptions of energy in biology, chemistry, and physics. *Science & Education, 23*(6), 1245–1267.

Langman, J. (2014). Translanguaging, identity, and learning: Science teachers as engaged language planners. *Language Policy, 13*(2), 183–200.

Lee, O., Quinn, H., & Valdés, G. (2013). Science and language for English language learners in relation to Next Generation Science Standards and with implications for Common Core State Standards for English Language Arts and Mathematics. *Educational Researcher, 42*(4), 223–233.

Lucas, T., Villegas, A. M., & Freedson-Gonzalez, M. (2008). Linguistically responsive teacher education preparing classroom teachers to teach English language learners. *Journal of Teacher Education, 59*(4), 361–373.

Martínez-Álvarez, P., Cuevas, I., & Torres-Guzmán, M. (2017). Preparing bilingual teachers: Mediating belonging with multimodal explorations in language, identity, and culture. *Journal of Teacher Education, 68*(2), 155–178.

McEneaney, E. H., López, F., & Nieswandt, M. (2014). Instructional models for the acquisition of English as bridges into school science: Effects on the science achievement of U.S. Hispanic English language learners. *Learning Environments Research, 17*(3), 305–318.

Moll, L. C., Amanti, C., Neff, D., & González, N. (1992). Funds of knowledge for teaching: Using a qualitative approach to connect homes and classrooms. *Theory into Practice, 31*(2), 132–141.

Moore, L. (2014). Language socialization and repetition. In A. Duranti, E. Ochs, & B. B. Schieffelin (Eds.), *The handbook of language socialization* (pp. 209–226). Malden, MA: Blackwell Publishing.

Mosqueda, E., & Maldonado, S. I. (2013). The effects of English language proficiency and curricular pathways: Latina/os' mathematics achievement in secondary schools. *Equity & Excellence in Education, 46*(2), 202–219.

National Center for Education Statistics. (2011). *The condition of education 2010. Indicator 6: Children who spoke a language other than English at home.* Washington, DC: U.S. Department of Education. Retrieved from http://nces.ed.gov/pubs2011/2011033.pdf

Perin, D. (2011). Facilitating student learning through contextualization: A review of evidence. *Community College Review, 39*(3), 268–295.

Reyes, I. (2009). English language learners' discourse strategies in science instruction. *Bilingual Research Journal, 31*(1–2), 95–114.

Ruiz de Velasco, J. & Fix, M. (2000). Overlooked and underserved: Immigrant students in U.S. secondary Schools. Washington, DC: The Urban Institute Press.

Solís, J. L. (2017). Adaptation and the language of learning science in a bilingual classroom. In J. Langman & H. Hansen-Thomas (Eds.), *Perspectives on discourse analysis and STEM education: Exploring English Learner interaction in the classroom* (pp. 195–215). New York, NY: Springer/Francis.

Solís, J. L., Bravo, M., & Mosqueda, E. (2017). Capitalizing on the synergistic possibilities between language, culture and science. In C. Buxton & M. Allexsaht-Snider (Eds.), *Supporting K-12 English language learners in science: Putting research into teaching practice* (pp. 178–205). New York, NY: Routledge Publishers.

Stoddart, T., Solís, J. L., Tolbert, S., & Bravo, M. (2010). A framework for the effective science teaching of English Language Learners in elementary schools. In D. W. Sunal, C. S. Sunal, & E. L. Wright (Eds.), *Teaching science with Hispanic ELLs in K–16 classrooms* (Vol. Research in Science Education, pp. 151–182). Charlotte, NC: Information Age Publishing.

Tharp, R. G., & Dalton, S. S. (2007). Orthodoxy, cultural compatibility, and universals in education. *Comparative Education, 43*(1), 53–70.

Williams, C. (1994). *Arfarniad o ddulliau dysgu ac addysgu yng nghyd-destun addysg uwchradd ddwyieithog* [An evaluation of teaching and learning methods in the context of bilingual secondary education]. (Unpublished doctoral dissertation). University of Wales, Bangor, Wales.

6. Transformative Practices Lending to Latin@s Participating in STEM in the EL Classroom[1]

ZAYONI N. TORRES AND ARIA RAZFAR

STEM, Gender, Racial and Language Ideologies

Why Latin@ ELs

Education reform has largely focused on the fields of science, technology, engineering and mathematics (STEM) (Zhao, 2009). Little evidence exists of changing teaching methods or that learners have shown increased interest in STEM (Breiner, Harkness, Johnson, & Keehler, 2012). Literature has documented links between teachers' ideologies and their influence on teaching methods (Bailey, Scantlebury, & Letts, 1997; Fennema & Peterson, 1985; Lee, Marks, & Byrd, 1994; Li, 1999; Thorne, 1993; Tolman & Porche, 2000). Teachers' ideologies are "tacit, often unconsciously held assumptions about students, classrooms and the academic materials to be taught" (Kagan, 1992, p. 65). The stances teachers take built upon these assumptions are *ideological stances.* For teachers of the Latin@ English Learner (EL) population in the U.S., these ideological stances become paramount to explore, given the current and historical political climate that disproportionately affects the Latin@[2] population, principally within schools (Valenzuela, 1999).

In this chapter, we explore the intersection of the gender, racial and language ideological stances of seven teachers who are a part of a long-term professional development program (i.e., PROJECT[3]). How do teachers explicitly construct gender, race and language in relation to STEM learning? and How do teachers' gender, racial and language ideological stances mediate curriculum and teaching methods? In the proceeding sections, we present our conceptual framework, background of this study, data collection and analysis, findings from two case studies and recommendations for professional development.

GiRL Conceptual Framework

We developed a conceptual framework focused on the intersection of gender, racial and language ideologies (Figure 6.1). We present a condensed version of key terms and categories that were most recurrent in our data set. First, gender ideologies (G) are an organizing framework that represents a gender order and how individuals align with that gender order or challenge it (Spencer, Porche, & Tolman, 2003). As follows, those behaviors that align with the gender order are valued and those that are counter are seen as deficient or resistant (Thorne, 1993). Two views of teachers addressing gender in their classrooms include *egalitarian* and *anti-sexist* (modified from Streitmatter, 1994). *Egalitarian* practices seek for the equal treatment of gender. For example, a PROJECT teacher assigned tasks to both boys and girls, although girls tended to be the ones assigned to take notes. The act of girls overwhelmingly taking secretarial roles reaffirm traditional gender roles. *Anti-sexist* practices actively push for gender equity. For example, a PROJECT teacher noticed in mixed gendered groups, boys were the ones assigned to be the breadwinner of the "household." The teacher challenged learners to consider that women can work and that men can stay home.

Figure 6.1. GiRL conceptual framework.

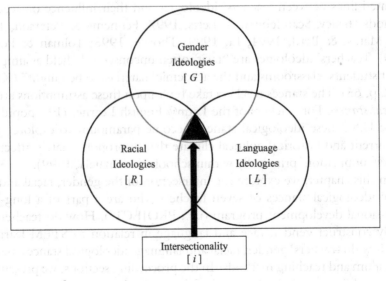

Source: Author

Second, racial ideologies (*R*) are an interpretive repertoire focused on *dominant racial ideologies* and *critical alternative racial ideologies* (Bonilla-Silva, 2010). *Critical alternative racial ideologies* challenge the racial order. For example, a PROJECT teacher challenged learners' notion that homeless African-American people simply do not work because they are lazy. Lastly, language ideologies (*L*) are a set of representations through language filled with cultural meaning for particular communities (Cameron, 2011). Themes across the literature are "where and how language originated, why languages differ from one another and what that means, how children learn to speak, and how language should properly be used" (Cameron, 2011, p. 583). Two language ideological stances are *English-Only*, where all materials and instruction are in English, and *heteroglossia*, where multiple languages are valued and used. In essence, this framework guided our selection and interpretation of the data set.

PROJECT

PROJECT targets K-8 teachers of ELs (Razfar, 2007). Over a seven-year span, 70 teachers participated in PROJECT. Teachers applied for acceptance. Consideration was given to teachers who had ELs in their classroom, were a part of a cohort of teachers (three or more at a school), and demonstrated an interest in conducting an action research project. Cross content and cross grade collaborations were encouraged. Therefore, in this chapter teachers of various subject area expertise and grade levels are included since teachers worked as cohorts. Over the course of 2½–3 years, teachers pursued an English as a Second Language/Bilingual Endorsement or Approval, master's degree and conducted a year-long action research project. Action research is research that educators conduct to solve their own problems and to improve their practice (McKernan, 1996).

During the action research portion of PROJECT, teachers developed, executed and analyzed three, four-week curricular units that drew on students' funds of knowledge (FoK) and integrated STEM concepts and literacy. Moll and González (1994) define FoK as "historically accumulated and culturally developed bodies of knowledge and skills essential for household or individual functioning and well-being" (p. 443). Teachers utilized tools grounded in research and theory to guide the planning, executing and analyzing steps for each unit. PROJECT is grounded in learning theories, is design based, and encourages teachers to see the intersection of FoK, STEM, gender, race and language.

In this chapter, we focus on cohorts of teachers at two K-8 public schools in the Midwest—Werth and Nugent. The demographics of Werth are 453 students enrolled with 89.6% Latin@, 7.5% Black, 1.5% White and 0.9% Asian. The population of Nugent is 1340 students enrolled with 98% Latin@, 1.1% African-American and 0.9% White. Teachers at Werth are Kamala, Bianca and Jesus. Teachers at Nugent are Aubrey, Candace, Maria and Jessica. Five teachers are Latin@, one is White and one is Pakistani (Table 6.1). Furthermore, six teachers are females and one teacher is male. Teaching experience ranges from 3 years to 20 years. All teachers speak English; six are bilingual. Three teachers teach 6th/7th grade language arts; one 7th/8th grade mathematics; one 5th grade science; one 4th grade general education; and one 2nd grade general education. Each classroom has at least two ELs and at least 90% Latin@s.

Table 6.1. Teacher demographics

Name	Race/ Ethnicity	Gender	School	Subject/ Grade	Years of Teaching Experience	Language(s) Spoken
Kamala	Pakistani	Female	Werth	6th/7th grade language arts	12 years	Urdu; English
Bianca	Latina	Female	Werth	7th/8th grade mathematics	12 years	Spanish; English
Jesus	Latino	Male	Werth	4th grade general education	20 years	Spanish; English
Aubrey	Latina	Female	Nugent	6th/7th grade language arts	3 years	Spanish; English
Candace	White	Female	Nugent	6th/7th grade language arts	10 years	English
Maria	Latina	Female	Nugent	5th grade science	5 years	Spanish; English
Jessica	Latina	Female	Nugent	2nd grade general education	3 years	Spanish; English

Source: Authors

Methods and Analysis

Data Sources

We conducted a qualitative, multiple case study (Yin, 2009). Data sources consist of video of classroom observations (9 per teacher), instructional materials for those lessons observed, teacher field notes (9 per teacher), researcher field notes (total of 63), individual reports (3 per teacher), group reports (total of 6), transcripts of weekly meetings (total of 50), focus group interviews (total of 8) and final reports (1 per teacher). We triangulated our data by drawing from multiple data sources during various points of the study. For example, weekly meetings and instructional materials took place before the implementation of each curricular unit. Video of classroom observations and teacher and researcher field notes were completed during each curricular unit. Lastly, individual reports, group reports, focus group interviews and final reports were completed at the culmination of each curricular unit.

For each of the three curricular units, the research team video recorded three lessons of approximately 1 hour each. This resulted in 63 hours of video recordings. Teachers and researchers provided field notes for each lesson. Each teacher analyzed the data they collected for each unit and wrote an individual report. Questions included: "Identify evidence of learning from the sociocultural point of view" and "What things would you change?" As a cohort, teachers produced a group report for each unit. Questions included: "Have the learning outcomes been achieved? If so, what is the evidence?" and "What missed opportunities for expansion did you identify?" A researcher met with a cohort of teachers on a weekly basis to discuss the progress of the curricular units. These meetings were audio recorded and transcribed. Focus group interviews were conducted throughout the action research project, semi structured and ranged in time from 1 to 1½ hours each. Among the questions were language questions (e.g., "how is your thinking of language changing?"), teaching questions (e.g., "have your views of teaching math and science changed") and action research questions (e.g., "what do you see as key issues or challenges in conducting action research?"). The final reports were completed at the end of the action research project. Teachers worked with the researcher to analyze data collected over the course of the three curricular units and to produce a publishable quality final report. The length of these final reports ranged from 45 to 61 pages each.

Analysis of Data

Drawing on the literature on gender, racial and language ideologies informed how we approached our data set. PROJECT encouraged teachers to see an intersection of gender, race and language; while researchers identified episodes in the data that showed this intersection. We developed qualitative codes from the data set, informed by the literature. Our codes ranged from concrete and topical categories (e.g., multiple language use, English only) to more abstract, conceptual categories (e.g., fragmentation of gender, invisibility of race). We coded through the data and determined the frequency of each code. By looking at the frequency of each code, we were able to recognize larger themes across the data set. After coding through the data set, another researcher coded part of the data set. This process allowed for interrater reliability (Suter, 2011), where we discussed any conflicting coding, until we achieved at least a 95% interrater reliability. We focused on those episodes in the data set that were coded as indexing an intersectionality of gender, racial and language ideological stances.

Findings

In this section, we highlight examples of the most recurrent themes— *egalitarian* and *anti-sexist* gender ideological stances, *critical alternative* racial ideological stance, and *English-Only* and *heteroglossia* language ideological stances. We explore examples from two case study teachers—Kamala and Aubrey. These teachers' examples were chosen because (1) they are both 6th/7th grade language arts teachers struggling to move to integrative curricular units and (2) the data for these two teachers were very rich to explore these ideological stances. These findings will help us to highlight the importance of teachers as reflexive of their ideological stances.

Ideological Stances in Curriculum

Academic Subject Areas and Instructional Materials

The curriculum, both school and non-school, shapes the worldview of individuals (Schubert, Schubert, Thomas, & Carroll, 2002). This worldview is "a living theory that guides [learners'] functioning, that embodies their information and misinformation about the world, how it works, and how to relate to it" (Schubert *et al.*, 2002, p. 500). PROJECT teachers were challenged to extract their learners' knowledge base and connect this non-school curriculum with the school curriculum. Here we refer to school curriculum as the academic subject areas (e.g., science, mathematics) and instructional materials. Non-school curriculum refers to learners' FoK. For Werth, teachers had benchmarks and standards that learners were required to meet, although the school did not have a scripted curriculum [weekly meeting, Werth]. Nugent also had benchmarks, and the school had particular programs/practices in place, such as Think Through Math, Stride Academy for Learning, Accelerated Reader, etc. [final report, Aubrey].

Principal, Interest, and Rate

The most recurrent themes for Werth were an *egalitarian* gender ideological stance, *critical alternative* racial ideological stance and *English-Only* language ideological stance. Kamala, Bianca and Jesus varied in how often and in what contexts diverse people (e.g., gender and race) were represented in curricular choices. During a unit on *the Great Depression and Cost of Living*, Kamala provided learners with a handout entitled "Borrowing Money Today: Simple Interest." All instructional materials were in English, indexing an *English-Only* language ideological stance. The handout consisted of an explanation of principal, interest, and rate and word problems. Kamala incorporated familiar names of Latin@ learners and teachers into the word problems, indexing a *critical alternative* racial ideological stance. There were 15 characters within these 10 problems. Of the 15 characters, 12 (or 80%) were male characters (e.g., Antonio, Adam, Daniel, Brian) and 3 (or 20%) were female characters (e.g., Anna, Amanda). During a video recorded lesson, Kamala selected two mathematics problems for students to solve.

> 1. *Farmer Anthony is borrowing $1,000 from Kamala-Todd [pseudonym] Bank as an operating loan to purchase plow's from John Deers. The APR on the loan is 6%. He plans to pay the bank off in 1 lump sum after 9 months. How much will he be paying back?*
> 2. *Marty [pseudonym] buys a pair of Jordans (Adult Size) for $159 at Foot Locker and charges it on his Visa credit card. Visa charges 21% interest. He decides to pay a lump sum (all together) after 8 months. Draw your own conclusions. [instructional material, Kamala]*

Both problems 1 and 2 have male main characters. Kamala's intent was to incorporate the mathematics into her lessons and to make the mathematics problems meaningful to learners, for example with the inclusion of Jordans [weekly meeting, Werth]. By incorporating males and females into the problems (e.g., Farmer Anthony and Kamala-Todd in problem 1 and Marty in problem 2), although positioning males overwhelmingly as the "mathematicians" within these problems (e.g., Farmer Anthony in problem 1 and Marty in problem 2), Kamala indexed an *egalitarian* gender ideological stance. She reaffirmed traditional views of "masculine" versus "feminine" fields.

Biology or Social Construct

The most recurrent themes for Nugent were an *egalitarian* gender ideological stance, *critical alternative* racial ideological stance and *English-Only* language ideological stance. During a unit on *Culture and Race*, Aubrey had learners participate in an activity that would challenge the concept of "race." All instructional materials were in English, indexing an *English-Only* language ideological stance. Aubrey posed questions for learners to grapple with race as a social construct, rather than a scientific fact [final report, Aubrey]. Aubrey wrote:

> Class began with a journal write. Students had to answer the following questions:
>
> 1. What is race?
> 2. How can we tell what race someone is?
> 3. Is it important to know what race a person is?
> 4. Is race in our genes? Part of our biological make up?
>
> Students answered these questions in about 15 minutes. Then I explained how the sorting activity worked and had kids log onto the website http://www.pbs. org/race/002_SortingPeople/002_00-home.htm. Students were eager to begin. As they sorted I asked them to write some reflections on sorting that was too easy or too difficult. Then, at the same time, we checked our answers as a class and students were instantly talking about what they got wrong and why. [field note, Aubrey]

The sorting activity included photos of diverse people and labels of race/ethnicity. Learners were required to match the photos with the racial label. Aubrey discussed her challenge in that she "*wanted kids to know that there was no DNA strand that was labeled Asian, Hispanic, White, or Black,*" although, "*didn't have the scientific background to teach it correctly*" [final report, Aubrey]. Aubrey's attempt to centralize race as a social construct rather than a scientific biological fact, indexed a *critical alternative* racial ideological stance. The online sorting activity also included an equal representation of males and females. This inclusion indexed an *egalitarian* gender ideological stance.

Ideological Stances in Teaching Methods

The Organization of Learning and Language Use

Teaching methods, in specific the organization of learning and language use, play a key role in the dynamics of the classroom space. Teachers sort and organize students and learning into more manageable groups and tasks (Schubert *et al.*, 2002; Streitmatter, 1994). This organization of learning includes: (1) how the activities are set up (e.g., individual, group, partner), (2) time dedicated to each mode of learning (e.g., teacher authority, conversational), (3) how students are seated (e.g., gendered grouping, EL grouping) and (4) roles students take up (e.g., assigned as note taker, expert role). Furthermore, the language used in classrooms conveys messages to students. These messages have implications for the dynamic of learning (Streitmatter, 1994).

Cost of Living and Division of Labor

The most recurrent themes for Werth were an *anti-sexist* gender ideological stance, *critical alternative* racial ideological stance and *heteroglossia* language ideological stance. Kamala, Bianca and Jesus made intentional moves in organizing learners. They were also cognizant of their and their learners' language use. Kamala encouraged learners to use their home language (in this case Spanish) and even repeated some key terms learners used. This practice indexed a *heteroglossia* language ideological stance. Kamala's way of grouping learners by mixed-gender indexed an *anti-sexist* gender ideological stance. However, this grouping had an unforeseen consequence. During a unit on *the Great Depression and Cost of Living*, learners explored the cost of living and working on minimum wage. Traditional gender roles came up related to the division of labor. Since only one learner from each partnership was going to work, in mixed-gendered partnerships, the male learner tended to be labeled the breadwinner.

> I think there was a lot of gender stereotypes going on. Especially when we were doing the, what can you afford in the 1920s. The division of labor. Especially if a boy and girl were grouped together on purpose. Well you're going to stay home because one person is going to work. So I'm going to make the money. The boy would make the money. And I think some things were said, "oh we can't afford that." So somebody's, Edward said to his partner and he brought it up to Melanie, which they were dating at the time ironically. And he's like, "you know, you need to go out and get a job I can't make all the money." It was interesting how they decided that he was going to go work and he decided that he was going to be the one to get that $5 a day job. [focus group interview, Werth]

Kamala addressed these misconceptions about gender and the division of labor by providing learners with counter-examples. She saw this as particularly important since women at home and men at work was common for this working-class Latin@ community [weekly meeting, Werth]. While respecting the culture of the learners and still challenging them to think otherwise of the division of labor, Kamala indexed a *critical alternative* racial ideological stance.

Scale for 6 Million

The most recurrent themes for Nugent were an *egalitarian* gender ideological stance, *critical alternative* racial ideological stance and *heteroglossia* language ideological stance. Aubrey, Candace, Maria and Jessica maintained the same mixed-gendered grouping throughout. For Aubrey and Maria, there was more of a focus on grouping ELs by mixed proficiency and academic ability. For example, Aubrey had a learner who was newly arrived from Mexico. She sat him with a learner who was fluent in both Spanish and English. The bilingual learner was key to the newly arrived learner understanding what was happening in the classroom.

During a unit on *Culture and Race*, Aubrey introduced the 6 Million Project—"*a math/art lesson to commemorate the 6 million people killed in the Holocaust*" [individual report, Aubrey]. Aubrey asked learners to pick their own design and medium for representing the number of people who were victims of the Holocaust [weekly meeting, Nugent]. Learners chose a scale and provided symbolism for their choices in materials. Learners made cross curricular connections. One example is a group of learners who drew two triangles on a poster paper—a smaller triangle inside a larger triangle—to represent those killed in the Holocaust [final report, Aubrey]. They filled the outer triangle with pennies, where 1 penny was equal to 15,000 people. The outer 15,000 pennies had stickers on them, representing the children who were killed. The pennies, to scale, totaled up to 1.5 million children and 4.5 million adults. Aubrey further explained:

> The students chose the shape of a triangle to represent individuals that were homosexuals, which were also killed during the Holocaust. They also used pennies to represent the value of individuals. We value money but we tend to toss out the pennies. While people's lives are valued, the Nazi's chose to devalue the lives of those they killed. [final report, Aubrey]

Aubrey incorporated the Holocaust and learners' understanding of the significant number of people killed because of ethnicity, which indexed a *critical alternative* racial ideological stance. Furthermore, Aubrey discussed the experiences of men, women and children in the Holocaust, indexing an *egalitarian* gender ideological stance. Learners were encouraged to use their home language (in this case Spanish) in discussions and Aubrey provided select learners with a further explanation in Spanish. This practice indexed a *heteroglossia* language ideological stance. Aubrey and her learners came to the conclusion that:

> By working with the numbers and creating a visual representation students really were forced to think about those numbers in more realistic terms. I think that for them and honestly me, this was a huge eye opener. I honestly told them, wow, I know that it's 6 million, and that's a lot, but you don't understand how many that is until you can really see what a million looks like. [final report, Aubrey]

Discussion and Recommendations

The findings of this study highlight the importance of teachers as active participants in their development. The intersection of FoK of learners and STEM concepts is as important as teachers' awareness of their gender, racial and language ideological stances. Here we provide recommendations for long-term professional development of teachers of Latin@ ELs. These recommendations are from PROJECT teachers, as well as our own. First, action research should be a central part of professional development. Aubrey recognized action research as *"research on my actions"* where teachers can *"analyze the elements of the lesson to duplicate"* what went well, as well as ensure that *"aspects that need improvement are met with a concrete plan"* [final report, Aubrey]. Second, cross-grade, content, and university-school collaborations are key. Aubrey found that by collaboration:

> We were able to hammer out concrete ideas to help one another integrate our curriculums and align them to a specific theme. We shared our successes and gained much needed serfdom and provided praises. We shared our failures and sought suggestions leaving the meetings confident to try again. It was during these discussions that we were able to draw connections across content and grade levels. [final report, Aubrey]

Third, teachers should be encouraged to integrate curricular units. This integration should include, but not be limited to STEM concepts and FoK. Werth school recommended that for the first unit teachers should:

> Elicit funds of knowledge to help them create a picture of the student body. This can be conducted through home visits, surveys, and discussions to help build a foundation for a curriculum that encompasses our students' [FoK]. [final report, Werth teachers]

Furthermore, they suggest that "*We must redirect our thinking and place importance on how students can practice investigative mathematics that they may encounter in their lives by problematizing, analyzing and criticizing it*" [final report, Werth teachers].

Lastly, throughout the action research process, researchers need to guide teachers in understanding how and in what contexts gender, race and language are or are not addressed. For example, we found variations in teachers' ideological stances across units, across lessons, and even across time frames/activities within a lesson. This finding is in alignment with Wood's (2013) study, which focused on the micro identities that became apparent in moment-to-moment positioning. In this chapter, we presented the most recurrent themes for two school cohorts a part of PROJECT. It is important to acknowledge that the messages, both implicit and explicit, that are conveyed to learners are important for STEM learning. In relation to curriculum, these messages were conveyed in (1) the content of the materials presented, (2) language the materials were presented in, and (3) the way certain racial and gendered groups were portrayed within these materials. In relation to teaching methods, these messages were conveyed in (1) how learners were seated, (2) whose input was valued, and (3) how the teacher and learners were positioned. Therefore, gender, race and language need to be a part of the discussion.

Notes

1. This study expands on the dissertation work of Torres, Z. (2015). *Three teachers' language, gender, and racial ideologies in practice in the English Learner classroom* (Doctoral dissertation). Retrieved from ProQuest Dissertations and Theses.
2. Latin@ refers to a population in the U.S. context with roots in Cuba, Mexico, Puerto Rico, South or Central America, or other Spanish speaking or Spanish-influenced cultures. The Latin@ population in this study is predominantly of Mexican descent.
3. All names are pseudonyms.

References

Bailey, B. L., Scantlebury, K., & Letts, W. J. (1997). It's not my style: Using disclaimers to ignore gender issues in science. *Journal of Teacher Education, 48*(1), 29–36.

Bonilla-Silva, E. (2010). *Racism without racists: Color-blind racism & racial inequality in contemporary America* (3rd ed.). Lanham, MD: Rowman & Littlefield Publishers, Inc.

Breiner, J. M., Harkness, S. S., Johnson, C. C., & Keehler, C. M. (2012). What is STEM? A discussion about conceptions of STEM in education and partnerships. *School Science and Mathematics, 112*(1), 3–11.

Cameron, D. (2011). Gender and language ideologies. In J. Coates & P. Pichler (Eds.), *Language and gender: A reader* (2nd ed., pp. 583–599). Malden, MA: Blackwell Publishers.

Fennema, F., & Peterson, P. (1985). Autonomous learning behaviors: A possible explanation of gender–related differences in mathematics. In L. Wilkinson & C. Marrett (Eds.), *Gender influences in classroom interaction* (pp. 17–35). Orlando, FL: Academic Press.

Kagan, D. M. (1992). Professional growth among preservice and beginning teachers. *Review of Educational Research, 62*(2), 129–169.

Lee, V., Marks, E., & Byrd, T. (1994). Sexism in single-sex and coeducational independent secondary school classrooms. *Sociology of Education, 67*(2), 92–120.

Li, Q. (1999). Teachers' beliefs and gender differences in mathematics: A review. *Educational Research, 41*(1), 63–76.

McKernan, J. (1996). *Curriculum action research: A handbook of methods and resources* (2nd ed.). London: Kogan Page Limited.

Moll, L., & González, N. (1994). Lessons from research with language minority children. *Journal of Reading Behavior, 26*(4), 439–456.

Razfar, A. (2007). *Transforming literacy, science, and math through action research (LSciMAct)*. Grant funded by U.S. Department of Education.

Schubert, W. H., Schubert, A. L. L., Thomas, T. P., & Carroll, W. M. (2002). *Curriculum books: The first hundred years* (2nd ed.). New York, NY: Peter Lang Publishing, Inc.

Spencer, R., Porche, M. V., & Tolman, D. L. (2003). We've come a long way—maybe: New challenges for gender equity in education. *Teachers College Record, 105*(9), 1774–1807.

Streitmatter, J. (1994). *Toward gender equity in the classroom: Everyday teachers' beliefs and practices.* Albany, NY: State University of New York Press.

Suter, W. N. (2011). *Introduction to education research: A critical thinking approach.* Thousand Oaks, CA: Sage Publications.

Thorne, B. (1993). *Gender play: Girls and boys in schools.* New Brunswick, NJ: Rutgers University Press.

Tolman, D. L., & Porche, M. V. (2000). The adolescent femininity ideology scale: Development and validation of a new measure for girls. *Psychology of Women Quarterly, 24*(4), 365–376.

Valenzuela, A. (1999). *Subtractive schooling: US Mexican youth and the politics of caring.* New York, NY: SUNY Press.

Wood, M. B. (2013). Mathematical micro-identities: Moment-to-moment positioning and learning in a fourth-grade classroom. *Journal for Research in Mathematics Education, 44*(5), 775–808.

Yin, R. K. (2009). *Case study research design and methods* (4th ed.). Thousand Oaks, CA: Sage Publications Inc.

Zhao, Y. (2009). *Catching up or leading the way: American education in the age of globalization.* Alexandria, VA: ASCD.

Part 3: Family and Community Involvement

7. Academy for Teacher Excellence: Promoting STEM Education and STEM Careers among Latinos through Service Learning

CYNTHIA LIMA, LORENA CLAEYS, AND PRANAV A. BHOUNSULE

Latino Underrepresentation in STEM

Increasing student enrollment in Science, Technology, Engineering and Mathematics (STEM) careers is considered one of the top priorities in education given the current shortage of STEM professionals, the expected growth in STEM occupations, and the relevance of STEM careers to maintain the US economically competitive (Museus, Palmer, Davis & Maramba, 2011; Taningco, Mathew, & Pachon, 2008). This priority is true for all students in the P-20 system, especially Latinos who are the fastest growing underrepresented population. The US Census Bureau predicts that the Latino population will double by 2050 (U.S. Census Bureau, 2014). Given the projected demographics and the shortage of STEM professionals, increasing the number of an underrepresented group in STEM who will constitute one third of the US population becomes a need. Which leads to the question, how do educators, policy makers, and other stakeholders across the US encourage Latinos to consider STEM careers? Different approaches are implemented to strengthen the STEM pipeline for Latinos, including targeted PK-12 STEM learning opportunities, access to more rigorous courses and dual enrollment (Contreras, 2011; Malcom, 2010). The Academy for Teacher Excellence (ATE) in the College of Education and Human Development (COEHD) at the University of Texas at San Antonio (UTSA) has conducted extensive work to strengthen the STEM pipeline for Latinos, for instance, providing service learning (SL) opportunities for undergraduate students. In this chapter, we first present an overview of the different SL efforts conducted by the ATE to strengthen the STEM pathways for Latinos; then we present the analysis and results of the impact of SL on academic and informal learning experience of two cohorts of Engineering undergraduates who conducted SL in Robotics clubs.

Pathways to Increase Latinos Participation in STEM

ATE's major focus is to create pathways to increase Latinos participation in STEM careers, specifically in STEM education. To achieve this goal, ATE has established strengths-based collaboration efforts with colleges across UTSA, in addition to public school districts, community colleges, and community organizations through informal learning opportunities for young learners— protégés. ATE aims to create a research-based model for enhancing and increasing protégés STEM awareness, knowledge, and aspirations by engaging teacher candidates and other undergraduate majors as mentors, promoters, and ambassadors in after-school informal learning experiences; which include: La *Clase Mágica (Magical Class-Bicultural-Bilingual Technology based after-school program)* (Flores, Vásquez, & Clark, 2014), *Nepohualtzitzin*-Ethnomatematics (Prieto, Claeys, & Lara González, 2015) and Robotics clubs (Schuetze, Claeys, Flores, & Sczeck, 2014). In general, the informal learning clubs, provide opportunities to teacher candidates—*aspirantes*, and other UTSA undergraduates from across departments in various colleges to engage in field experiences and/or SL opportunities for mentoring and promoting STEM education and STEM-related careers among. Important to note is that during the 2015–2016 academic year, 66% of the 710 undergraduate students participating in one of the three SL opportunities described were Latino.

ATE's primary collaborators in the creation and implementation of informal learning clubs are high need schools with large numbers of Latinos and English learners. Other ATE partner community organizations with a shared mission to promote a college going culture and facilitate access to college among Latinos and other underrepresented youth in our community include: the Alamo STEM Workforce Coalition, BiblioTech, Cáfe College, *College en la Comunidad*, Hispanic Network of Texas—Latinas in Progress Programs, Latinas SciGirls, the Martinez Women's Center, and San Antonio College Access Network. Over the years, ATE has partnered with these and other organizations to collaborate and leverage resources to reach out to young Latino learners and their families through information sessions, university sponsored events, informal learning experiences, and parent-family summits.

Service Learning and Field Experience as Pathways to STEM Education

In creating and strengthening pathways for STEM Education, ATE collaborates with the Department of Bilingual-Bicultural Studies (BBL) and the Department of Mechanical Engineering to engage bilingual *aspirantes* and other teacher candidates in field experience, and undergraduate students in service learning. Service learning (SL) is an approach utilized to engage *aspirantes* and other undergraduate majors in the three informal learning clubs to mentor protégés and to promote a college going culture in underserved communities. ATE creates innovative transdisciplinary SL opportunities where noneducation majors work with *aspirantes* to become mentors to protégés. Participating mentors get hands-on experiences working with protégés in elementary and middle schools that are highly populated by Latino and English learners. As a result, undergraduates' community SL experiences are connected to the local needs, which often strengthen the STEM knowledge and skills of future educators, in addition to promoting STEM education and STEM-related fields in schools located in underserved communities. With the many academic, financial, and personal demands that college students often face, specifically Latinos, ATE provides the following support services as part of the SL experience: textbook lending, college and career guidance, and psychosocial emotional support. The research-based informal learning experiences designed by ATE (Claeys, Lares, & Flores, 2016) allows *mentors* to serve the community, especially Latinos learners, at the same time that they are provided with guidance to enhance their education and career journeys.

In addition to students volunteering to participate in SL, ATE collaborates with the College of Engineering to integrate SL as an option in one course. Robotics SL is implemented after-school in a semi-structured informal learning environment, which provides opportunities for reflection for the participating Engineering mentors. The First Lego League (FIRST) drives the structure and rigor of the Robotics club since participants spend most of the time learning, preparing, researching, and strategizing for the annual challenge at the FIRST Competition. Schuetze *et al.* (2014) found that there is a better understanding in STEM, in addition to the reciprocal learning benefit for all undergraduates involved and protégés when they work in preparation for the FIRST Competition. Participation in the robotics club not only provides affirmation toward STEM education and career goals, but also fosters aspirational and self-efficacy on everyone engaged (2014). Bhounsule, Chaney, Claeys, and Manteufel (2017) also found academic benefits among mechanical engineering undergraduates who engaged in a SL experience. They indicated that benefits included a letter grade difference, improved communication, presentation skills, and a sense of satisfaction to be able to give back to the community, in addition to getting young learners interested in engineering. These findings are consistent with the results of the meta-analysis in SL conducted by Conway, Amel, and Gerwien (2009), in which SL experiences were found to have a moderate impact on students' outcomes. We believe that SL opportunities address the national need to increase the ethnic and gender representation of professionals in STEM when *aspirantes* and other undergraduates serve as mentors to protégés in underserved communities.

The field experiences for *aspirantes* are part of: BBL 4063-Bilingual Approaches to Content-Based Learning and BBL 3403-Cultural and Linguistic Equity for Schooling in which *aspirantes* mentor elementary and middle level protégés *in La Clase Mágica* and/or the Nepohualtzitzin-Ethnomathematics informal learning clubs. Over the years, these type of field experiences have offered *aspirantes* and protégés opportunities to learn in a playful informal manner, not only culture, language, content, and multiliteracy skills, but also the ancient and modern technological tools such as the nepohualtzitzin, computers, and mobile devices. Also, the engagement of *aspirantes* in these field experiences have served to strengthen, not only the STEM pathways and a college going culture, but the long-term partnerships between UTSA and public schools in our community.

Service Learning: Examining Student Learning
The SL experience developed by ATE is based on the core elements of SL that have been identified in the literature and Engeström's expansive learning framework (Engeström, 2009). The term "service-learning" has been used in different research studies with different meanings. According to Furco (2003), SL has been defined as a program, pedagogy, experience, and a philosophy. The diversity of the terms has its origin on the implementation approaches and conceptualization of SL, in addition to the fact that SL happens in specific settings with different foci. Nevertheless, Howard (2003) identifies *community service* as the element that distinguishes SL from other types of experiential learning. Considering community as a key element, ATE embraces SL as "a teaching and learning strategy that integrates meaningful community service with instruction and reflection to enrich the learning experience, teach civic responsibility, and strengthen communities" (National Service-Learning Clearing House, 2011).

Research demonstrates that SL does enrich the learning experience of students, promotes civic responsibility; and that reflection is needed to enhance SL experiences and community service (Astin, Vogelgesang, Ikeda, & Yee, 2000; Conway *et al.*, 2009). Undergraduates who participate in the SL experience immerse themselves in the informal learning clubs at a public school. Each club is representative of the community and the school culture in terms of the structure set by the trained volunteer sponsors who lead the sessions, including the enhanced learning opportunities that learners acquire and transfer to the classroom, among others. Each session is different from the previous as protégés prepare for the annual First Challenge, putting together new strategies to plan and prepare for the competition. The authors consider that the informal learning opportunities fostered through the Robotics clubs are constantly changing, thus consistent with Engeström expansive theory of expansive learning, which is learning acquired in organizations that are not stable (1987, 2009). The theory of expansive learning (Engeström, 2009) "focuses on learning processes in which the very subject of learning is transformed from isolated individuals to collectives and networks" (p. 5). Thus, all participants interact with a community around a common challenge to be solved, to create a new notion of the interactions. The theory draws from the work of Vygotsky and Leont'ev among others whose concept of the zone of proximal development, and object-oriented theory respectively serve as foundations for expansive learning. As a result, Robotic clubs provide participants the space in which learning occurs as a community of learners interacting to solve problems using different tools and instruments leading to expansive learning and the construction of a new collective and network.

Methodology

Participants

ATE promotes SL and recruits undergraduate participants across UTSA Colleges through classroom presentations, information sessions, a promotional video, and email communication with faculty. In this study, we examine the academic and career impact of the SL program on two student cohorts who served as mentors in the Robotics clubs. The first cohort includes students from various colleges who voluntarily signed up to participate in a two-semester SL experience. The second cohort is a group of Mechanical Engineering majors who participated in a one-semester SL experience as part of an elective class. Mentors who signed up to do SL in the Robotics club during the 2015–2016 academic year worked with students in grades 2–8 in high need schools located across San Antonio, TX. Each school counts with volunteers in charge of sponsoring, planning, and organizing the Robotics informal learning club to include protégés from different grade levels to work collaboratively in small groups with the mentors.

Cohort 1: Two-semesters of SL. The first cohort considered for the analysis included 41 mentors recruited from the College of Education and Human Development, College of Science, and College of Engineering. Participants ethnicity included 65% Latino, 19% Caucasian, 10% African-American, and 6% other; and gender 46% females and 54% males. The SL commitment required the completion of 10 hours per semester at one of the 15 high need public elementary and middle schools located across five independent school districts. The average student demographics for the school districts was 74% Latino and over 40% English learners.

Cohort 2: One-semester of SL. The second cohort considered for this analysis included 33 students from a Mechanical Engineering class who opted to conduct SL (10 weekly sessions of 60–90 minutes) to receive 25% of their final grade. Mentors were learning robotics using LEGO Mind storms with their protégés and in their own university Robotics class. The cohort was 39% Latino, 36% Caucasian, 12% Asian-Pacific Islander and 10% African-American; 12% female and 88% male. Undergraduate students in this Cohort served as mentors to protégés in 10 high need public elementary schools located across four independent school districts.

Research Design

We used a mixed method approach to examine students' perceptions and different experiences during their participation in the SL. A survey (Crano & Brewer, 2002), and a phenomenological approach (Marshall & Rossman, 2014) were implemented to identify the impact of the robotics SL on students self-perceptions of (a) the benefits of the comprehensive technological, counseling and mentoring support provided by ATE on their academic success, (b) the extent to which the program promoted development of skills needed for college success (e.g., teaching and leadership skills), and (c) the success of the SL program in fostering awareness of the need of STEM learning opportunities for underrepresented students (see Table 7.1). Given the focus of the study on the holistic learning experience and impact of the SL on all students who participated in the program, the cross-sectional survey was implemented online at the end of the SL experience to both cohorts.

One of the challenges of SL research is the lack of instruments that can apply to diverse approaches of SL implementation. Thus, ATE researchers designed a 24-item survey to be implemented after students complete the SL experience. The survey addresses the three aspects listed in the previous paragraph, collects students' background information (e.g., gender, ethnicity, teaching experience), and includes a set of open-ended questions to allow undergraduate mentors to reflect on their motivation to volunteer for the SL experience and their expectations. The first set of survey questions are intended for students to reflect on the impact that support services students can access as part of the SL program, for instance: book and technology lending, counseling services, mentoring, workshop sessions and guidance to navigate the educational system; including awareness of and preparation for graduation requirements. These questions also aim to elicit students' knowledge of how the provided services support their academic success and persistence in college. The second set of questions addresses the SL objective of promoting undergraduate students' development of academic content and skills relevant to their major, including self-perceptions of the STEM knowledge and skills developed. The open-ended questions at the end of the survey address the initial motivation and expectations of students. According to expansive learning, the learner develops new knowledge and applies it in practice. Thus, the open-ended questions would constitute a window to examine how participating in the SL experience helped students develop a new knowledge of what it means to be a mentor and what it means to do Engineering in the context of problem solving with young Latino learners in underrepresented public schools.

For this study, we used a representative sample (n=15) of both cohorts (46% White, 29% Hispanic). The selection of this sample was based on the completeness of the surveys submitted. Given that the survey is answered online, the researchers are not able to identify the reasons why students partially completed or did not complete the survey.

To support students' reflective participation in the program, and further our understanding of the student learning that happens in the informal learning club setting and experiences as Robotics club mentors, Cohort 2 responded to a longitudinal set of open-ended questions. The set of 9 reflection questions were administered throughout the semester.

Table 7.1. Research design for the robotics service learning 2015–2016 cohorts

Cohort Number	Type of Service-Learning Experience	Data Collection Methods
Cohort 1 (n=41)	Service—learning experience (2 semes-ters—20 hours)	- Survey answered at the end of SL
Cohort 2 (n=33)	Service learning for credit (10 weekly sessions of 60–90 minutes)	- Survey answered at the end of SL - Structured reflections (Set of 2–3 questions answered monthly during SL experience)

Source: Authors

Data from the survey was analyzed descriptively to examine the frequency of responses, which revealed: (1) the extent to which the comprehensive set of services provided by ATE (e.g., book lending, coaching, mentoring, etc.) as part of the SL experience have an impact in students' academic lives, (2) the various dimensions of students' transformations, for instance, whether students became advocates or might become future advocates of STEM careers, changes in their conceptions about what it means to be a mentor, and (3) their initial perceptions and motivation to volunteer for SL in the Robotics club. Given that the set of questions related to initial perceptions and motivations were open-ended, responses were transcribed and coded for emergent themes (Miles, Huberman, & Saldaña, 2013). Data from structured reflections was transcribed and coded for themes that reflected their construction of their roles as mentors in the context of problem solving with young Latino learners in underrepresented public schools.

Results and Discussion

Survey Results

Self-Perceptions of the Benefits of the Program. The comprehensive set of services SL mentors have access to when volunteering were found to be an important academic support for 20%, who reported that they could not have been able to complete their college degree without the services provided. From this group of students, 80% identified the experience as an opportunity to learn about their community and give back. In addition, almost 50% of this group indicated that the project staff provided personal and academic support when needed. The survey indicates that the comprehensive set of services provided by ATE (textbook lending, career guidance and psychosocial emotional support) to undergraduate students involved in the SL experience constituted a personal and academic support system that is key to achieve completion of their college degrees and to overcome challenges inherent to being a student. Given that one of the main motivations of the students to serve as mentors to young learners is the desire to be an inspiration and a role model for them, having a support system behind them can potentially foster their sense of community.

Development of Knowledge and Skills. We consider students expressed rationales to serve as mentors in the Robotics club relevant because they indicate undergraduate students' confidence about how to teach and what it means to be a mentor in SL. Nevertheless, these two conceptions changed as mentors engaged with their protégés, as shown by the finer analysis of Cohort II structured reflections. We analyzed students' rationales to sign up to serve as mentors in the Robotics club for emergent themes to identify what motivates students to engage in the SL experience. Four categories emerged from the analysis. The first category, *support students to go into STEM careers*, includes responses addressing the desire to provide support to underrepresented students and promote careers related to Robotics. The second category, *be an inspiration to young learners*, represents students' interest in becoming an inspiration for all learners. The interest in inspiriting is rooted in undergraduates' previous experiences with adult mentors, or previous experiences serving as mentors in ATE's SL program. Another group of students expressed that SL was a good opportunity to work with young learners in informal settings. Finally, a group of students were motivated to be mentors in the Robotics club to learn about robotics. Some of the students who volunteered for the SL were from the COEHD, and were not likely to be familiar with Robotics. College of Engineering mentors showed confidence in their content knowledge and their ability to teach protégés. However, as mentors engaged in the Robotics clubs with their protégés, they identified various aspects of teaching and skill development that required changing to successfully interact with protégés. This is shown in the survey results indicating that 66% of the students expressed that they had opportunities to develop skills that are relevant to their career, including teaching and leadership. In addition to developing skills, students also reported an increased interest in STEM careers.

Awareness of the Need of STEM for Underrepresented Students. Overall, results of the survey for both Cohorts indicate that SL has positive effects on more than 60% of the mentors as they reported developing awareness of the need to advocate for quality STEM education for Latinos, low income, and other underrepresented students. These outcomes are similar to the ones that have been reported in the literature as discussed by Celio, Durlak, and Dymnicki (2011). The fact that students reported increased awareness of the need of STEM learning opportunities for Latinos and underrepresented students, learning of knowledge and skills, and the comprehensive set of services provided by ATE were considered fundamental for their academic success, indicating that ATE's SL program generated positive outcomes in at least 60% of the students who responded the survey. This is consistent with the positive academic outcome reported by Bhounsule *et al.* (2017) for Cohort II students. The structured reflections of Cohort 2 provided a more detailed insight into mentors learning as they engaged with their protégés.

Structured Reflections

Development of Knowledge and Skills. Two of the five categories that emerged from the analysis of Cohort II structured reflections are similar to the ones expressed by both cohorts in the Survey: the desire to be an inspiration to young learners and learn about Robotics. The third category represents the mentors' desire to support protégés of Robotics knowledge. Mentors responses classified under this theme reflect their self-confidence in their engineering and technology knowledge, how they can use this resource to support the development of protégés' knowledge, and get them excited about robotics and technology. For instance, one of the mentors expressed: "I had never before taught kids about this kind of concepts. It taught me how to express my ideas to kids and teach them." Another mentor elaborates: "I feel like I have the opportunity to show the students how fun the field of engineering is...." A group of mentors selected the SL option because they already enjoyed teaching children. Finally, learning about student thinking emerged as the fifth category. Opposite to the desire of teaching and sharing their knowledge with students, mentors whose response is categorized under this theme expressed their interest in deepening their knowledge about how students solve Robotics problems. Responses to the survey and the responses to the structured reflections are consistent, and show that these cohorts of Engineering students were excited for the opportunity to share their knowledge and get students excited about their field of knowledge. As a result, mentors were serving as promoters of engineering careers and role models to protégés.

Overall, mentors showed confidence in their ability to teach students Robotics, or be an inspiration to students so they could go into STEM careers. However, initial assumptions of their knowledge about how to teach Robotics were challenged and modified as they engaged with protégés. Engaging in problem solving in an informal and expansive learning setting supported the transformation of mentors' self-perceptions, awareness of need for more Latinos in STEM, and Robotics knowledge. In the context of the informal learning Robotics club and in their roles as mentors, undergraduate students identified the need to further develop their Robotics and Engineering knowledge to be able to communicate core ideas to their protégés. Recognizing the need to deepen the knowledge and adapt it to serve the students is illustrated in the following reflection: "I think the most challenging aspect of being a mentor would be to convey what I know in ways the kids will understand." Even more, mentors modified their thinking to communicate ideas to students in the context of the problem. Thus, mentors are supporting the process of solving problems that might be also new for some of them. The knowledge mentors developed in this process is related to ways in which their content knowledge must be shaped to facilitate their protégés' problem solving process, and to solve the actual problem. The LEGO League challenge created a common space in which mentors and protégés interacted and co-constructed new knowledge in their respective roles as mentors and protégés. In terms of the expansive learning theory (Engeström & Sannino, 2010), the learning that happened for the mentors was twofold: constructing an identity as mentors, and constructing new meanings for the Robotics knowledge to facilitate the process of problem solving. A key aspect of undergraduate students development of a mentor identity and skills, was being able to develop a relationship with their protégés, for which they needed to develop effective communication skills. This relationship was considered necessary to also engage students in the problem-solving process. In general, mentors engaged in diverse interactions with their protégés, however one theme that was common to most of their reflections was being able to help students work through the challenge, which included providing hints, ideas, building teamwork skills and explaining content relevant to the problem.

Conclusion

The study presented in this chapter offers a finer grain analysis of one of the efforts conducted by the Academy for Teacher Excellence to increase Latinos representation in STEM by engaging Latino young learners—protégés in underrepresented communities and undergraduate mentors in informal learning opportunities. The research-based service-learning in an informal and expansive learning experience successfully supports the promising increase for Latino representation in STEM in different ways. First, by partnering with public schools located in lower income communities with high percentage of young Latino learners, provides awareness and access to STEM education and STEM careers. Second, it enhances the preparation of the Engineering student cohorts considered in this analysis—most of which are Latinos, by providing them with opportunities to deepen the content knowledge acquired in their coursework and expanding their academic and professional knowledge and skills through mentor–protégé interactions. From the expansive learning theory stance, strategizing for the annual competition creates the space in which mentors and protégés interact, leading to a mutual transformation of the community in which mentors and protégés are part of. Through their active engagement in this common space, it is evident that mentors and protégés benefited from the development of communication structures that facilitated the establishment of rapport, new conceptualizations of the Robotics content, and the creation of an identity as SL mentors for undergraduate students and as future STEM professionals for protégés.

Overall, we surmise that SL experience impacts both mentors and protégés by creating a community of learners in which both learn from each other coconstructing knowledge in a creative and innovative way. Solving real-world challenges presented by the First Lego League offers the exploration of scientific topics, thus increasing interest in STEM-related careers. Implications for university scholars and researchers including school administrators, educators and community stakeholders include collective networks of university-school-community partnerships to engage in research-practice partnerships to further explore the impact of service learning in underrepresented communities largely populated by young Latino learners in an effort to promote STEM education and STEM careers.

References

Astin, W., Vogelgesang, J., Ikeda, K., & Yee, A. (2000). How service learning affects Students. *Higher Education*. Paper 144. Retrieved from http://digitalcommons.unomaha.edu/slcehighered/144

Bhounsule, P., Chaney, D., Claeys, L., & Manteufel, R. (2017). *Robotics service learning for improving learning outcomes and increasing community engagement.* Proceedings of the 2017 American Society for Engineering Education (ASEE) Gulf-Southwest Section Annual Conference at The University of Texas at Dallas, Dallas, TX.

Celio, C. I., Durlak, J., & Dymnicki, A. (2011). A meta-analysis of the impact of service-learning on students. *Journal of Experiential Education, 34*(2), 164–181.

Claeys, L., Lares, K., & Flores, B. B. (2016). *Academy for teacher excellence: Expansive learning as innovative STEM informal learning opportunities.* Poster presented at the

Science & Mathematics Teaching Imperative (SMTI) National Conference, San Antonio, TX.

Contreras, F. (2011). *Achieving equity for Latino students: Expanding the pathway to higher education through public policy.* New York, NY: Teachers College Press.

Conway, J. M., Amel, E. L., & Gerwien, D. P. (2009). Teaching and learning in the social context: A meta-analysis of service learning's effects on academic, personal, social, and citizenship outcomes. *Teaching of Psychology, 36*(4), 233–245.

Crano, W. D., & Brewer, M. B. (2002). *Principles and methods of social research.* Mahwah, NJ: Taylor & Francis.

Engeström, Y. (1987). *Learning by expansion.* Helsinki: Orienta Konsultit.

Engeström, Y. (2009). *Expansive learning: Toward an activity-theoretical reconceptualization.* Retrieved from http://pagi.wikidot.com/engestrom-expansive-learning licensed under Creative Commons Attribution-NonCommercial-ShareAlike 3.0 License.

Engeström, Y., & Sannino, A. (2010). Studies of expansive learning: Foundations, findings and future challenges. *Educational research review, 5*(1), 1–24.

Flores, B. B., Vásquez, O. A., & Clark, E. R. (2014). *Generating transworld pedagogy: Re-imagining La Clase Mágica.* Lanham, MD: Lexington Publishers, Rowman Littlefield Publishing Group.

Furco, A. (2003). Issues of definition and program diversity in the study of service-learning. In S. H. Billig & A. S. Waterman (Eds.), *Studying service-learning: Innovations in education research methodology* (pp. 13–33). New York, NY: Routledge.

Howard, J. (2003). Service-learning research: Foundational issues. In S. H. Billig & A. S. Waterman (Eds.), *Studying service-learning: Innovations in education research methodology* (pp. 1–12). New York, NY: Routledge.

Malcom, L. E. (2010). Charting the pathways to STEM for Latina/o students: The role of community colleges. *New Directions for Institutional Research, 148.* doi:10.1002/ir.359 Retrieved from https://facstaff.necc.mass.edu/wp-content/uploads/2012/03/charting_the_pathways_to_stem_latina_students.pdf

Marshall, C., & Rossman, G. B. (2014). *Designing qualitative research.* Thousand Oaks, CA: Sage.

Miles, M. B., Huberman, A. M., & Saldaña, J. (2013). *Qualitative data analysis.* Thousand Oaks, CA: Sage.

Museus, S. D., Palmer, R. T., Davis, R. J., & Maramba, D. (2011). Special Issue: Racial and ethnic minority student success in STEM education. *ASHE higher education report, 36*(6), 1–140.

National Service-Learning Clearing House. (2011). *What is service-learning?* Retrieved from http://servicelearning.org/what-is-service-learning

Prieto, L., Claeys, L., & Lara González, E. (2015). Transnational alliances: La Clase Mágica-nepohualtzitzin ethnomatemathics club. *Journal of Latinos and Education, 14*(2), 125–134.

Schuetze, A., Claeys, L., Flores, B. B., & Sczeck, D. (2014). LCM as a community based expansive learning approach to STEM education. *International Journal for Research on Extended Education, 2*, 1–19.

Taningco, M. T. V., Mathew, A. B., & Pachon, H. P. (2008). STEM professions: Opportunities and challenges for Latinos in science, technology, engineering, and mathematics. A review of literature. *Tomás Rivera Policy Institute*.

U.S. Census Bureau. (2014). *Population projections.* Retrieved from https://www.census.gov/population/projections/data/national/2014.html

8. Math, Music, and Arts, a Community-Based Approach: Improving Outcomes for At-Risk Hispanic Students

BEVERLEY ARGUS-CALVO, CLAUDIA SALDAÑA CORRAL, AND OLGA M. KOSHELEVA

Introduction

Hispanics are the nation's largest minority group representing 16.4% of the population in the U.S. (Motel & Patten, 2012). According to data reported from the Pew Research Center (2015), "[as] of 2013, 28% of Mexican immigrants were the single largest source country for the nations' foreign born of the immigrant population" (p. 67), and have become the largest racial/ethnic minority group in the United States; as with other minority populations they suffer from educational disenfranchisements such as disproportional representation in special education, high dropout rates, educational underachievement in grades K–12, and inequitable access to and retention in college (APA, Presidential Task Force on Educational Disparities, 2012). Results reported by the National Assessment of Educational Progress (2009), indicate the mathematics proficiency in the United States is at alarmingly low levels: just one-third of eighth graders reach the proficient or better level. Although overall progress is evidenced for both White and Hispanic 4th and 8th graders, Hispanics, in general, still lag significantly behind their White counterparts (Murphey, Madill, & Guzman, 2017). As our nation becomes economically dependent on innovations from the fields of science, technology, engineering, and math (STEM) there is an urgency to increase proficiency skills for all Latin@ students to remain competitive in a modern economy (Murphey et al., 2017). Furthermore, a recently published report by the National Academies of Sciences, Engineering and Medicine (2017) indicates that one of the reasons that Latin@ and English Learners (ELs) children may not be meeting the national standards can be attributed to the varying opportunities that children experience due to the familial social and economic standing including access to skilled teachers and enriched educational opportunities. The NASEM (2017) report addresses how the struggles that children, parents, and family face as immigrants learning in different cultural environments impact their academic success. The need for schools situated in underresourced communities to recognize the cultural and human capital that marginalized communities unknowingly pose is critical when addressing the significant academic gaps identified for Hispanic students.

In spite of this grim picture, there are community-based programs where policies and practices embrace Hispanic school-age children, their families, schools, and community. This chapter presents how music and art can be used as mediating tools for elementary Hispanic students to construct cognitive, academic and social meanings through participation in Touching Lives of Children with Music (TLC), an afterschool community-based music and arts program.

Music and Arts-Based Programs

Music and arts-based programs have been proven to be beneficial for at-risk children for several reasons. First, according to the Facts and Figures Navigator prepared by Americans for the Arts (2015), "a student involved in the arts is four times more likely to be recognized for academic achievement" and "low-income students who are highly engaged in the arts are more than twice as likely to graduate college as their peers with no arts education" (p. 4). At the national level, academic progress is rooted in gains measured by test scores. Yet the fundamental activities that keep children's emotional and cognitive health in balance have greatly decreased (Heath, 2015). Specifically, during the era of No Child Left Behind Act school reform led to an increase of skill-based instruction in schools serving predominately low-income families living in underresourced communities.

Furthermore, Heath (2015) has strongly advocated for music and arts-based after-school programs that promote high learning demands for children in underresourced communities by establishing that learning that takes place in nonformal environments which she refers to as the third learning environment, "which takes place beyond the classroom and home is generally left unattended, minimally supported, and almost completely un-examined" (Heath, 2001, p. 10). She specifically addresses how children living in poverty and in underresourced communities benefit from programs such as *El Sistema* a community-based program based on Dr. Abreu's model (Wakin, 2012) for providing free classical music education to underserved and impoverished children of Venezuela. Third, children participating in either choral or instrumental music-based programs develop social emotional skills. These concepts have been studied by social, behavioral, cognitive, and neuroscientists (Heath, 2015). Empirical evidence that Social Emotional Learning (SEL) interventions are linked with increased academic outcomes and child well-being are reported by Zins, Weissberg, Wang, and Walberg (2004) and have been established as skills that lead to future adult success in children (Heath, 2015). Skills such as self-monitoring, self-efficacy, persistence, self-control, and social competence are skills children learn through participation in music and ensemble activities (Heath, 2015).

Relationship between Mathematics and Art

Art in itself is a broad term that can include visual arts such as painting, drawing, sculpture and design, architecture, music, crafts, and poetry (Sharp as cited in Björklund & Ahlskog-Björkman, 2017). Björklund and Ahlskog-Björkman (2017) state:

> Mathematics is a complex knowledge area, involving not only mathematical objects such as concepts, principles and symbols, but also procedures such as the skills needed to master these concepts, principles and symbols to solve problems both abstract and practical through measuring comparing, and calculating. (p. 6)

Furthermore, Björklund and Ahlskog-Björkman (2017) suggest that "learning mathematics leads to understanding meaning-making whereby art and aesthetical expression contribute to visualizing mathematical ideas" (p. 11). Research conducted to identify how math and art are related have yielded multiple results (Catterall, Dumais, & Hampden-Thompson, 2012). Specifically, recent studies by Willis (2016) and King (2016) show that there is an increase in test scores for students in elementary and middle school students who receive music education. Other studies identify that children involved in music education develop skills essential for life-long success acquired through their participation in music and arts-based programs (Heath, 2001).

Reiterating that art in itself is defined in broad terms and can take on different meanings, we refer to Booth's (2001) definition of art "to make stuff you care about" (p. 5). It is the process of learning not the end product in itself. In order for children to care about and make the cognitive and emotional connections with academic learning, foundations of SEL must be considered in any setting. Student engagement in third environments as defined by Heath (2001) (e.g., afterschool, extended learning, or extracurricular activities) enhances the learning process when directed toward individual learning and meaning-making between the interactions and communication amongst and between students, adults, and their environment.

Understanding the Community and Art in Context

Cultural Historical Activity Theory (CHAT) (Engeström, 2001; Welch, 2007; and Viera, 2017) serves as the theoretical framework for analyzing the data to understand how the complex and dynamic social contexts (the community) in which learning takes place are understood by the subjects involved in this study (e.g., the students, TLC teaching artists (n=6), program directors (n=2) community volunteers (various throughout the year), El Sol Symphony Orchestra (ESSO) staff (n=2), school staff, and parents). The activity theory analysis consists of the following: The context (e.g., schools, community settings including museums, performing arts centers, university setting), and the mediating artifacts (e.g., music instruction, performances), the division of labor (e.g., how is curriculum selected, internal organization of roles and responsibilities of students and staff), the rules (e.g., school, program, community organization policies), and the object of the activity (e.g., SEL, collective-musical skill development, nonformal learning of academic skills). As data continue to be analyzed, emerging activity theories represent the subjects and their contexts to better understand how students understand and make meaning of their learning experiences.

Following we discuss the community and TLC providing data that highlight the context of the study. Thereafter is a discussion that establishes the benefits of music and arts-based programs for vulnerable children living in underresourced communities, and the socioemotional skills identified in the research that leads to cognitive development and effective learning. We then present examples of how TLC's programming and related community-based field trip activities complement student understanding of mathematical concepts in nonformal learning environments while acquiring (SEL) skills.

Methods

Context

Located on the Rio Grande in the far western edge of Texas along the borders of Mexico and New Mexico, El Sol is a bustling urban area of over 800,000 people (U.S. Census Bureau, 2010), more than 81% of whom are Mexican in origin. El Sol's sister city in Mexico has a population of more than 1.5 million, making this the largest metropolitan area along the almost 1989 mile U.S.–Mexico border (Guest Life, 2017). More than 73% of El Sol's households speak Spanish as the language of preference at home. Over 23% of the families in El Sol fall below the federal poverty levels (U.S. Census Bureau, 2010).

Additionally, in the city of El Sol there are several school districts which includes El Sol Independent School District (ESISD) and Hacienda (ISD) which are part of the study. Understanding the social and emotional needs of children growing up in these vulnerable settings requires that programs purposefully enhance student learning in multiple contexts.

Touching Lives of Children through Music (TLC)

The mission of El Sol Symphony Orchestra (ESSO) is to assure that superior concert music is made available to entertain and educate the multicultural community of the greater El Sol region. It is also the only professional symphony within a 300-mile radius presenting a 9-month performance season. The ESSO has over 10 education and outreach programs that serve children and youth in the region. Committed to the expansion of its programs to the local youth, in 2013, in collaboration with El Sol ISD (ESISD), these institutions launched the first after-school program which was inspired by the El Sistema movement, whose intended outcomes are (a) to empower at-risk children, (b) to improve their sense of community and (c) improve a sense of opportunity through immersive music learning and performing. In 2015 the second TLC program was established in Hacienda ISD. TLC uses music and arts-based education as a vehicle for children to acquire valuable tools of teamwork, self-confidence, leadership, and academic success.

At this time TLC serves a total of seventy-five 3rd through 5th grade girls and boys at two different schools. Per capita income of El Barrio community is below $9000 per year and of Colonia is below $7600. The cultural make-up of both communities is over 98% Hispanic, of which approximately 90% speak only Spanish in the home. While El Barrio is a highly transient community, the Colonia is generational with families rarely venturing outside of the area. El Barrio's history, as an entry point into the U.S. from Mexico, contributes to 95% of the region's population being of Hispanic descent and 56% speaking little or no English, therefore putting the students in this specific area at an academic disadvantage.

The data presented in this chapter are a subset of a larger ethnographic study that aims to understand how music and art can be used as mediating tools for elementary Hispanic students to construct cognitive, academic and social meanings through participation in TLC. Data collection has been ongoing since 2016 and includes semi-structured and focus group interviews with teaching artists (n=5), students (n=10), parents (n=6), and museum of art docents (n=4). Monthly observations during programming, student performances (n=10), and field trip activities (4 museum visits and 1 visit to El Sol University (ESU) have been conducted and documented by a research team consisting of two PhD professors and a doctoral student, TLC teaching artists and staff. Student surveys have been collected and analyzed after each field trip and student performances (n=150 individual survey responses) and parent mid-term questionnaires (n=19) have been obtained. Data from these surveys provide written comments and reflections about participant experiences. Specifically, we present the case of a subset of the data collected and analyzed to date that demonstrates how mathematical concepts embedded in nonformal learning settings and how they are experienced and understood by the students.

At Border Elementary, any student is eligible to participate in TLC as long as parents complete the application and demonstrate a commitment by signing an agreement to the program requirements (e.g., attend concerts, encourage student practice at home by providing a practice space, attend monthly parent meetings, attend student performances, participate in community activities, and ensure that their child is picked-up in a timely manner). At East Elementary, selection of students is based on the recommendation from the school's counselor, principal (or assistant principal), and parental request. Student participants have been identified as students who may be considered at-risk by school/district standards and would benefit from participation in TLC. Now in its fourth year, TLC has had over 150 elementary-age boys and girls who have participated from both schools ranging in academic and musical abilities. Currently, each site has 30 to 35 students. TLC activities takes place on Monday through Thursday from 3:15 to 5:30 p.m. Students participate weekly in three distinct activities: (a) two to four hours of academic tutoring provided by TLC staff and community volunteers, (b) one hour of unstructured outside-play time, and (c) six to eight hours of musical instruction (musicianship, piano, and string instruments—violin, violas, cellos, and double base). Students also perform in local community cultural venues and attend four fieldtrips to El Sol's Museum of Art (ESMA).

Findings

Four distinct activities have been identified that illustrate how math related concepts are embedded in daily practice and field trip experiences. Along with learning conceptual concepts students inherently develop social emotional skills.

Developing a Sense of Caring through Responsibility

A deep sense of responsibility is built in the students as they are held to caring for their instruments, practicing at home, and attending concerts outside of school activities. All students are assigned an instrument which is theirs to keep throughout the school year with the commitment from the student and their parents that they will be cared for and returned at the end of the school year. Prior to students taking their instrument home, a community building activity is planed with the goal of engaging families in collectively building paper instruments. These paper instruments provide students an opportunity to learn how to respect and care for them before receiving real instruments. During the observation where students were creating a paper violin out of cardboard and foam pieces (September 8, 2016), it was noted that they spoke about the parts of the violin (e.g., body, F holes, neck and fingerboard, bridge, peg box, and scroll) as well as they informally explored the geometric shapes required to build the violin. The concept of symmetry was reflected in comments made by students during this activity (e.g., how both sides of the violin were the same and the F holes were mirror images of each other). An and Capraro (2011) emphasize the importance of creating classroom experiences where student can explore mathematical concepts in nonthreatening environments. Such is the case in TLC, where students are introduced with vocabulary and concepts on a daily basis, and are observed to use these terms in other activities.

Making Connections with Fractions

In an observation conducted (May 24, 2017) during instructional time the teaching artist, Mr. Juan stopped the students to correct them on a piece they were practicing. At one particular instance, there was some confusion between one measure and another. He asked the students if the section they were playing was the same, similar, or equal to the previous measure. One student noticed that there were half notes that were not in the previous measure that made the section similar but not the same. Right after this interaction, a 4th grade student thought about what he had said and raised her hand and asked, "*¿Esto también es como math?*" [Is this also like math?] and Mr. Juan quickly responded, "yes, this is all math and science!"

Musical measures resemble fractions that students study in their math classes. According to the National Math Advisory Panel (2008) report, "difficulty with fractions (including decimals and percents) is pervasive and is a major obstacle to further progress in mathematics including algebra" (p. xix). Students in TLC get exposed to the concept of whole, half, quarter, eighths, and sixteenth notes and physically practice variations of notes through application as they learn how to play their instruments and read music daily during programming. Mr. Juan provides students the opportunity to practice and apply vocabulary that is commonly used during music and math instruction. Goral and Wiest (2007) state that when students make conceptual connections they become better mathematical learners.

Children living with families and in impoverished communities are often limited in their opportunities to explore and participate in enriched language-based activities (Heath, 2015) that allows for students' curiosity to expand. Curiosity serves as motivation to learn beyond the contexts of their homes, schools and immediate community. Saldaña and Kosheleva (2016) presented data on how TLC students explored music and math concepts when presented with complementary learning activities using Cuisenaire Rods and Xylophone Resonator pipes during some of the academic tutoring periods of the program. The authors demonstrated that when students were provided with the time to explore with manipulatives, spontaneous connections were made with music and mathematical concepts. Using the observed examples of students connecting ideas from music education to mathematical concepts extends the opportunities for children to see that mathematical concepts are applied in different settings. Therefore, a variety of significant mathematical concepts (National Council of Teachers of Mathematics [NCTM], 2000) can be taught in conjunction with musical educational activities.

Field Trips: Extended Learning Opportunities

Field trips provide experiences that encourage children to observe and explore outside environments providing them with the possibility to connect their learning experiences, discover through their curiosity, and encourage their capacity of questioning and reflection. Budgetary constraints limit schools to one field trip per year. Many of the children participating in TLC have limited opportunities for attending cultural and educational events outside of their immediate communities. TLC has extended the opportunity for students and families to visit and watch their children perform in El Sol's most prestigious cultural venues such the museum of art and performing art theaters.

El Sol Museum of Arts (ESMA) Creating and Discovering Art. TLC students visit El Sol's Museum of Art (ESMA) four times during the school year during school hours. The director of ESMA works in close collaboration with TLC program directors and they coordinate music and visual art activities through a program called Arts Beats, which was developed for children and families who resided in El Sol. The Arts Beats activities play an important role for the students in TLC. Activities during the field trips to the museum are carefully planned to connect art and music, through community and social performances, thus supporting TLC's program goals. During the museum visits, children learn about works of art, history about the artist, art styles, and vocabulary (e.g., tone, rhythm, color, line, perspective, depth, aesthetics), which serves to help students express their feelings and perceptions in conjunction with listening to and playing music. For example, in 2016, students had the opportunity to play a student-led musical composition for a famous Mexican sculptor whose works includes large geometric shapes. During one of the visits to the ESMA, the lesson focused on identifying the geometric shapes in several images of this sculptor's work. The teaching artist then discussed how many sides and angles the shapes had and what connections they could make with music beats and tempo. The students noticed that triangles were used often in the large sculptures. From that, collectively the agreed on a three tempo beat in representation of the three angles found in triangles. Students explored, wrote, and played different 3-beat compositions. Mr. Juan composed two different pieces of music that were then performed by the students in front of the sculptor, members of the Mexican Consulate, and general public. This is a clear example of how students took mathematical concepts and connected them to making music. Simultaneously, they demonstrated their social skills by performing in front of known dignitaries and artist. Their participation in the music ensemble has taught them to work together toward one common goal—the performance. While many students may not have a conscious understanding of their individual roles in the ensemble, ten of the students reported in their surveys that they felt nervous because they might make a mistake as stated by one of the girls "*Me senti nerviosa proque era la unica violin y porque me iva a equivocar*" [I felt nervous because I was the only violin and I was going to make a mistake] (survey, 3rd grade EL student, April 2017).

El Sol University (ESU) Career Day. A collaborative effort by TLC staff, the research team, and faculty and staff from the colleges of Liberal Arts and Engineering from ESU planned a full-day visit with the purpose of experiencing a day in the life of a college campus. Sixty-five eager students participated from both of the school sites. Their trip included visiting the ESU Art Museum, attending band orchestra, and choir classes, visiting and experiencing the 3D printing lab, and participating in planned leadership activities in the Engineering department. For most students it was their first visit to a college campus. Their experiences were documented through their comments and reflections in the student surveys they completed the following day. A total of 39 surveys were collected after the visit to ESU.

During the visit to the music department, the TLC students saw ESU student musicians' practicing, studying, and socializing; they learned about new instruments, and they were especially excited when they saw their own music instructors in class. Three of the teaching artist are students seeking music education degrees. Permission was obtained for the students to observe their ESU classes. Thirty percent (n=11) of the students' open ended survey responses specifically addressed seeing their teachers as students. The students related to them as they saw how the professors corrected their students posture, and were asked to repeat sections of the music over and over again. One of the students specifically stated: "*I like this event because on the orchestra they were 6 bases, 6 big. I saw a little confused because one women not put the correctly fingers. It make me feel sad because they will playing beautiful*" (survey, 3rd grade EL student, February, 2017).

The students proceeded to visit the 3D Printing Lab. There students had the opportunity to work on a computer and they had a mini lesson on how to use a 3D modeling program. They were also able to see 3D printers, printing, and samples of objects that had been printed by others. Forty-six percent (n=18) of the students' open-ended survey responses stated that visiting the 3D printing lab was one of the highlights of the day. The opportunity to get hands-on experience and to see the printers was something they had only heard about. In particular, they expressed interest as they listened to one of the graduate students working in the lab tell them that he had been a musician in middle and high school and now he had designed and printed out an electric violin which he designed and played for them. Lao, Motter, and Patton (2016) state that "Students gain digital media skills empowering them to understand that everyone can learn how to use the computer as an expressive art medium" (p. 34). Next the students visited the Technology and Engineering department where students watched career activity presentations aimed to encourage children to start thinking about opportunities for future career choices. The ESU provided the infrastructure and space, in which children could one day see themselves as students and to become musicians, artists, and engineers.

The last stop of the field trip was at the College of Engineering where faculty and staff prepared two different leadership and team building activities for the students, Activity 1: Engineering design challenge: Building the tallest tower activity and Activity 2: Leadership activity: Crossing the river of lava. Of all the activities during the day these were reported as the most fun by half (49%) of the students. In their comments, they identified that they liked the challenge of working together as a team to meet a goal, and helped each other, and specifically stated that they had fun.

Student surveys for this visit indicated that 38 (9%) of the students liked the field trip to ESU and 34 (85%) said that they learned something new. In particular, the comment by a 4th grade girl summed up the experience the students had: "*A mi me gusto porque hisimos muchas cosas como escuchamos a la orchestra, nos dieron bolsitas de EPU vimos unas 3D imprimidores, estuvo muy chido y mas porque comimos pizza estuvo tan rico que me llene y nos tomamos fotos con otra escuela. Cuanodo yo este grande voy a ir a EPU porque hay es donde aprende de cómo ser una sientifico y todavía mas emocionante fue el mejor dia de mi vida*" [I liked it because we did a lot of things like listening to the orchestra, they gave us EPU bags we saw some 3D printers, it was really cool especially because we ate pizza it was so good that I got full and we took a picture with the other school. When I grow up I will go to EPU because there is where you learn how to be a scientist and still more exciting is that it was the best day of my life.]

The collaboration between the ESSO through TLC and ESU provided opportunities that are indirectly supporting children who are considered to be at-risk academically. Consequently, nonformal learning environments provide students spaces where they can apply skills they are learning in formal academic settings.

Discussion

Research (Americans for the Arts, 2015) indicates that the active involvement of children and youth in art-based programs leads to the development of socioemotional skills that link academic and/or future adult success (Heath, 2015; Zins *et al.*, 2004). Furthermore, cognitive and social skills are further developed nonformal and formal contexts (Heath, 2015). Student engagement in third environments have the opportunity to enhance learning process when interactions with adults and extended learning experiences, such as field trips, are directed toward individual learning and meaning-making.

The preliminary findings of this study have not specifically addressed if and how specific mathematical skills are gained by the students participating in TLC. However, what is evident is that students engaged in TLC activities have multiple opportunities in developing critical social emotional skills that are linked to academic success. In times when educational resources are being cut and participation in extracurricular activities are limited for students living in underresourced communities, change will only come if community organizations and schools engage in collaborative efforts to extend learning opportunities for vulnerable students. We have presented how TLC and community organizations such as the ESSO, ESMA and ESU have created bridges in working together with the purpose of providing access to students and their families to a world beyond classroom and school walls (Daml, 2017). Art connected with other disciplines such as mathematics, technology, sciences within the nonformal education spaces creates a holistic circle between ART and STEM and STEM and ART. Although art placed against science, technology, and mathematics may seem as significantly disconnected fields of study, research has documented that art, in the broad sense of the word, works as a bridge to achieving a better understanding of the difference between the mathematical and aesthetical perspectives (McAdoo, 1991 as cited in Björklund & Ahlskog-Björkman, 2017).

To date, we have found that TLC has had a positive influence for the students and their families situated in two vulnerable settings. As data continue to be analyzed, we aim to gain a deeper meaning and clearer understanding of how music and art act as mediating tools for constructing cognitive, academic and social meanings. Thus far, data indicate that these programs create possibilities and opportunities for students living in underresourced communities to thrive.

References

American for the Arts. (2015). Facts and figures navigator. Retrieved from http://www.americansforthearts.org/sites/default/files/AFTA_Navigator_Facts-and-Figures_lo.pdf

American Psychological Association, Presidential Task Force on Educational Disparities. (2012). *Ethnic and racial disparities in education: Psychology's contributions to understanding and reducing disparities.* Retrieved from http://www.apa.org/ed/resources/racial-disparities.aspx

An, S. A., & Capraro, M. M. (2011). *Music-mathematics integrated activities for elementary and middle-grade students.* Irvine, CA: Education for All.

Björklund, C., & Ahlskog-Björkman, E. (2017). Approaches to teaching in thematic work: Early childhood teachers' integration of mathematics and art. *International Journal of Early Years Education, 25*(2), 98–111.

Booth, E. (2001). *The everyday work of art: Awakening the extraordinary in your daily life.* Bloomington, IN: iUniverse.

Catterall, J. S., Dumais, S. A., & Hampden-Thompson, G. (2012). *The arts and achievement in at-risk youth: Findings from four longitudinal studies.* Washington, DC: National Endowment for the Arts. Retrieved from http://arts.gov/sites/default/files/Arts-At-Risk-Youth.pdf

Daml, M. (2017). Using community events to enlive STEM education. *Teaching Children Mathematics, 23*(6), 376–378.

Engeström, Y. (2001). Expansive learning at work: Toward and activity theoretical reconceptualization. *Journal of Education and Work, 14*(1), 133–156.

Engeström, Y. (2009). Expansive learning: Toward and activity-theoretical reconceptualization. In K. Illeris (Ed.), *Contemporary theories of learning: Learning theorists. In their own words* (pp. 53–73). London: Routledge.

Goral, M., & Wiest, L. (2007). An arts-based approach to teaching fractions. *Teaching Children Mathematics, 14*(2), 74–80.

Guest Life. (2017). Retrieved from http://www.guestlife.com/media/GuestLife/El-Paso/The-411-On-El-Paso/The-411-Fascinating-Facts/

Heath, S. B. (2001). Three's not a crowd: Plans, roles, and focus in the arts. *Educational Researcher, 30*(7), 10–17.

Heath, S. B. (2015). Museums, theaters, and youth orchestras advancing creative arts and sciences within underresourced communities. In W. G. Tierney (Ed.), *Rethinking education and poverty* (pp. 177–199). Baltimore, MD: Johns Hopkins University Press.

King, M. (2016). *Comparing the effects of elementary music and visual arts lessons on standardized mathematics test scores* (Doctoral dissertation, Liberty University).

Lao, C., Motter, J., & Patton, R. (2016). Tech-Savvy girls: Learning 21st-century skills through STEAM Digital Artmaking. *Art Education, 69*(4), 29–35.

Motel, S., & Patten, E. (2012). *The 10 largest Hispanic origin groups: Characteristics, rankings, top counties.* Pew Research Center. Retrieved from http://www.pewhispanic.org/2012/06/27/the-10-largest-hispanic-origin-groups-characteristics-rankings-top-counties/

Murphey, D., Madill, R., & Guzman, L. (2017). *Making math count more for young Latino Children.* Child Trends Hispanic Institute.

National Council of Teachers of Mathematics (NCTM). (2000). *Principles and standards for school mathematics.* Reston, VA: NCTM.

National Academies of Sciences Engineering and Medicine (NASEM). (2017). *Promoting the educational success of children and youth learning English: Promising futures.* Retrieved from http://nationalacademies.org/hmd/Reports/2017/promoting-the-educational-success-of-children-and-youth-learning-English.aspx

National Mathematics Advisory Panel (2008). The final report of the National Mathematics Advisory Panel. (p. xix). Retrieved from https://www.scribd.com/document/2912664/NMAP-National-Math-Advisory-Panel-Final-Report-2008

Pew Research Center. (2015, September). *Modern immigration wave brings 59 million to U.S., driving population growth and change through 2065: Views of immigration's impact on U.S. society mixed.* Washington, DC. Retrieved from http://www.pewhispanic.org/2015/09/28/chapter-5-u-s-foreign-born-population-trends/

Saldaña, C., & Koshcleva, O. (2016). Students learning about music-math connections by playing with Cuisenaire rods. *Journal of Mathematics Education, 9*(2), 97–108.

U.S. Census Bureau. (2010). *American fact finder community facts.* Retrieved from https://factfinder.census.gov/faces/nav/jsf/pages/community_facts.xhtml

Viera, J. (2017). *Emergent bilinguals' engagement in an online mathematics course utilizing an intelligent tutoring system* (Doctoral dissertation, University of Texas at El Paso).

Wakin, D.J. (2012). *Venerated high priest and humble servant of music education.* Retrieved from http://www.nytimes.com/2012/03/04/arts/music/jose-antonio-abreu-leads-el-sistema-in-venezuela.html

Welch, G. (2007). Addressing the multifaceted nature of music education: An activity theory research perspective. *Research Studies in Music Education,* 28(1), 23–37.

Willis, G. (2016). *Impact of music education on mathematics achievement scores among middle school students* (Doctoral dissertation, Welden University).

Zins, J. E., Weissberg, R. P., Wang, M. L., & Walberg, H. J. (Eds.). (2004). *Building school success through social and emotional learning: Implications for practice and research.* New York, NY: Teachers College Press.

9. Acceso la Ciencia: *Expanding STEM Learning Repertoires in Rural Latino Communities through Informal Science Activities*

ANNE E. CAMPBELL AND MICHAEL S. TREVISAN

This chapter discusses summative evaluation findings and shares lessons learned from *Acceso la Ciencia: Bringing Informal Science to Rural Migrant Latino Families and Communities* (ACCESO). ACCESO was a five-year, three million dollar Informal Science Education (ISE) Broad Implementation grant funded by the National Science Foundation (NSF). ACCESO brought bilingual informal science activities and information about STEM careers to Latino communities, parents, and youth in eastern Washington state. The chapter provides an overview of project design and goals, evaluation methodology, and activities development and implementation. It examines the reciprocal relationships between ACCESO staff, rural Latino agricultural workers and parents, MESA students, and the Pacific Science Center (PSC) in Seattle in the development of interactive bilingual science exhibits and shows. It concludes with a discussion of critical project components, themes, lessons learned, and key outcomes.

ACCESO was based on two prior NSF ISE grant projects and the partnership developed from those projects between the Yakima Valley/Tri-Cities MESA (Mathematics, Science, and Engineering Achievement) currently, in it's 33rd year, science and engineering faculty at Washington State University (WSU) Pullman and Tri-Cities campuses, the PSC, and Radio KDNA, a Spanish radio station located in the Yakima Valley. The design was also informed by prior research. Malcom (2007) suggested that issues of access and opportunity, rather than choice, were significant challenges for Latino youth participation in STEM programs. Azmitia *et al.* (1994) and Delgado-Gaitán (1991) documented the importance of establishing and strengthening links between students' at-home and out-of-school learning experiences with students' academic progress and persistence in school. Sosa (1997) found that that Latino parents have high educational aspirations for their children but often felt marginalized from their children's school. He argued that collaborative relationships between parents and educators in which parents were partners in program development and decision-making processes were effective ways to strengthen the home-school link. Moll (1992); González, Andrade, Civil, and Moll (2001); and González, Moll, and Amanti (2005) documented the importance of identifying "household and community knowledge" (p. 257) and the ways in which that knowledge was expressed in community practices.

Project Design, Goals, and Materials Development

Based on the above research and the prior ISE grant projects, ACCESO was designed to create a community "infrastructure" that would increase access and opportunities for the Latino community's engagement in informal science that would support the development and implemention of specific experiences. The purpose was to encourage Latino/a students to develop an interest in STEM, as well as support their pursuit of college-level STEM programs and degrees. One goal was to link funds of knowledge with respect to agricultural sciences and community practices in rural migrant communities to the development of interactive bilingual exhibits and informal science activities delivered to those communities.

Paramount to the design and implementation of ACCESO was the need to develop culturally relevant activities and identify venues for program development, delivery, implementation, and evaluation (Yalowitz & de la Hoz, 2009). To this end, ACCESO employed the functional collaborative approach developed by Hallman (Campbell, 2007; Hallman, Campbell, & Ernst, 1992). This approach to building community partnerships identified and acknowledged the expertise of all stakeholders and partners in the project. An assumption made was that leadership and participation would be fluid as needs emerged. Thus, the expertise of any partner might be be required to complete project elements.

As ACCESO became an established informal science outreach project within the Latino community, its mission evolved and collaboration with commuity partners increased to 30 organizations fundamental to the project's success. These included Pacific Northwest National Laboratories (PNNL), Battelle NW, U.S. Fish and Wildlife Services, LIGO Hanford Observatory, Friends of Mid-Columbia River Wildlife, and Pasco School District. Many of these collaborators provided bilingual printed materials for intern training purposes or materials to distribute at ACCESO events. In addition, four colleges and universities provided campus tours for the ACCESO interns.

Goals

The outcomes proposed by the project were "proximate" rather that ultimate. We argued that informal science learning experiences and parental involvement were critical influences needed to support students' STEM interests and learning as they move through the STEM education "pipeline." Project goals aligned with the NSF GPRA Strategic Plan 2001–2006 (National Science Foundation, 2000):

1. broaden the participation of underrepresented groups (e.g., gender, ethnicity, disability, geographic, etc.) who are excited about STEM and who pursue STEM activities both in- and out-of-school;
2. promote linkages between informal and formal education, creating a synergy that strengthens STEM education in many learning environments;
3. include students (e.g., K–12) as participants in the proposed activities as appropriate;
4. develop new approaches (e.g., use of information technology and connectivity) to engage underserved individuals, groups, and communities in science and engineering;
5. bring informal science programs and activities to areas that are currently without, or minimally reached by, STEM opportunities (e.g., rural and inner city environments);
6. encourage parents and other primary caregivers to support their children's STEM endeavors in the home and elsewhere; and
7. strengthen STEM education, as well as ISE programs and its supported activities, through applied research about informal learning.

To achieve these goals ACCESO proposed a model that would increase family involvement in informal science directly through project-supported family science festivals, family science and math Saturday/Sundays, and family science workshops (Heil, Amorose, Gurnee, & Harrison, 1999a, 1999b). Central to the model was the development of bilingual informal science activities and materials that were community-based and culturally relevant.

Materials Development

The PSC staff had primary responsibility for product development. One of the most important was creation of two sets of portable bilingual exhibits and two bilingual shows. Prototypes were made by the PSC curriculum and exhibit developers and tested on PSC guests, as well as the intended audience for the project. Through a variety of questions regarding the participants' experience with the shows and exhibits, the development team gathered information to improve the exhibits' experience, content, and design. The exhibits were housed in wooden suitcase-type boxes. Inside the cover of each case were bilingual graphics that explained how the exhibit worked. Exhibits included an interactive element, which correlated with the best method of conveying the main topic and the learning objective of the exhibit. They were designed to be appropriate for all ages and could be set up in a variety of locations and venues, outdoors or indoors, and they were an integral part in engaging the public.

The first exhibit, *Harvesting Science/Cosechando la Ciencia*, was developed in the second year of the grant and finalized at the beginning of the third year. It included 15 bilingual agricultural exhibits that focused on the kinds of crops grown in Washington, the ways in which climate and soil influence the types of crops grown, and methods used to irrigate, harvest, and deliver crops to market. Related exhibit topics included conservation and use of water and today's atricultural technologies.

The second set of exhibits, *Minds at Work/Mentes Trabajando*, was designed in year three. It followed the same structural design as the first set but covered different topics and learning objectives. These interactive exhibits were designed to introduce a variety of engineering and science careers found in Washington State, to the Latino public in a way that demystified those careers and made them accessible through hands-on examples. To illustrate, one exhibit highlighted Boeing and demonstrated the different things an aeronautical engineer considers when designing and building airplanes. The visitor combined different airplane body and wing models to make an airplane with a stable center of gravity. The interactive problem solving approach created an understanding of, and a way for visitors to see themselves in, those professions. It also stimulated visitor thinking about the science topics illustrated in the exhibits.

Two bilingual shows were developed to further promote interest, literacy and understanding of the science terms and concepts introduced by the exhibits. The shows were presented by the ACCESO high school interns and engaged audiences through fun, hands-on demonstrations, typically requiring the help of audience volunteers. During the development phase, props and show content were tested and prototyped with various audiences. The first show, *Secret Scientist/Científico Secreto*, used agriculture as a gateway to explore various science concepts such as soil science, hydrology, chemistry and ecology. The show demonstrated how science and technology are woven throughout everyday agricultural practices. The second show, *World Wide Science/Ciencia Mundial,* followed an "interview-the-scientist" format where the host introduced the audience to four different scientists. The scientists shared science activities they enjoyed as a child and their path to college. The highlighted scientists included: a chemist, an engineer, a volcanologist and an oceanographer.

Finally, more than 50 bilingual take-home science activities, and hundreds of interactive make-it-take-it activities were developed to use at community events and distributed to parents for their use at home. Many of these activities aligned with the LASER science education reform initiative implemented in Washington state in the late 1990s. These activities provide parents direct experiences with various science concepts related to the LASER curriculum. In addition, two take home bilingual guides were designed to promote shared learning between parents and their children. Each guide centered on a specific theme. One detailed the process of seed germanitation; testing seeds and changing related variables to see how they affect seed growth; testing the PH of soil by taking soil samples; and learning about different varieties of apples by exploring type, texture, taste, color, and size. The second focused on science careers in Washington state and the day-to-day activities of scientists in fields such as chemistry, engineering, and biology. The guides established links between the exhibit content and a variety of experiments and applications linked to the highlighted disciplines.

Methodology

The values and related research methods of ethnography provided the theoretical framework guiding the design and implementation of qualitative evaluation activities (Bernard, 2002; Wolcott, 1999). Ethnographic data collection began year one and continued throughout the project. It included observations, discussions and informal surveys with project interns and parents, questionnaires and interviews with project partners and ACCESO staff, conversations with community members' who attended ACCESO events, and informal evaluations of project activities. Data collection was facilitated by the fact that one of the external evaluators and most of the ACCESO staff were bilingual, and all the staff members were from the Latino community.

During year one, ACCESO staff and the evaluators developed a project logic model (Frechtling, 2002) and identified key evaluation points and activities, as well as the variety of data sources needed to document program implementation (Frechtling, 1995, 2002; Friedman, 2008). Evaluators worked to develop trust, "[establish] rapport, and [learn] to act so that people [went] about their business as usual when [they] showed up" (Bernard, 2002, p. 324). They participated in regularly scheduled staff meetings, retreats and field trips with project partners, and phone conferences with ACCESO and PSC staff. They took fieldnotes during these meetings, conducted follow-up interviews with ACCESO staff, and maintained files that included meeting minutes, some e-mails, agendas, flyers, and other documents (e.g., handbooks, training materials, etc.) generated as a result of implementation activities. An archive of materials developed and/or distributed at ACCESO events was also compiled.

In years one and two, participant observation and fieldnotes taken at events were primary sources of data collection. Fieldnotes were of a moderate level of detail (Dobbert, 1984). They were used to develop event evaluation questionnaires for years three, four, and five of the grant. They guided interviews with interns and staff regarding the grant implementation. *Grand tours* (Spradley, 1979) at events included a map that detailed the layout of the exhibit area, the exhibits and their locations, persons acting as docents for the exhibit area, and tables manned by ACCESO partners. Also noted were the types of handouts distributed and kinds of interactions conducted in various sections of the event area. Fieldnotes were recorded during and immediately fleshed out following all events. Periodic running records were made at community events to document traffic flow and the numbers of parents and children at the various interactive displays, family science activities, or information tables. Fieldwork activities included ethnographic interviews (Spradley, 1980) with ACCESO staff and community partners, e-mail correspondence, and documentation of ACCESO activities using artifacts—such as flyers, meeting agendas, etc.—provided by staff.

In years two through five, formal record keeping logs were implemented to document the following information: dates, kinds of activities, attendance numbers, ACCESO or partner staff and interns participating in the activities, and materials distributed at the events. The logs were used to categorized the kinds of training, outreach, and dissemination activities conducted throughout the year. Audio taped interviews in English and Spanish were conducted with ACCESO staff and some parents. Structured and open-ended bilingual evaluation questionnaires were administered at childcare provider workshops, parent family fieldtrips, and intern training sessions. In year five, focus group interviews with interns were conducted.

Intern Questionnaires and Forms

In year three, formal questionnaires were developed for interns to evaluate the training sessions in which they participated and provide feedback to improve them. A comprehensive questionnaire was created in year three and administered in years four and five to gain an understanding of the interns' overall ACCESO experiences.

Other Data Sources

In year two, raffles were introduced and conducted each year of the grant at every community event. From the raffle entry tickets, lists of participants were developed for each event, and overall event attendance was estimated. Evaluators compiled a list of community agency representatives that participated in outreach events and created an artifact file of flyers, handouts, and materials provided by the different agencies. Finally, they read training materials developed for parents and interns and listened to audio files of the KDNA radio programs and ads developed in Spanish specifically for the ACESSO grant. A c.d. collection of the radio advertising was compiled.

A bilingual open-ended questionnaire for parents to evaluate events and provide feedback for improving them was developed and piloted in Year 3. The questionnaire was revised and administered at five caregiver workshops and parent specific events. A total of 325 questionnaires were completed in Years 4 and 5. Finally, a standardized bilingual workshop evaluation form (STARS Formulario de Evaluacion) was piloted at the Childhood Caregiver conferences. A total of 90 STAR forms were completed in Years 4 and 5.

Critical Project Components and Lessons Learned

Intern Leadership Training, Development, and Mentoring

ACCESO supported the development of student interest in and pursuit of STEM education through an environment designed to support informal science learning, provide access to important science and engineering related experiences, and provide access to critical resources. A key component of this environment was the on-going training, development, and mentoring of project interns.

Science Interpretation Training Workshops. In year one, high school juniors and seniors were recruited as ACCESO interns. The PSC implemented a science interpretation training program for them based on the PSC's formal training workshops designed for front-line staff, volunteers, and members of other relevant PSC departments. The materials used for the workshops presumed some awareness or experience with existing models for informal science interpretation. The interns were not familiar with those models, and their feedback indicated the need for additional training. Based on this information, the order of the trainings was reorganized for years two through five. The PSC training materials were adapted by PSC and ACCESO staff and made more culturally appropriate for the ACCESO interns. Based on the interns input in year two, new training topics were identified and delivered in years three, four, and five.

In years two through five of the project, interns observed at the PSC, participated in PSC programs, and worked closely with its front line staff and volunteers. The PSC workshops were one to two hours and included a training curriculum, supply bin and workshop packet for the interns. Workshops included the following:

1. *Making Meaning:* Interns were encouraged to reflect on the value of interpretation by connecting their own powerful memories of informal learning experiences with their interpretive role as ACCESO interns. They learned to promote meaningful learning experiences for those interacting with the ACCESO exhibits and shows.

2. *Customer Service:* Four keys to customer service were introduced and discussed: service, attitude, consistency and teamwork. Interns role-played turning negative situations into positive ones and strategies to be proactive in providing excellent customer service.

3. *Explainer 101:* Interns were introduced to and practiced four simple steps for successful interpretation: how to be approachable, how to initiate conversation, how to use one's unique "Explainer Toolkit," and how to politely end the conversation.

4. *Questioning Strategies:* Interns learned effective questioning techniques in their role as science interpreters. They role-played both as a teacher and as a student, worked through several learning interactions, guided a learner to a desired learning objective, and compared the use of questioning versus lecturing.

In addition to the above workshops, interns observed the PSC floor staff and live science show presenters, shadowed exbibit interpreters, and interacted with teen interpreters working on the center floor. They visited other informal education institutions such as Woodland Park Zoo, Seattle Aquarium, Seattle Art Museum, Discovery Park and the Space Needle where they learned more about the science presented in ACCESO exhibits, as well as other STEM topics. These trips showed interns that informal science interpretation can take many forms and may be presented in various venues.

ACCESO also provided opportunities for interns to tour research facilities at LIGO, Northwest Labs, PNNL, and WSU Tri Cities, work with scientists, and participate in internships. Interns also completed team building activities and attended organizational meetings designed to develop leadership skills. In addition to these scheduled events, they worked at home to practice interpreting exhibits for the different events in which they participated. They met four times a year for more than 20 hours to work on presentations and to prepare for the annual ACCESO Showcase Event attended by parents, families, WSU faculty, PSC and ACCESO staff. At the Showcase, the interns presented portions of the two bilingual shows and a selection of exhibits from each of the two shows. They individually prepared and presented a Power Point that documented their experiences and the impact that participation in ACCESO had on them.

Community and Family Participation

ACCESO was designed to increase family involvement in informal science directly through project-supported family science festivals, family Saturday/ Sundays, and family science workshops. Project partners collaborated to create activities that introduced formal science concepts and terminology and created an environment that encouraged STEM interests and learning by providing parents with science activities they could do with their children. Activities and data from parent interviews and evaluation forms completed at caregiver workshops indicated that parents were using the activities at home for birthday parties and during leisure time with children. One parent implemented the activities a the preschool where she worked. Informal interviews documented parent learning on the fieldtrips and with the interactive exhibits and Family Science activities.

In year one, five ACCESO parents volunteered to help at community events. The same challenges the interns had were evident in training the parents to facilitate learning at the events. They were unfamiliar with informal science interpretation models and needed specific mentoring to develop needed skills. With the unused funds carried forward from the first year of the grant, parent training sessions were developed to facilitate their learning and to enhance their comfort with informal science activities. Additional funding from Radio KDNA provided parents with opportunities to experience informal science learning with trips to the PSC, boat trips up Hanford Reach, and visits to LIGO and the Columbia River Exhibition of History, Science and Technology (CREHST), Museum in Pasco, WA. Parent responses to the trips were very positive. Most had never visited Seattle or the local science museums before. ACCESO gave them their first opportunity to visit these resources in a nonthreatening way with a bilingual interpreter. Parents indicated that they made additional trips to CHREST and PSC with other family members.

College Preparedness Workshops. At the secondary level, materials related to college preparedness and persistence and course selection in high school were developed and distributed at community events. Informal data was collected from parents who came to future events and shared how they had used the materials with their children. Evaluation forms, completed following workshops presented by ACCESO staff related to college preparedness, financial aid and completing college applications indicated that parents felt more confident in their ability to support their children in the college application process.

Themes, Lessons Learned, and Key Outcomes

To understand the impact of the project on student interns, the external evaluator led a focus group year five of the project with current interns and several who were attending college (N=14). The focus group discussion was audio taped. A follow-up questionnaire provided additional data and two face-to-face interviews were conducted with in Pullman. Several themes were evident in participants' responses regarding the internship experience.

Leadership

Interns continually mentioned developing leadership skills and confidence as a positive aspect of the ACCESO project. Sample responses included the following:

> "The Questioning training helped me learn how to interact with kids and strangers too."
> "We had a lot of responsibility. I think we matured. We learned commitment. We gained confidence through risk taking and presenting the shows."
> "I am using these skills in college. I joined a club. I wouldn't have done that before...too shy before. It had also given me great communication and leadership skills."

Pride and Accomplishment

The second theme that was evident in the intern interview responses was the feeling of accomplishment and enjoyment that interns got from teaching science through the exhibits. For example,

> Every time I am at events doing exhibits, I feel like these kids are coming to my exhibit end up learning something by the time they leave. I feel like I am seriously teaching them something. For example, there was this one time when I had showed a kid about our exhibits and made him participate. After I was done, the kid came back with his friends, and he taught them all he had learned from me.

Ability to Make Observations and Interact with Public

In addition to developing leadership skills, confidence, and a sense of accomplishment, interns developed the ability to make observations about their interactions with the public and were able to adjust their interaction style to more effectively interact with children, parents, and community members. They learned when to approach someone and when to stand to the side and just let them explore. When asked what their observations were about the way the public engaged with them or the exhibits, they were able to articulate their insights:

> They are very tentative. So we have learned how to draw them in and show them that science can be fun. I've noticed that the more comfortable I get with them; the more they open up to me!

Appreciation

In the focus group discussion and the written evaluations, the interns expressed their appreciation for having had the opportunity to participate in ACCESO and for the skills they had developed and experiences and opportunities they were given through the project.

> The most rewarding experience I've had as an ACCESO intern would be having the feeling that I have showed something to and met new people in my community. Its great having the experience to surprise or make people laugh with what I teach or talk about. Just being part of ACCESO has been my greatest reward, makes me feel like a part of something.... I can go on and on from what I have gotten out of being an ACCESO intern. It's really been the greatest thing for me.
>
> There have been many rewarding experiences I have had with ACCESO. However, I think that being able to take on new challenges and explore the world and opportunities that we have makes you realize that you can do something great with your life while also helping out the community, and it makes you feel great.

Throughout the ACCESO project, intern feedback was solicited and used to improve project activities. One important area that benefitted from intern feedback was that of interpretation training. Surveys were administered after all science interpretation and show trainings to gauge the impact and effectiveness of the training materials. Participants were asked four to five questions regarding their experience and identified training strategies worked best and those that did not work. This information was then used to inform changes and improve programming. Year two interns wanted more training in memorization, enunciation and overall performance strategies. The next year of show training included a day of activities that addressed this area and gave the program interns a variety of resources to improve the overall show performance.

Lessons Learned

Findings indicate strong potential for projects like ACCESO that are placed-based (Gruenewald & Smith, 2008), grounded in community funds of knowledge and "rich with everyday science phenomena" to support science learning. The following lessons learned from the five-year study of the ACCESO project are offered for others to consider in the development of community-based, culturally relevant, informal science education activities for groups underrepresented in STEM.

Lesson 1: Critical Role of Community Partners. Community partnerships with 15 STEM related and 15 additional agencies, businesses, and research organizations were critical to the success of ACCESO. These partnerships enabled ACCESO staff, interns, parents, and community members to offer a wider variety of informal science activities and resources to the community, than might otherwise have been possible. Partners provided bilingual materials, funded family field trips, and disseminated information about STEM careers at community events. When the interns requested more training in the science behind the activities, WSU faculty, LASER, Battelle, CHREST, and other STEM partners provided workshops to develop the interns' scientific understanding.

Lesson 2: Culturally Relevant Bilingual Activities. Place-based bilingual exhibits, shows, and activities built on local cultural capital and area resources, enabled ACCESO to bring informal science to the Latino communities. Bilingual exhibits depicted local agriculture, engineering projects, and bioscience topics present throughout the region. The text of the bilingual exhibits and materials taught community members the formal science behind the daily agricultural activities in which many participated. Parents took a leadership role in explaining science concepts based on their daily work to their children. Family science nights included children and parents, and caregiver workshops that acknowledged the critical role that women have in educating the children in the community.

   Lesson 3: Ability to Adapt and Add New Activities. One of the strengths of ACCESO was the flexibility of the staff and their ability to adapt to meet the needs of the Latino community. This flexibility was illustrated in the development of additional parent workshops held at the high schools or individually that provided information on STEM careers, strategies to plan high school courses and match them with desired careers, the college application process, and financial aide. Flexibility also included the addition of workshops specifically designed for Latino/a caregivers on the use of informal science activities in daycare settings, and the development of science workshops requested by the interns to develop their understanding of the concepts illustrated by the bilingual exhibits.

   Lesson 4: Community Participation. A key factor related to ACCESO's success was the fact that by the third year of the project every staff position (Director, Science Educator, Parent Outreach Coordinator, Intern Coordinator, and Community Liaison) was held by a bilingual member of the rural migrant and more established Latino communities that ACCESO was designed to serve. Additionally, the inclusion of a bilingual evaluator provided for greater participation of Spanish speaking parents and children in the evaluation of ACCESO events. Finally, the use of a functional collaborative approach to ACCESO's design and implementation authentically included project partners, parents and student interns in all phases of project design, product development, and activities implementation.

Key Outcomes

During the five years of the grant, ACCESO partners sponsored or participated in a total of 188 events attended by approximately 22,175 parents and students. Two major outcomes were increased parental awareness of and involvement in science education and careers and an increase in the number of Latino students pursuing undergraduate degrees in STEM. A total of 25 high school students participated as interns in ACCESO from 2008 through 2012. Four decided not to continue as interns after a year due to personal reasons, but all four of the 25 graduated from high school. Of the 21 interns who actively participated in ACCESO, five ACCESO seniors graduated in 2009, and all five attended college. Three pursued STEM related careers. Of the six who graduated in 2010, five attended college, four pursued STEM related careers, and three have scholarships. Four graduated in 2011, three attended college and pursued STEM related careers. In 2012, four interns were in high school and all planned to attend college. Three will pursue STEM related careers. Two graduates were unable to attend college due to financial reasons. They are working and hope to attend college in the future. In total, 100% of the 21 interns graduated from high school, 80% are attending college, and of those 76% are pursuing STEM related careers. These numbers reflect the larger statistics for Yakima Valley/Tri Cities MESA, a primary partner with ACCESO. In 2009, 83 MESA seniors graduated including the five ACCESO interns. Of those 83, 96% are attending college, 68% were pursuing STEM related careers, and 33% had scholarships.

Concluding Remarks

The successful development and implementation of ACCESO depended on the strong collaboration between the stakeholdes and organizations involved in the project. Each brought unique expertise, which enhanced and contributed to achieving the goals and objectives. Pacific Science Center's bilingual exhibits, shows and interpreter trainings were central in developing the culturally relevant activities that increased Latino students', families' and communities' involvement with informal science education. The interns and parents played a critical role as bilingual science interpreters of the exhibits and as cross-cultural liaisons with the Latino/a community members who attended ACCESO events. ACCESO staff who were located at WSU Tri Cities in Richland, WA, coordinated and implemented ACCESO's outreach and training activities. In collaboration with WSU faculty, they created the infrastructure and support needed to develop and deliver the events and maintain critical contact with ACCESO community partners. As a result, ACCESO became a community project, not just a project delivered to the community.

The evaluation was a major component of the project and played a central role in the documentation of outcomes, some of which were challenging and illusive to capture. The evaluation design allowed for mid-course changes to project materials and various activities, based on feedback from participants and stakeholders. And given that the project was complex, worked toward being culturally responsive and relevant, with many moving parts, the qualitative research strategies used in the evaluation provided rigor and sensitivity to documenting outcomes and lessons learned. Our evaluation approach has much to offer similar projects that seek to develop interest in science learning and grounded in a specific cultural context.

References

Azmitia, M., Cooper, C., Garcia, E., Ittel, A., Johanson, B., Lopez, E., ... Rivera, L. (1994). *Links between home and school among low-income Mexican-American and European-American families*. Berkley, CA: Center for Research on Education, Diversity and Excellence. Retrieved from http://escholarship.org/uc/item/1n9843b7

Bernard, H. R. (2002). *Research methods in anthropology: Qualitative and quantitative approaches*. Walnut Creek, CA: Altimira Press.

Campbell, A. E. (2007). Retaining American Indian/Alaskan Native students in higher education: A case study of one partnership between the Tohono O'odham Nation and Pima Community College, Tucson, AZ. *Journal of American Indian Education, 46:* 19–41.

Delgado-Gaitán, C. (1991). Involving parents in school: A process of empowerment. *American Journal of Education, 100*, 20–24.

Dobbert, M. (1984). *Ethnographic research: Theory and applications for modern schools and societies*. New York, NY: Praeger.

Frechtling, J. A. (1995, January). The search for footprints: Nontraditional approaches to evaluating NSF programs. In J. A. Frechtling (Ed.), *FOOTPRINTS: Strategies for nontraditional program evaluation* (pp. 1–2). Rockville, MD: Westat, Inc.

Frechtling, J. (2002). *The 2002 user friendly handbook for project evaluation*. Arlington, VA: NSF, Directorate for Education and Human Resources, Division of Research, Evaluation and Communication. Retrieved from http://www.nsf.gov/ pubs/2002/ nsf02057/nsf02057.pdf

Friedman, A. J. (Ed.). (2008). *Framework for evaluating impacts of informal science education projects: Report from a National Science Foundation workshop*. Washington, DC: National Science Foundation Directorate for Education and Human Resources, Division of Research on Learning in Formal and Informal Settings. Contract Number GS-10F-0482P.

González, N., Andrade, R., Civil, M., & Moll, L. (2001). Bridging funds of distributed knowledge: Creating zones of practice in mathematics. *Journal of Education for Students Placed at Risk, 6*(1), 115–132.

González, N., Moll, L. C., & Amanti, C. (2005). *Funds of knowledge: Theorizing practices in households, communities, and classrooms*. Mahwah, NJ: Lawrence Erlbaum Associates.

Gruenewald, D. A., & Smith, G. A. (2008) *Place-Based Education in the Global Age*. Mahwah, NJ: Lawrence Erlbraum Associates.

Hallman, C., Campbell, A., & and Ernst, G. (1992). Development and implementation of FLES summer institutes in Florida: A functional-collaborative effort. *Foreign Language Annals, 25*(3), 245–254.

Heil, D., Amorose, G., Gurnee, A., & Harrison, A. (1999a). *Family science*. Portland, OR: Foundation for Family Science.

Heil, D., Amorose, G., Gurnee, A., & Harrison, A. (1999b). *Ciencia para la familia*. Portland, OR: Foundation for Family Science.

Malcom, S. (2007). Broadening participation in STEM: Challenges and opportunities. *The Opportunity Equation*. Prepared for the Carnegie-IAS Commission on Mathematics and Science Education. Retrieved from: http://opportunityequation.org/mobilization/broadening-participation-stem

Moll, L. (1992). Bilingual classroom studies and community practice: Some recent trends. *Educational Researcher, 21*(3), 20–24.

National Science Foundation. (2000). *NSF GRAP plan 2001–2006*. Arlington, VA: NSF. Retrieved April 28, 2017 from https://www.nsf.gov/pubs/2001/nsf0104/nsf0104.pdf

Sosa, A. S. (1997). Involving Hispanic parents in educational activities through collaborative relationships. *Bilingual Research Journal, 21*, 2–3.

Spradley, J. P. (1979). *Participant observation*. New York, NY: Holt, Rinehart and Winston.

Spradley, J. P. (1980). *The ethnographic interview*. New York, NY: Holt, Rinehart and Winston.

Wolcott, H. (1999). *Ethnography a way of seeing*. Walnut Creek, CA: Altimira Press.

Yalowitz, S. & de la Hoz, J. (2009). ¿Como se dice "Evaluation?" The significant difference of culturally appropriate evaluation. Paper presented at *Expanding Informal Science for Latinos* Conference, Albuquerque, NM.

Part 4: Student Engagement

10. Using Cogenerative Dialogues to Create a Constructivist Science Internship for Hispanic High School Students Living in Poverty

PEI-LING HSU

In the decade from 2000 to 2010, the Hispanic population in the United States grew by 43%, from 35.3 million to 50.5 million (Passel, Cohn, & Lopez, 2011), representing 16% of the total US population. Researchers predict that this population will triple by 2050 and will represent 29% of the total US population (Passel & Cohn, 2008). However, researchers also have identified the phenomenon of vanishing Hispanic populations in higher education (Saenz & Ponjuan, 2009).

In particular, research indicates that Hispanic students, as well as African-American and Native American students, face the greatest difficulty in enrolling in and graduating from science and engineering programs (Huang, Taddese, & Walter, 2000). The national average for college readiness among all high school students in the United States is 32%, compared to 38% for Asian students, 37% for white students, 20% for African-American students, 16% for Hispanic students, and 14% for Native American students (Greene & Forster, 2003). Most high school students with low socioeconomic status are especially not college ready because they come from families with limited economic, educational, and social resources, seldom have role models of college graduates in their life to look up to, and often receive poor-quality K–12 schooling (Zambrana & Zoppi, 2002). Given the growth of the Hispanic population in the United States and the current challenges faced by Hispanic students, it is crucial to understand that, without effective interventions, a problematic pipeline will exist that keeps most Hispanic students out of higher education (Chapa & De La Rosa, 2006). It is therefore important to conduct studies that can inform us how to help Hispanic high school students with low socio-economic status to pursue higher education in general and science education in particular.

Next Generation Science Standards recommend that teachers should help students learn science more authentically to support their acquisition of scientific literacy (NGSS Lead States, 2013). Programs designed for students to work with scientists have been suggested as one of the most productive activities for helping students both to learn science authentically by engaging in open-inquiry activities (National Research Council, 1996) and to experience diverse aspects of science practice in problem-solving contexts with a high degree of complexity (Lee & Songer, 2003). Although these types of science internships provide valuable opportunities for students to directly experience science in authentic settings, two important issues emerge during students' interactions with scientists.

First, scientists are deemed to be knowledgeable experts who hold higher status and power in society than do students. In collaborations with scientists, power-over issues are a pervasive phenomenon. Research shows that lay people are often unable to successfully challenge the continual privileging of scientists' technical expertise (Kerr, Cunningham-Burley, & Tutton, 2007). It is therefore not surprising to see power-over issues in student–scientist partnerships. Without an explicit structure and appropriate support, students may be intimidated by scientists and feel they are denied a chance to express their needs and ideas.

Second, the jargon and complex concepts of scientific language tend to be a barrier to communication. It is common for scientists' outreach activities to become lectures, with the public acting as passive listeners (Davies, 2009). As a result, the teaching involved in a science internship tends to involve an authoritative repertoire in which students passively receive instructions from scientists.

To address these issues and challenges, this study set out to transform student-scientist partnerships into constructivist learning environments by incorporating *cogenerative dialogues* (Roth, Tobin, & Zimmerman, 2002) to improve communications and interactions between high school students and scientists.

Constructivist Learning Environment and Cogenerative Dialogues

Increasingly, research is investigating how to provide constructivist learning environments for students. Studies have indicated that the learning environment is a strong factor in determining and predicting students' attitudes toward science (Lawrenz, 1976; Simpson & Oliver, 1990; Talton & Simpson, 1987). Teaching has traditionally been seen as a process of "transmitting" knowledge to students' heads. The traditional classroom environment often emphasized the authority of teachers' knowledge as a means to control the content and timing of student learning activities. In contrast, more and more scholars support the view of social constructivism, which deems learning as a sense-making process involving active negotiation and consensus building with the people and contexts around the learners. A constructivist classroom is a learner-centered environment in which the past experience of the students is respected, construction of knowledge is interactive, inductive, and collaborative, and questions are valued. The teacher in such a classroom acts as a facilitator, provides students with a variety of experiences from which learning is built, and maximizes social interactions among learners so that they can negotiate meaning (Ozkal, Tekkaya, Cakiroglu, & Sungur, 2009). Research shows that if students are given support to exercise their autonomy and control in learning, negotiate meanings among peers, and conduct open-ended inquiry, they tend to develop higher interest in tasks, use more self-regulatory strategies, and demonstrate higher academic performance (Kingir, Tas, Gok, & Vural, 2013).

To help create a constructivist learning environment, cogenerative dialogues (cogens) serve as a potentially productive tool to transform the partnership between students and instructors. Cogens are conversations among different stakeholders about their collective experiences, with the goal of reaching collective decisions about the rules, roles, and responsibilities that govern their shared activities (Roth *et al.*, 2002). Cogens offer participants a safe, respectful space in which to articulate their ideas and needs and address issues involved in their partnerships. Topics for discussion might include the partnership's goals, roles for each participant, content to be learned and discussed, places to work, activities, assessments, and ways to improve. Cogens have been shown to be a powerful means of helping students and teachers address various issues in urban education, which is a difficult environment due to poverty and other social problems (Emdin, 2011).

Basically, cogens can be conducted regularly in school classrooms with a diverse group of stakeholders, such as teachers, students, researchers, and school administrators. Three central principles guide cogens: (1) participants are given equal turns and times to talk; (2) participants show respect and listen attentively in conversations; and (3) a plan of action for addressing identified issues is generated from the conversations and implemented in further practice (Emdin, 2011). Because of their inclusive and democratic nature, cogens appear to be a potentially effective means to create a constructivist learning environment and improve student-scientist partnerships.

Research Context

Work with a Scientist Program and Participants

The Work with a Scientist Program was housed at the University of Texas at El Paso, which is located at the United States–Mexico border. It involved 36 high school students (11th graders) recruited from three Title I schools, which have high percentages of children from low-income families (these particular three schools have 48, 57, and 81% of their students coming from low-income families). Students who were interested in participating in the program submitted an application with teachers' recommendations and were interviewed and selected by the program according to students' knowledge of and commitment to the program. These 36 internship students, of whom 71% were coded as economically disadvantaged, were divided into four groups, and each group worked with one lead scientist and their research team for seven months. These four scientists included a chemist, a neurologist, and two immunologists. From January to May, internship students came to the university every other Saturday to learn about scientific thinking (e.g., how to frame a research question, design an experiment, and find solutions). From June to July, internship students worked with the scientists daily for 30 days on open-inquiry scientific projects. The students also presented their project proposals at the end of June and their final project results at the end of July to the scientists and to their families, school teachers, and friends. During these seven months, students and scientists conducted cogens regularly to address issues and concerns for improving internship teaching and learning.

Cogen Practice in the Science Internship

In each of the four laboratory teams, the cogens involved four groups of stakeholders, consisting of the lead scientist, one to three science teaching assistants, nine high school students, and one cogen mediator who was an educational research assistant who had received training for mediating cogens. Before the program, educational researchers held a cogen training workshop to help the scientists and science teaching assistants understand the purpose and logistics of cogens. At the first cogen session with the high school students, the educational research assistants held another cogen training session to explain the purpose and timeline of cogen practices in the program.

Throughout the program, students had cogens with scientists and research assistants regularly.

During the first five months in the spring semester, students worked with scientists and conducted cogens every other Saturday afternoon from 1:00 p.m. to 4:00 p.m. (science practice for the first two hours and cogens for the third hour). In the six weeks of the summer program, students participated in scientific practice every weekday from 9:00 a.m. to 4:00 p.m., with a one-hour lunch break, and conducted cogens twice a week to address issues and share experiences with each other.

In accordance with cogen rules (Emdin, 2011), each person had equal turns and times to talk, each person showed respect and listened attentively in conversations, a plan of action was generated for addressing issues to be implemented in further practice, and video clips of collective practice were available for discussion. For each cogen, a sandwich structure was used to discuss (1) the implementation of consensus generated from the previous cogen, (2) issues/positives/topics this week (e.g., questions, positive experiences, other topics), and (3) the quality of today's cogen (assessed by randomly checking three items from a list of 40 cogen heuristics (Tobin & Alexakos, 2013). The dialogues included identifying issues and then generating solutions to address the issues and improve the group's scientific practice. Students were active participants in the cogens, which provided opportunities to reflect on and discuss scientific practices, such as project design, data collection, and resolution of challenges associated with their investigations.

Method and Data Sources

The purpose of this study was to investigate high school students' perceptions of the unique learning environment of a university internship that incorporates the pedagogical tool of cogenerative dialogues. Mixed methods were used to collect both quantitative and qualitative data, including surveys, interviews, real-time video recordings, and field notes. For quantitative data, a quasi-experimental design was used to involve an experimental (internship) group and a control (no-internship) group. The internship group included 33 high school students who completed the seven-month internship (out of the 36 who started the internship), and the no-internship group consisted of 20 high school students who took advanced placement physics (AP physics) classes in school. The 33 internship students (28 Hispanics, 2 Asians, 2 Whites, 1 Black) included 11 males and 22 females, whereas the 20 no-internship students (17 Hispanics, 3 Blacks) were 8 males and 12 females.

The Constructivist Learning Environment Survey (CLES; Taylor & Fraser, 1991) was administered to all 53 students as a pre- and posttest. The CLES in this study was a 28-item measure in which participants indicated their responses to statements on a Likert scale with five points (i.e., "very often," "often," "sometimes," "seldom," and "never") on important aspects of a constructivist learning environment (e.g., "In the internship [or, AP physics class], I ask other students about their ideas"; "In the internship [or, AP physics class], I think hard about my own ideas"). For qualitative data, internship students' journals were collected and individual interviews about their internship experience were conducted. Ethnographic data (e.g., field notes, video recording) were also collected throughout the seven-month internship program.

Students' Perceptions of the Learning Environment

To investigate students' perceptions of the learning environments in the university internship and at school, students' gain scores on the pre-CLES and post-CLES, using the General Linear Model procedure in SPSS 21.0 and univariate ANOVA, were compared between the internship group and no-internship group. The analysis showed that students in the internship group had greater gains from pre to post (n=33, pre=3.45, post=3.81, gain=0.36), compared to those in the no-internship group (n=20, pre=3.16, post=3.21, gain=0.05, p=0.003). These findings suggest that students who participated in the internship strengthened their perceptions of constructivist learning over the course of the program to a greater extent than students in the no-internship group. Particularly, female internship students had greater gains from pre to post (n=22, pre=3.49, post=3.92, gain=0.43), compared to those in the no-internship group (n=12, pre=3.34, post=3.27, gain=-0.07, p=0.001). Such differences, however, were not observed among male internship students (n=11, pre=3.42, post=3.70, gain=0.28) and male no-internship students (n=8, pre=2.99, post=3.16, gain=0.17, p=0.48).

Students' journals and interviews also support the view that the internship was a more constructivist learning environment. At the beginning of the internship, students understood that they were expected to have autonomy in their scientific work. Although they may have found it "frightening," they believed they could make it with the support of scientists and assistants.

> I'm also learning that what we're doing now will be all on our own, that we don't need as much supervision as previous states; we're going to have to conduct our own project and research into that like a real scientist. It's a little frightening, because I'm barely getting the feel for it, and eventually, we're going to have to

dive off the deep end with everything. But overall, I know we can take it, that's why we're in this program; to learn and to be more independent in the ways we see science. (St 16)

In the middle of the internship, students commented that they felt "comfortable" with each other and had become more "independent" in their work. They enjoyed the autonomy and were proud of being able to work independently.

> We are slowly getting more comfortable with each other and we are also being more aware if we make a mistake we will be upfront with it. The students' relationship with the mentors is getting stronger in ways that we are more comfortable than before. We are also slowly getting more independent in the lab and we are starting to feel better in doing things by ourselves. We used to be very dependent on our scientist and although we aren't completely independent, we are slowly assimilating ourselves into working on our own. (St 17)

Some students compared the learning environments of the internship and school. They felt that teachers in school usually cover the "basics" of science and teach by "textbooks" (St 23). Thus, students felt that sometimes they just memorized the knowledge in textbooks and did not understand the scientific practices in a deeper, contextualized manner. Occasionally, if experiments were involved at school, students were expected to follow certain procedures to confirm "what you already know" or do "the same project someone else did" (St 23).

Thus, students stressed that the internship was a very different learning environment from school. For example, if one expressed too many ideas, they might be judged and labeled as a "nerd" at school.

> Whereas if I were to do that in high school, I'd be a "know-it-all." I'd be the nerd. It's very judgmental in high school, whereas in college it's like, "Wow. That's a good idea," or, "Yeah, we'll try that. We'll see if works." And then when I came here, and how Dr. MacDonald and how the RAs and how everyone, like, all my lab mates, they were all so willing to hear my opinions, they were willing to test my theories, they were willing to, you know, I would try to throw out different ideas as to how to commence with an experiment, and they would listen to that. (St 14)

While showing too much interest in learning might result in being judged negatively in high school, in the internship, students commented that "you're able to put that knowledge to practice" and "you're able to apply what you learned to a real-life application" (St 26). As a result, students emphasized that they felt heard and respected in the science internship because their ideas were encouraged and accepted.

Students' Experience of Cogens with Scientists

During the cogens with scientists, students discussed various topics about the science internship, including issues and solutions about personal needs (e.g., being hungry), oral instruction (e.g., pace is too fast), teaching materials (e.g., unclear PowerPoint), group communication (e.g., lack of communication), science knowledge (e.g., not having sufficient knowledge) and practice (e.g., not having equal turns), equipment (e.g., that it takes time to run data), data analysis (e.g., unclear guidelines), presentations (e.g., anxious about public speaking), etc. The following episode illustrates how participants communicated during cogens after two hours of internship practice that focused on the chemistry concept of solvents. The scientist mentioned that one possible area the group might improve upon was engaging "the students' thinking about the topic of the day."

> Scientist: Yeah, one maybe comment or not really an issue/a concern, I think we need to engage more some of the students' thinking about the topic of the day.
>
> Mediator: What, what do you mean by that? Can you rephrase it?
>
> Scientist: Thinking, meaning, just for example, an example where we were talking about solvents, okay, ethanol is a solvent. We talked about mixability, how we mix the two solvents, that's not mixable or mixable is one layer versus two. The thinking for me is deeply thinking about why those two solvents will like each other, why the mechanism behind or rationalize behind the why. The question is why. It's not just accepted one plus one equals two, but indeed it equals two because it makes sense.
>
> ...
>
> Mediator: And then why would that be important? To make sure that when you're asking your questions, you're asking why for Dr. Scott to go more into, to create your learning.
>
> Student 1: It like slows down the whole learning process for everybody, not just you. So don't be kind of selfish to not to listen
>
> Student 2: To clear understanding
>
> Mediator: Okay. So what I'm hearing for the solution is that we need to be asking more questions, asking why if we don't understand, but in conjunction with making sure that it's because we're being attentive, and just simply say we just don't understand, to be more clear.
>
> Student 2: Yes.
>
> Mediator: Okay.
>
> Scientist: Or alternatively, slow down the speed of the presentations or the discussions to allow to everybody being on the same train. Right?
>
> Student 3: Yes.
>
> Student 4: Um, because that is actually one of the things or like concerns, is like I'm not a slow learner, it's the fact that, I need it to be kind of said, and then explained, and then said again, and then re-explained, and so if it goes a

bit slower, it'd be easy because I was having a bit of a hard time understanding, and so that's why I was like, I needed a little bit slower than just like here is, here is this, and then slight explanation, look it up and like a little bit more explanation.

Mediator: Okay, so a slower pace with more explanation. Anybody else? That's a really good point. So take your time and do not rush it. We really want you to think this out, because when we come to finding the solution, this is how we're going to implement it for your next internship. So if it's a half, fast done job because you don't agree with it, it's not gonna help you.

Student 5: I feel like another issue may be that sometimes when you're learning something, sometimes you don't get it right away. Like you don't understand it completely, but everybody else does, so sometimes you feel like you should agree too, because you're like, Well, everybody else gets it, I don't. Why am I gonna be the only one to speak up and say, Oh, I don't understand this, and then slow everybody else's pace down. Sometimes I feel like that, like maybe like it's a little bit too fast, like the process is too fast so maybe it should slow down, because others don't really voice their opinions.

After hearing the scientist's suggestion that "we need to engage more some of the students' thinking," high school students started to share their opinions and eventually agreed on the solution that students should ask more questions, especially questions that foster critical thinking. While all the students agreed with this solution, the scientist also suggested another solution: "or alternatively, slow down the speed of the presentation or the discussion to allow to everybody being on the same train." This alternative solution resonated immediately with students, who expressed that a slower pace would really help their comprehension of the instruction.

The episode above shows that the cogens involved equal turns in talking, listening to each other's voice, and collective efforts in brainstorming solutions to improve the internship teaching and learning. Students felt that "cogen is empowering" students to have voices (St 4) and can help scientists and students to "work together" (St 1) as a team. Importantly, students felt "cared" for by the scientists and even commented that they felt "like a family during cogen."

[What] greatly fascinated me is that they not only care about our safety, but also how we feel. Cogen rules are to help better everyone and make us all equal. The scientists made it very clear that they care about our participation and opinions just as much as everyone else. I like to know that the scientist believes in all of us and cares. (St 10)

I feel like a family during cogen. When in a family, you always have to talk to each other, that is the whole point of a family. So like, converse with each other, and actually get a grasp of different values and ideas. Cogen is basically like a place where you work as a family together. (St 16)

The bonding and care that students felt during cogens really helped them maintain their interest in science. For example, one student shared during a cogen that she might decide to drop out of the program because of her low self-esteem and feelings of being less than her peers. However, she ended up completing the program because of the support and encouragement she received from the scientist and her peers during cogens. Students also articulated that cogens provided opportunities for participants to receive feedback or constructive criticism and to recognize areas for improvement. Students interpreted this feedback as a springboard to improve themselves: "Cogen has given me the opportunity to learn about myself and fix the wrong things I have done" (St 2). Students' comments suggest that cogen is a useful tool to empower students to speak up and articulate any questions or concerns, and, at the same time, to help scientists listen to students' ideas and voices. The team atmosphere during cogens fosters a constructivist learning environment where participants' voices are heard and respected.

Conclusion and Discussion

The purpose of the study was to incorporate the pedagogical tool of cogens in a science internship and investigate Hispanic high school students' perceptions of the science internship learning environment. The results show that the internship students in the study perceived the science internship as a constructivist learning environment, especially for female students. Students reported that cogens empowered them to express their voices and concerns and positively enhanced their communications with scientists. These findings suggest that the constructive learning environment of the science internship provides agency and structure that allow students to learn science constructively.

Scientists working with students often encounter teaching difficulties (Mumba, Mejia, Chabalengula, & Mbewe, 2010) and express a need to improve their teaching and communication skills for the purpose of working with students (Hsu & Roth, 2010). The use of cogens would likely address the inevitable issues of power-over, complexity of scientific language, and teaching difficulties that often occur when scientists work with high school students. Conducting cogens regularly in science internships allows both scientists and students to address any emergent or unexpected issues and concerns and to diminish the gaps between scientists and students gradually. In this study, cogens acted as a successful "in-between space" (Bhabha, 1994) to foster dialogues among members of distinct communities of practice.

Importantly, cogens' unique nature provides an intimate, supportive space that allows students to "feel like a family in cogens." That is, during cogens, science professionals are no longer "speaking to" students in a one-way form, but are "working with" students as a team to improve teaching and learning in a two-way form of communication. Thus, students may ask any questions they are interested in and scientists may open themselves more to share their personal stories with the students. In fact, researchers have found that if students learn how scientists achieve through failures and struggles, they may feel more connected to scientists. In addition, understanding the struggles and vulnerabilities of scientists may improve students' motivation and academic performance in science (Lin-Siegler, Ahn, Chen, Fang, & Luna-Lucero, 2016). Through these conversations in cogens with scientists, students may also gain aspirational capital (Yosso, 2005), which enables students to hope and dream for their future even while knowing that challenges are ahead. As reported in this study, for Hispanic students, especially those with low socioeconomic status, bonding with their instructor and peers can play a central role in fostering and maintaining students' interest in science.

Acknowledgments

This material is based on work supported by the National Science Foundation under Grant No. DRL 1322600. Any opinion, findings, and conclusions or recommendations expressed in this material are those of the authors and do not necessarily reflect the views of the National Science Foundation.

References

Bhabha, H. K. (1994). *The location of culture*. New York, NY: Routledge.

Chapa, J., & De La Rosa, B. (2006). The problematic pipeline: Demographic trends and Latino participation in graduate science, technology, engineering, and mathematics programs. *Journal of Hispanic Higher Education, 5*(3), 203–221. doi:10.1177/1538192706288808

Davies, S. R. (2009). Doing dialogue: Genre and flexibility in public engagement with science. *Science as Culture, 18*, 397–416. doi:10.1080/09505430902870591

Emdin, C. (2011). Citizenship and social justice in urban science education. *International Journal of Qualitative Studies in Education, 24*, 285–301. doi:10.1080/09518398.2010.539582

Greene, J. P., & Forster, G. (2003). *Public high school graduation and college readiness rates in the United States*. New York, NY: Center for Civic Innovation, Manhattan Institute. Retrieved from http://www.manhattan-institute.org/pdf/ewp_03.pdf

Hsu, P.-L., & Roth, W.-M. (2010). From a sense of stereotypically foreign to belonging in a science community: Ways of experiential descriptions about high school students' science internship. *Research in Science Education, 40,* 291–311. doi:10.1007/s11165-009-9121-5

Huang, G., Taddese, N., & Walter, E. (2000). *Entry and persistence of women and minorities in college science and engineering education* (NCES Rep. No. 2000–601). Washington, DC: U.S. Government Printing Office.

Kerr, A., Cunningham-Burley, S., & Tutton, R. (2007). Shifting subject positions: Experts and lay people in public dialogue. *Social Studies of Science, 37*(3), 385–411. doi:10.1177/0306312706068492

Kingir, S., Tas, Y., Gok, G., & Vural, S. S. (2013). Relationships among constructivist learning environment perceptions, motivational beliefs, self-regulation and science achievement. *Research in Science & Technological Education, 31*(3), 205–226. doi:10.1080/02635143.2013.825594

Lawrenz, F. P. (1976). Student perception of the classroom learning environment in biology, chemistry and physics courses. *Journal of Research in Science Teaching, 13,* 351–353. doi:10.1002/tea.3660130405

Lee, H.-S., & Songer, N. B. (2003). Making authentic science accessible to students. *International Journal of Science Education, 25,* 923–948. doi:10.1080/09500690305023

Lin-Siegler, X., Ahn, J. N., Chen, J., Fang, F.-F. A., & Luna-Lucero, M. (2016). Even Einstein struggled: Effects of learning about great scientists' struggles on high school students' motivation to learn science. *Journal of Educational Psychology, 108*(3), 314–328. doi:10.1037/edu0000092

Mumba, F., Mejia, W. F., Chabalengula, V. M., & Mbewe, S. (2010). Resident scientists' instructional practices and their perceived benefits and difficulties of inquiry in schools. *Journal of Baltic Science Education, 9,* 187–195.

National Research Council. (1996). *National science education standards.* Washington, DC: National Academy Press.

NGSS Lead States. (2013). *Next generation science standards: For states, by states.* Washington, DC: The National Academies Press.

Ozkal, K., Tekkaya, C., Cakiroglu, J., & Sungur, S. (2009). A conceptual model of relationships among constructivist learning environment perceptions, epistemological beliefs, and learning approaches. *Learning and Individual Differences, 19*(1), 71–79. doi:10.1016/j.lindif.2008.05.005

Passel, J. S., & Cohn, D. (2008). *U.S. population projections: 2005–2050.* Washington, DC: Pew Hispanic Center.

Passel, J. S., Cohn, D., & Lopez, M. H. (2011). *Census 2010: 50 million Latinos/Hispanics account for more than half of nation's growth in past decade.* Washington, DC: Pew Hispanic Center.

Roth, W.-M., Tobin, K., & Zimmerman, A. (2002). Coteaching/cogenerative dialoguing: Learning environments research as classroom praxis. *Learning Environments Research, 5*(1), 1–28.

Saenz, V. B., & Ponjuan, L. (2009). The vanishing Latino male in higher education. *Journal of Hispanic Higher Education, 8*(1), 54–89.

Simpson, R. D., & Oliver, J. S. (1990). A summary of major influences on attitude toward and achievement in science among adolescent students. *Science Education, 74*, 1–18. doi:10.1002/sce.3730740102

Talton, E. L., & Simpson, R. D. (1987). Relationships of attitude toward classroom environment with attitude toward and achievement in science among tenth grade biology students. *Journal of Research in Science Teaching, 24*, 507–526. doi:10.1002/tea.3660240602

Taylor, P. C., & Fraser, B. J. (1991). *CLES: An instrument for assessing constructivist learning environments.* Paper presented at the annual meeting of the National Association for Research in Science Teaching, Lake Geneva, WI.

Tobin, K., & Alexakos, K. (2013). *Coteaching heuristic (I|Other).* New York, NY: The City University of New York.

Yosso, T. J. (2005). Whose culture has capital? A critical race theory discussion of community cultural wealth. *Race, Ethnicity, and Education, 8*(1), 69–91. doi:10.1080/1361332052000341006

Zambrana, R. E., & Zoppi, I. M. (2002). Latina students: Translating cultural wealth into social capital to improve academic success. *Journal of Ethnic & Cultural Diversity in Social Work, 11*(1–2), 33–53. doi:10.1300/J051v11n01_02

11. Behavioral Roots of Latin@ CS Engagement

Don Davis and Gabriela Rivera

The underrepresentation of Latinos in Computer Science (CS) is disconcerting seen from social, fiscal, and design perspectives. The numbers of Latino males completing CS degrees is problematic as only 3% of CS graduates are Latino males whereas Latino males constitute 17.9% of the population (NSF, 2017). Even more troubling, Latinas are especially underrepresented among CS graduates. Although Latinas represent approximately 20.8% of the population between the ages of 18 and 24, only 2.3% of CS graduates are Latinas (NSF, 2017).

Beyond issues of social equity, Latino underrepresentation in CS becomes increasingly problematic as Latinos become the majority, which is projected to happen by 2044 (Colby & Ortman, 2015). Namely, the increasingly important CS-grounded tech sector may likely fail to adequately address the needs and interests of Hispanic communities (Tornatzky, Macias, & Jones, 2002), the fastest growing demographic in the US (Dowd, Malcom, & Macias, 2010).

Moreover, for many Latino students, there are additional obstacles, including fiscal and familial concerns, that can impede exposure to and potential interest in CS (*cf.* Varma, 2007; Zambrana & Zoppi, 2002). As with other demographics underrepresented in CS, a lack of childhood opportunities to engage with CS limits later participation (*cf.* Margolis, Goode, Holme, & Nao, 2008). Consequently, there is a push to increase CS engagement opportunities for Latina/o and other underrepresented students (*cf.* Gates *et al.*, 2011).

Self and Identity

The targeted fostering of identity is of particular concern in broadening participation, especially with regards to CS, as subtle and less subtle identity clues can suggest to students that they do not belong in CS (e.g., Teague, 2009). Though for underrepresented students, such as Latinas, interest may simply relate to exposure to and familiarity with CS (Varma, 2006, 2007). Furthermore, there are pragmatic benefits to supporting students' identification with future CS-related careers, i.e., the CS selves that students see as possible (Cuero & Kaylor, 2010; Davis, Yuen, & Berland, 2014; Dunkel & Anthis, 2001).

However, many articulations of *self* are "mentalistic," meaning that they are unobservable and unmeasurable, making interventions that target identity and self impractical (Stewart, 2013). By contrast, from a behavioral lens, *self* can be operationalized as "discrimination of one's own behavior" (Dymond & Barnes, 1997). More specifically, nonverbal and verbal behavior are deeply intertwined, and relationships between these two can produce *self*-relations that influence patterns of behavior that comprise skill and identity trajectories. For instance, having a family member that is supportive of tinkering or computer-related behaviors, or having a role model in the CS field, can shape an individual's behavior and increase the likelihood of developing a CS identity and related career trajectory (*cf.* Davis *et al.*, 2014). In order to effectively increase participation in CS, it becomes necessary to build on students' behavioral assets, namely those patterns of behavior that can best support CS identity trajectories.

Makerspaces

Consequently, educators, researchers, and community activists are increasingly acknowledging and examining the affordances of makerspaces for broadening STEM interest and STEM-related identity trajectories, especially for underrepresented students (Barton, Tan, & Greenberg, 2016; Brahms, 2014; Shin, 2016). Makerspaces are public, often community-driven formal spaces where students can be exposed to new forms of equipment, can learn the necessary skills for projects that require electronics and programming, and work with knowledgeable others to complete personally relevant projects (Davis & Mason, 2017). Such open-ended, community-situated spaces are advocated as providing many different pathways to CS and other STEM skill and interest trajectories, as they provide authentic and personally relevant contexts for engaging with underlying concepts, communities of practice, and related technologies (e.g., Blikstein, 2013).

The more authentic, community-oriented makerspace approach may be more beneficial for some Latinos, as researchers have noted certain assets, i.e., patterns of prior conditioning and resulting behavioral repertoires, common to Latino communities that may support students' greater CS success (*cf.* Smokowski, Rose, & Bacallao, 2010). Among these cultural assets are an emphasis on family life and interest in cultural heritage (Smokowski *et al.*, 2010). These assets are particularly relevant to makerspace supported learning, as makerspaces support community and familial projects in addition to many other personally and culturally relevant projects (Brahms, 2014).

Consequently, we have sought to behaviorally examine whether and how the CS-related identity behavioral repertoires of the Latina/o students in this study were engaged during a makercamp designed to increase CS interest. Namely, the research question guiding this study was: For the CS novice Latina/o students participating in this study, what are the observable interactions related to identity and skill trajectories emitted during participation in an introductory CS makerspace experience?

Methodology

This study was grounded in radical behaviorism to facilitate greater social justice. Simply stated, behavioral methods rely on observable data and the functional analysis of behavior (*cf.* Lahren, 1978), which provides a better pathway to social justice. Namely, as Moore (2003) suggests, much traditional psychology, whether it be cognitive psychology, neuroscience, psychopathology, or personality theory are based on mentalisms that provide an echo chamber for "...pernicious social-ism of racism and sexism" (p. 192). By contrast, behavior analysts take the distinct perspective that social injustice is the aggregate product of problematic behaviors being socially reinforced; this distinction is important as it shifts the focus to external factors—and does not place blame on those being oppressed (Moore, 2003; *cf.* Ahl, 2006).

More specifically, this study used a behavioral phenomenological approach (Day, 1977; Lahren, 1978; McCorkle, 1978) to investigate novice Latino/a engagement in a makerspace and avoid problematic mentalisms and other examples of deficit thinking that attribute problematic character traits to students (Valencia, 2012). Moreover, the behavioral phenomenological methodology was selected because it provides a behavioral, but more qualitatively nuanced, nonexperimental method for investigating novel phenomena, which made it well suited for initial behavioral investigations into makerspace experiences for Latina/o students (Davis & Mason, 2017; McCorkle, 1991). As with other small n and qualitative studies, it would be inappropriate to generalize the findings presented here to large populations; rather findings provide starting points for further experimental research (*cf.* Creswell, 2014). Also, the more intense focus on a smaller group of participants, as in this study, highlights nuance and variability that larger studies obfuscate (Cooper, 2007). Here, as with other behavioral studies, researchers seek to identify relationships in participants' histories, their behaviors, and how the environment increases or decreases those behaviors. Additionally, students' self-articulated histories are used to contextualize their experiences at the makercamp.

Makercamp

The activities described here took place at a makerspace near downtown in a large, predominately Hispanic central Texas city. The makercamp presented in this study recruited participants from makerspace regulars and the general public, as is common with makerspace classes. The makercamp consisted of two consecutive weekends of approximately 4.5 hours each day. Makercamp activities focused primarily on using the Raspberry Pi, a credit-card sized computer, to program interactions with the physical world, such as lights, buzzers, and motors.

In total, the makercamp had seventeen participants registered, six of whom were involved in a larger research study. Here, the current research focuses on the three high-school-aged students identified as Latina/os, Osiel, Yesenia, and Sara (pseudonyms). The three participants were recruited, for a much larger study, from the school and classroom of the researcher. Two of the three participants attended non-CS classes with the researcher. The third participant had participated in a Pre-AP CS course and knew the researcher in the context of the magnet program. The three students in this study were familiar with one another as they were in the same magnet program.

During the camp, students worked primarily in pairs. First, they programmed with Scratch, a drag-and-drop programming language, and then on the last day, students used Python, a text-based programming language.

Data Collection

The primary researcher conducted semi-structured audio interviews, typically 15- to 30-minutes in length, with each participant. The interviewer directed questions so as to evoke each participant's description of self and their relation to CS-related topics, including careers, making, and family. Also, participants were audio and video recorded while attending the camp. Participants wore a lanyard with a cassette-tape recorder attached for audio, and there were three cameras focused on the areas where participants were seated.

Audio from the makercamp was then transcribed to be further analyzed for verbal behavior, including the conditions that preceded and followed statements, i.e., antecedents and consequences. Though both verbal and physical behavior were examined, verbal behavior was given special attention because verbal behavior forms the basis for complex problem solving and identity-related behaviors (Barnes-Holmes, Hayes, & Dymond, 2001; O Hora & Barnes-Holmes, 2000).

For verbal behavior, antecedent stimuli, events occurring before the participants' statements, were coded as *other's verbal behavior*, participant is responding to someone else's verbal speech, *environment*, other physical stimuli relating to participants' immediate surroundings, and *motivating operations*, a want or need, such as hunger or thirst, causing responses to become more rewarding. Consequences, the result of the participant's verbal behavior, were scored as either social, such as "small talk," or physical, such as requesting and receiving a physical object. Also, whether a student explicitly referred to them self as an individual or part of a group was coded as another measure for engagement (*cf.* Fies & Langman, 2011).

Video recordings were analyzed with partial interval recording to identify physical on-task behaviors, including *pragmatic actions* with real-world effects such as moving a water bottle, and *epistemic actions*, such as gesturing or movement to help articulate speech (Kirsh & Maglio, 1994), and off-task behaviors, including cell phone use. Intervals were one-minute long, wherein, if the behavior was observed at any point during the interval, it was scored as occurring, i.e., partial interval recording. In keeping with the aforementioned social justice motivations for using behaviorism, researchers refrained from speculating on internal states (*cf.* Mason, Davis, & Andrews, 2016).

Osiel

In interviews, Osiel identified himself as someone who was "not afraid of anybody" and follows this statement up with "when you grow up, [you] just do what you want and don't be afraid of what anybody else is going to say about you." Osiel states that his peers might label him using curse words, homophobic slurs, and hateful words. Such aversive experiences with others are replicated throughout Osiel's interviews, when he, possibly unknowingly, repeatedly describes a lack of reinforcement from friends and family regarding computer and STEM-related professions. He notes that when speaking about the makercamp with his family, "they were like not that interested, like usual." Furthermore, Osiel relates few and mostly negative experiences when describing his family in relation to technology.

Osiel indicates that his friends say that he will never reach his career goal, being a surgeon, because he does not receive "the best grades." However, even with these punishing statements, he still asserts the importance of his family and friends as "things that make [him] happy." Osiel, also, indicates his peers do not interact with CS and technology. His interviews reveal a history of punishment through verbal comments from peers, friends, and family, regarding many topics including CS and technology-related pursuits.

School for Osiel also appears not to be a reinforcing environment that facilitates completion of school work or a perception of success. He states, "Sometimes I don't work out my problems with my studies" or "do…homework a lot," and that he "barely passed" his courses.

Despite many identified aversive experiences, Osiel does suggest that elements of making and technology can be rewarding. For example, he describes, "I feel like when you create something on a computer, you feel like excitement. I guess like you're happy that you actually make something cool on a computer instead of just making something on paper that is not as interesting." However, in a follow-up interview, Osiel concludes that he would only go into computer programming if he did not "like medical stuff anymore" or "broke [his] leg or something."

An Analysis of Osiel's Speech and Other Behavior

During Osiel's only day (day 1, approximately 4 hours) at the makercamp, he only spoke 84 times. Though he seldom spoke, much of his communication was socially motivated. All of Osiel's interactions were identified as having social consequences and many with physical consequences as well. Overall, 79.8% (67/84) of Osiel's utterances were preceded and most likely prompted by other's verbal behavior. The sparsity of his communication reveals that he rarely initiated conversations with others at the makerspace, suggesting a reduced susceptibility to the social and physical contingencies afforded by the makerspace and that the makerspace's contingencies did not reinforce his verbal behavior. Further, Osiel attended only one of the four days, which highlights that his participation was particularly important to consider when refining makerspace style interventions. It should be noted that Osiel missed the second weekend for a family trip. Namely, it is students who respond less positively for whom the environment should be reconsidered.

Osiel spoke quite infrequently with few utterances (n=84) mentioning himself, alone or in combination with others, in relation to anything even less frequently (n=22). His statements had a mean length of 5.2 words, a median length of 4 words, a mode of 1 word, and a maximum utterance length was only 34 words. The "not present" interpretation of Osiel's behavior is further illustrated by his tallied behavior frequency. Namely, Osiel frequently engaged in off-task behavior, looking at his cell phone during 46% of the timed intervals during the makercamp, i.e., meaning that he looked at his phone at least once a minute 46% of the time. Subsequently, when asked if he had taken out his cell phone at the makerspace, he explained,

> Yeah, like, I would be confused…I felt like a little awkward because people were doing like they know what to do. And I was like kind of in my own world with like "I don't know what to do." And so I would just like get on my phone. And be like "okay, just wait until someone tells you something."

This escape behavior was, however, not unique to the makerspace environment. When Osiel was asked if the cellphone behavior was the same in his classes, he affirmed, "when I don't know what to do on assignments, sometimes I will just take my phone and get distracted."

Yesenia

Yesenia identified herself as "that weirdo in the corner who doesn't talk and is pretty smart." She also describes herself self-determined in relation to school, noting that for "school work, I refuse to fail" and that she does not "give up. I just ask someone for help…I refuse to fail." She elaborated on her personal history, explaining "well, my parents are strict. If I don't get a certain grade every report card, they're going to punish me for it." When asked how she was punished, she detailed that she had "a lot of technology at home. So they're going to take away that, take away all my privileges, and they recently started ignoring me."

Yesenia suggests that her immediate family does not exhibit a positive relationship to or interest in technology. She quotes her family as describing technology as "wasting my eyesight on something that…they don't think will get me anywhere." Similarly, Yesenia depicts her family as expressing little interest in the makercamp, explaining "they're just like 'oh, you're going here? Okay. We'll drop you off and pick you up." The depicted lack of interest from her family would be unlikely to directly increase the reinforcing value of technology and making for Yesenia. Further, Yesenia portrays her family's relationships to technology as primarily aversive.

During interviews, Yesenia articulates a preference for making, such as "digital art stuff," over CS and programming. She states that she enjoys making things with computer and technology, because "it's entertaining." When asked about how this relates to peers, she states that they say creating things using technology is "cool." Yesenia's articulation of peers who find making reinforcing suggests greater susceptibility to the social reinforcers provided by communities that support making behaviors. Moreover, Yesenia's descriptions of CS, technology, and making suggest a history of related reinforcement, but not exerting strong control. For example, she notes that programming "could be a hobby" for her. Though, she did not "see [herself] doing this for a job" and elaborated that CS was "fun, just not overly fun." However, she does say that she would like to work as a video game designer.

An Analysis of Yesenia's Speech and Other Behavior

During Yesenia's time (3 days, approximately 12 hours) at the makercamp, she produced few verbal episodes (62, 114, 105), with short mean lengths (3.5, 3.9, 4.3), with increasing maximum lengths of 22, 23, and 36 words. Overall, many of Yesenia's utterances had other's verbal behavior as a noticeable antecedent (96.8%, 60/62; 85.1%, 97/114; 95.2%, 100/105), indicating she did not initiate conversations with others at the makerspace. Almost all (>99%) of Yesenia's interactions were identified as having social consequences, with few identified physical consequences (12.9%, 8/62; 12.3%, 14/114; 8.6%, 9/105) emphasizing the speak-only-when-spoken-to nature of her conversations.

Yesenia spoke only infrequently with few utterances each day (n=62, 114, 105) referring to her herself less frequently (n=15, 24, 26). Though Yesenia indicated that she had a cellphone, it was rarely visible. She only engaged in observable off-task behavior, such as looking at her cell phone, 2.7% of the time. Probing Yesenia' perceptions of cell phone use and related academic escape behavior, the interviewer recounts to Yesenia that some students indicated that they took out their cellphones to await further instructions if confused. Yesenia was asked if she engaged in such behavior. She replied,

> No, they're dinguses...Because they could just try for themselves. Usually, if you just mess with it a little, you should get what you want, even though you weren't trying to.

She was asked to explain what "messing with it" entailed. She expounded, "you see a code, you just mess with different settings until you get a result." Yesenia was then asked to discriminate why she had engaged in changing things whereas some other students had not. She posited "they're lazy" and added, "they're quitters." The interviewer then prompted Yesenia to explain why the others were quitters and she was not. She elaborated,

> What makes them quitters is that they think they can just stop whenever they want, 'cause they know they'll get the answers delivered right to them on a silver plate instead of working for it.

She explained that she had learned from her parents "if you don't do anything, you're not going to get anything in return."

Sara

During her interviews, Sara identified herself as "someone who likes to create things" using several types of methods such as animation programs, programming, and creating things out of junk. She stated that she enjoys playing massively multiplayer online (MMO) games, from which she appears to receive a significant amount of reinforcement.

Sara's frequent descriptions of familial making suggest that she has a history of reinforcement and likely increased susceptibility to the contingencies of reinforcement afforded by maker communities for behaviors involving making, CS, programming, and technology. She explicitly articulates multiple examples of her mother, brother, and older sister as makers. Further, she notes that her peers are "amazed" by her ability to code and make things. Sara distinctly indicates that progressing and learning about technology is reinforcing, elucidating "[the animation program] is very hard to [use], but as I move on and I get more programs and more and more I'm able to expand what I like to do."

In relation to school, Sara states the makercamp environment was "much more fun," but may only be for people who are interested in creating things. During her final interview, she indicates that she would like to pursue studying CS, "because I like this stuff and I would like to learn even more than I know already," even though she failed her second-semester introductory CS course.

An Analysis of Sara's Speech and Other Behavior

Sara was more verbose than other participants with more daily utterances (377, 633, 727, 706), commonly longer utterance means (10.8, 9.4, 9.4, 12.8), longer maximum utterance lengths (of 247, 299, 127, and 244 words).

As the makercamp progressed, Sara spoke even more frequently. Her speech was increasingly prompted by others' verbal behavior, from 77.5 to 93.5% of statements. Although environmental stimuli often preceded Sara's utterances, they less commonly preceded her VB as the camp progressed. Few utterances were attributed to motivating operations, i.e., wants or needs, as the direct identifiable antecedents. Sara's contingencies were also most commonly social, quite frequently a combination of social and physical, whereby the consequences were rarely only physical.

Sara referred to herself, alone or in coordination with others, most frequently (37.1%, 140/377; 32.2%, 204/633; 42.6%, 310/727; 50.0%, 353/706). She also engaged in off-task behavior, looking at her cell phone, during 19.5% of the intervals of her makercamp attendance. When asked whether she used her cell phone in class. She explained that she did not "because I can get in trouble if I use it during class, plus you can get it taken away, and it is a distraction."

An Examination of Participants' Contingency Histories and Self

A core tenet of behaviorism is that three elements determine behavior: prior experiences, the current situation, and phylogenetic susceptibility to reinforcement (e.g., Skinner, 1953). During the makercamp, each participant's unique personal history noticeably influenced their relationships and responding identifiably with respect to prior experiences with school, family, CS, and making. Here, verbal and physical behaviors and engagement are not exclusive and should be considered together.

When comparing participants, Osiel and Sara have stark differences in their data. Sara spoke, on three of the four days she attended, over seven times as much as Osiel during his only day of attendance. Yesenia and Osiel had similarly low frequencies of speaking; however, when comparing off-task behavior, Osiel engaged in self-described escape behaviors at a much higher rate—with a 46% chance of looking at his phone each minute. Yesenia and Sara, attending three and four days of camp respectively, engaged in off-task behaviors at significantly lower rates, suggesting that they were more "present"—engaged and reinforced by the makerspace activities. It is perhaps worth noting that given the frequency of their speech, both Osiel and Yesenia could be considered "quiet"; it was their observable off-task behavior that was more revealing of escape and engagement. Given Osiel's self-articulation, limited speech, and frequent off-task behaviors, it is unsurprising that he did not return to the makerspace. By contrast, Sara's frequency of speech and low levels of off-task behavior and Yesenia's low rates of off-task behavior reflect more likely susceptibility to reinforcement for articulated CS identities and skills.

Lessons Learned from Osiel

For example, Osiel identified little support from his family and his peers within the school setting. His articulated lack of prior reinforcement was evident in his limited verbal and physical engagement with the makerspace and susceptibility to its contingencies of reinforcement. Attesting to the effects of antecedent experience, Osiel indicated that his frequent escape behaviors had been learned at school. Similarly, Osiel depicted his and his family's relations to technology, CS, and making as primarily negative experiences. Given his self-reports, it is unsurprising that Osiel attended to his phone the most, during 49% of the intervals of day one, out of the three participants and only attended one of the four classes. Osiel's lack of engagement, attendance, and resorting to escape-maintained behaviors could be due to lack of suggests the need for more targeted social and task-related reinforcement.

Osiel's most commonly articulated self is one of distinction from academic contexts. Such self-articulation and related responding cannot facilitate his higher education medicine goals or CS interest. By contrast, Osiel did express reinforcement during more creative endeavors such as digital art. Using Osiel as a case example, for makerspace activities to support CS or maker identity trajectories, they should be framed in coordination with creative and exploratory aspects—even more so than presented at the camp. Furthermore, Osiel and others similar to Osiel would benefit from targeted, specific conversations with near peers who affirm their interests and connections to CS and making.

Lessons Learned from Sara

Sara presented a stark contrast to Osiel. She evidenced participation in several communities, including her family, peers, and gaming community, that facilitated pathways to technology and making identities increasing her likelihood to engage in and discuss such behaviors. Her descriptions of past experiences illustrate her pathway to a game programming identity. Moreover, Sara engaged in the most verbal behavior, had limited cell phone usage while attending the camp, and took home a Raspberry Pi when provided the opportunity. Sara's divergent experience highlights that, with little adaptation, makerspace environments can be more conducive in maintaining CS and maker interest for individuals with related interactional histories. For example, Sara would most likely have benefited more from the makercamp by reifying longitudinal

career and project goals in coordination with experienced makers and culturally relevant role models.

Lessons Learned from Yesenia

Yesenia differed from both Osiel and Sara. Whereas Osiel mainly articulated a
lack of reinforcement for himself and Sara indicated frequent prior reinforcement of maker, CS, and technology-related behaviors, Yesenia's description
was more ambivalent. On the one hand, her parents actively questioned her
interest in technology, and on the other, she described reinforcement emanat-
ing from her peers with regards to technology-related topics.

While attending the makercamp, Yesenia did not speak much. However,
Yesenia describes her *self* as a resilient individual, which behaviorally speaking
describes someone acclimated to an intermittent schedule of reinforcement[1]
like those evidenced by professionals. Her self-articulated identity provides a
helpful impetus, i.e., rule-governed behavior or meta-discriminative stimulus,
for engaging with extended problem-solving tasks. Moreover, she explicitly
connects her identity to systematic tinkering, which has been suggested to
be key in the early acquisition of CS skills (Berland, Martin, Benton, Petrick
Smith, & Davis, 2013; Martin, 2009). Yesenia would benefit from targeted
activities that prompt Yesenia's articulation of self in relation to CS and frame
CS in relation to her identified interests such as game development.

Limitations

As with other small n and qualitative studies, this study has limited replicability. Given the nuanced approach and the nature of individuals, replicability
is not the goal for such studies. More so then, a limitation of this study is
the discrimination training of the researchers and access to participants. The
behavioral and relational discriminations of neither researcher are perfect and
are products of their unique interactional histories. Another possible limitation is that the interviews were conducted by a non-Latino male, which may
have influenced the veracity, framing, and length of participants' responses.

Recommendations

Identifying strategies to assist Hispanic students, Hug, Thiry, and Tedford
(2011) noted that near-peer tutoring (modeling) and mentored lab activities
with Hispanic student mentors bolstered Hispanic students' CS success. The
study presented here highlights the relevance of Hug *et al.* (2011) viewed

through a behavioral lens. Namely, providing personally relevant role models, whether it be family, peers, or others, can increase the likely reinforcement of CS and making-related activities, which can then facilitate the necessary social contingencies for Latino students in CS and maker-related behaviors. The communities and improved opportunities for engagement can then in turn support more longitudinal CS identity and skill trajectories—potentially increasing the number of Latino students pursuing CS-related careers.

However, makerspaces and related activities will not help unless students have access to these resources, made available in personally and culturally relevant manner (*cf.* Brahms, 2014), which is problematic as underrepresented students typically have significantly fewer opportunities to explore CS and CS-related topics at younger, more impressionable ages (Margolis *et al.*, 2008; *cf.* Tai, Liu, Maltese, & Fan, 2006). If schools, communities, and other stakeholders work in coordination to provide maker-rich CS-related activities, students will be more likely to develop the requisite verbal communities, e.g., maker communities, that provide frequent opportunities for members increase their related use of technical language and articulations of self. Such communities can then facilitate more longitudinal CS identity and skill behaviors, possibly leading to higher matriculation and retention in CS-related fields for underrepresented students.

Indeed, CS and maker communities may be more significant than fluency building activities; as such activities do not necessarily build students' interest in studying CS or their interest in CS careers (Hug *et al.*, 2010). This should be less surprising in light of the findings presented in this study that highlight the dominant role of social interactions and social reinforcers in CS exploration activities—even for students who speak infrequently. Therefore, it is crucial to develop social, relevant makerspaces that can provide the needed verbal communities to grow students' perceptions of self as potential computer scientists (Dunkel & Anthis, 2001; Fordham & Ogbu, 1986; Lee & Hoadley, 2007; Markus & Nurius, 1986). Moreover, by targeting individuals at a younger age, longer contingency histories related to CS can be developed, which in the end, would require a much longer period of time for these behaviors to extinguish or, in layman's terms, would create greater CS resilience.

Note

1. Here, it is especially important to utilize behavioral definitions for terms such as resilience so as to avoid the problematic mentalistic and eugenic baggage that they are otherwise burdened with (*cf.* Bennett *et al.*, 2004).

References

Ahl, H. (2006). Motivation in adult education: a problem solver or a euphemism for direction and control?. *International Journal of lifelong education, 25*(4), 385–405.

Barnes-Holmes, D., Hayes, S. C., & Dymond, S. (2001). Self and self-directed rules. In S. Hayes, D. Barnes-Holmes, & B. Roche (Eds.), *Relational frame theory: A post-Skinnerian account of human language and cognition* (pp. 119–140). New York, NY: Kluwer Academic.

Barton, A. C., Tan, E., & Greenberg, D. (2016). The makerspace movement: Sites of possibilities for equitable opportunities to engage underrepresented youth in STEM. *Teachers College Record.*

Bennett, G. G., Merritt, M. M., Sollers, J. J., III, Edwards, C. L., Whitfield, K. E., Brandon, D. T., & Tucker, R. D. (2004). Stress, coping, and health outcomes among African-Americans: A review of the John Henryism hypothesis. *Psychology & Health, 19*(3), 369–383.

Berland, M., Martin, T., Benton, T., Petrick Smith, C., & Davis, D. (2013). Using learning analytics to understand the learning pathways of novice programmers. *Journal of the Learning Sciences, 22*(4), 564–599.

Blikstein, P. (2013). Digital fabrication and 'making' in education: The democratization of invention. In J. Walter-Herrmann & C. Büching (Eds.), *FabLabs: Of Machines, Makers and Inventors.* (pp. 1–21). Bielefeld: Transcript Publishers.

Brahms, L. J. (2014). *Making as a learning process: Identifying and supporting family learning in informal settings* (Doctoral dissertation). Retrieved from Proquest Dissertations Publishing. (UMI No. 3582510).

Colby, S., & Ortman, J.M. (2014). *Projections of the Size and Composition of the U.S. Population: 2014 to 2060* (Current Population Reports, P25-1143). Washington, DC.: U.S. Census Bureau.

Cooper, J. O. (2007). *Applied behavior analysis* (2nd ed.). Upper Saddle River, NJ: Pearson/Merrill-Prentice Hall.

Creswell, J. W. (2014). Research questions and hypotheses. In J. W. Creswell (Ed.), *Research design: Qualitative, quantitative, and mixed methods designs* (4th ed., pp. 139–154). Los Angeles, CA: Sage Publications, Inc.

Cuero, K., & Kaylor, M. (2010). Engaging in travesuras: A Latino fifth-grader's disassociation from the schoolboy label. *International Journal of Multicultural Education, 12*(1), 1–15.

Davis, D., & Mason, L. L. (2017). A behavioral phenomenological inquiry of maker identity. *Behavior Analysis: Research and Practice, 17*(2), 174–196.

Davis, D., Yuen, T., & Berland, M. (2014). Multiple case study of nerd identity in a CS1 class. In *Proceedings of the 45th ACM Technical Symposium on Computer Science Education* (pp. 325–330). New York, NY: ACM.

Day, W. F. (1977). On the behavioral analysis of self-deception and self-development. In T. Mischel (Ed.), *The Self: Philosophical and Psychological Issues,* (pp. 224–249). Oxford, England: Blackwell.

Dowd, A. C., Malcom, L. E., & Macias, E. E. (2010). *Improving transfer access to STEM bachelor's degrees at Hispanic serving institutions through the America COMPETES Act.* Los Angeles, CA: University of Southern California, Rossier School of Education.

Dunkel, C. S., & Anthis, K. S. (2001). The role of possible selves in identity formation: A short-term longitudinal study. *Journal of Adolescence, 24*(6), 765–776.

Dymond, S., & Barnes, D. (1997). Behavior-analytic approaches to self-awareness. *The Psychological Record, 47*(2), 181–200.

Fies, C., & Langman, J. (2011). Bridging worlds: Measuring learners' discursive practice in a part sim supported biology lesson. *International Journal of Science and Mathematics Education, 9*(6) 1–24.

Fordham, S., & Ogbu, J. (1986). Black students' school success: Coping with the burden of acting white. *Urban Review, 18*, 176–206.

Gates, A. Q., Hug, S., Thiry, H., Aló, R., Beheshti, M., Fernandez, J., … Adjouadi, M. (2011). The computing alliance of Hispanic-serving institutions: Supporting Hispanics at critical transition points. *Transactions of Computing Education, 11*(3), 1–16.

Hug, S., Thiry, H., & Tedford, P. (2011). Learning to love computer science: peer leaders gain teaching skill, communicative ability and content knowledge in the CS classroom. In *Proceedings of the 42nd ACM Technical Symposium on Computer Science Education* (Vol. Dallas, TX, USA, pp. 201–206). New York, NY, USA: ACM.

Kirsh, D., & Maglio, P. (1994). On distinguishing epistemic from pragmatic action. *Cognitive Science, 18*(4), 513–549.

Lahren, B. L. (1978). *An exploratory functional analysis of stimulus control in descriptive verbal behavior* (Doctoral dissertation, University of Nevada, Reno).

Lee, J., & Hoadley, C. (2007). Leveraging identity to make learning fun: Possible selves and experiential learning in massively multiplayer online games (MMOGs). *Innovate, 3.*

Markus, H., & Nurius, P. (1986). Possible selves. *American Psychologist, 41*(9), 954–969.

Margolis, J., Goode, J., Holme, J. J., & Nao, K. (2008). *Stuck in the shallow end: Education, race, and computing.* Cambridge, MA: The MIT Press.

Martin, T. (2009). Rethinking the concrete to abstract shift: A theory of physically distributed learning. *Child Development Perspectives, 3*(3), 140–144.

Mason, L. L., Davis, D., & Andrews, A. (2016). Mentalistic explanations for autistic behavior: A behavioral phenomenological analysis. *Behavior and Philosophy, 43*, 62–84.

McCorkle, M. (1978). *A radical behaviorist study of "women's experience of conflict"* (Doctoral dissertation, University of Nevada, Reno).

McCorkle, M. (1991). A retrospective account of some qualitative research. *The Qualitative Report, 1*(2), 1–10.

Moore, J. (2003). Behavior analysis, mentalism, and the path to social justice. *The Behavior Analyst, 26*(2), 181–193.

National Science Foundation, Division of Science Resources Statistics. (2011). *Women, Minorities, and Persons with Disabilities in Science and Engineering: 2011* (Special Report NSF 11–309). Arlington, VA.: National Science Foundation, Division of Science Resources Statistics. Retrieved from http://www.nsf.gov/statistics/wmpd/

O Hora, D., & Barnes-Holmes, D. (2000). Stepping up to the challenge of complex human behavior: A response to Ribes-Iñesta's response. *Behavior and Philosophy, 29,* 59–60.

Shin, M. (2016). *A makerspace for all: Youth learning, identity, and design in a community-based makerspace – ProQuest.* East Lansing, MI: Michigan State University.

Skinner, B. F. (1953). The controlling environment. In B.F. Skinner (Ed.), *Science and human behavior* (pp. 129–140). New York, NY: The Free Press.

Smokowski, P. R., Rose, R. A., & Bacallao, M. (2010). Influence of risk factors and cultural assets on Latino adolescents' trajectories of self-esteem and internalizing symptoms. *Child Psychiatry & Human Development, 41*(2), 133–155.

Stewart, I. (2013). A recent behavior analytic approach to the self. *European Journal of Behavioral Analysis, 14*(2), 271–283.

Tai, R. H., Liu, C. Q., Maltese, C., & Fan, X. (2006). Planning early for careers in science. *Science, 312,* 1143–1145.

Teague, D. M. (2009). A people-first approach to programming. In M. Hamilton & T. Clear (Eds.), *Proceedings of the Eleventh Australasian Conference on Computing Education – Volume 95* (Vol. Wellington, New Zealand, pp. 171–180). Darlinghurst, Australia, Australia: Australian Computer Society, Inc.

Tornatzky, L. G., Macias, E. E., & Jones, S. (2002). *Latinos and information technology: The promise and the challenge.* Claremont, CA: The Tomás Rivera Policy Institute.

Valencia, R. R. (2012). *The evolution of deficit thinking: Educational thought and practice.* New York, NY: Routledge.

Varma, R. (2006). Making computer science minority-friendly. *Communications of the ACM, 49,* 129–134.

Varma, R. (2007). Women in computing: The role of geek culture. *Science as Culture, 16*(4), 359–376.

Zambrana, R., & Zoppi, I. M. (2002). Latina students: Translating cultural wealth into social capital to improve academic success. *Journal of Ethnic & Cultural Diversity in Social Work, 11*(1/2), 33–53.

12. Latin@ Students' Perspectives on Learning Real-to-My-Life Mathematics

Patricia Maria Buenrostro

It has been well documented that Latin@ students (and other marginalized racial-ethnic groups) continue to engage in STEM fields of study at disproportionately lower rates (National Science Foundation, 2006). The literature points to various barriers that might explain and contribute to Latin@s underrepresentation and interest in pursuing STEM-related degrees. Some of these barriers include inadequate K–12 academic preparation in STEM-related subjects, insufficient postsecondary academic and moral support, and financial and familial responsibilities (Taningco, Mathew, & Pachon, 2008).

There is an overwhelming narrative that STEM implies a career in contributing to helping secure the U.S. prominence as a global power (Martin, 2003; Secada, 1989). The presumed crisis over the U.S. global standing in technological advantage and innovation has created a demand for more workers entering the labor force with STEM-focused degrees. However, I argue, as others have, that mathematical literacy can and should serve an alternative, justice-oriented vision in today's world. Perhaps by expanding our understanding of possible STEM-related careers to include explicit goals toward creating more equity on the planet and less power differentials between groups, we might bring more socially conscious students into the fore.

The notion that mathematics or STEM-related disciplines can serve a purpose other than maintaining a U.S. competitive edge in global relations is not new. In this chapter, I draw on both a theoretical framing of mathematics education and an exemplary urban high school mathematics class that promoted an explicit stance toward justice. Students in the focal class looked to each other for intellectual support as they collectively persevered through challenging mathematics in order to interrogate relevant social problems impacting their families and communities. I begin with the theoretical framework upon which the class was designed and carried out followed by a description of the class and students' perspectives on learning mathematics as a tool for understanding and transforming their social reality.

Theoretical Framing: Critical Mathematics Education

Critical mathematics (CM) education has its roots in critical pedagogy and has great overlap with the concept of teaching mathematics for social justice (TM-fSJ). I use both terms interchangeably to signify the notion that mathematics as a disciplinary lens can serve social, economic, and political justice goals. A major goal of CM education is to use mathematics (and other subjects) to interrogate and transform issues of sociopolitical (in)justices impacting disenfranchised communities. At the same time, critical mathematics educators are committed to a mathematics education program that "seeks to engage students, socially marginalized in their societies, in cognitively-demanding mathematics in ways that help them succeed in learning that which dominant ideology positions them to believe they are incapable" (Powell, 2012, p. 27). Hence, CM education seeks to equip students with the mathematical skills and dispositions needed to succeed academically while also enabling students to see how certain social, economic, and political structures create and uphold inequities.

Gutstein (2003, 2006, 2013, 2016) is only one of many scholars that has written and contributed to the concept of teaching mathematics for social justice purposes. However, I choose to focus on his scholarship precisely because the focal class curriculum was based on his theoretical framing. Notwithstanding, Gutstein has built upon the scholarship of many pedagogues within and outside of critical pedagogy including African-American scholars and revolutionaries within a U.S. and global context, Marilyn Frankenstein, an adult mathematics educator who has committed her lifetime to advancing the importance of critical mathematics literacy (Frankenstein, 2009), and Paulo Freire, one of the most influential contributors to the theory and practice of critical pedagogy.

Freire (1970/1999) coined the terms *reading the world* and *reading the word* as two dialectical processes that lead to critical consciousness and reflective action. In short, through his literacy campaigns, Freire's pedagogical aims were to engage adults in learning how to read the word (literacy) through a practice of reading the world (critical read of society) with the goal of writing the world (transformative action). Similarly, Gutstein's teaching of mathematics for social justice has entailed learning to *read the mathematical word* (classical mathematical knowledge) and learning to *read the world with mathematics* (using mathematics to unpack relations of power) as two dialectical processes. Gutstein (2003) defined reading the world with mathematics as able

> To use mathematics to understand relations of power, resource inequities, and disparate opportunities between different social groups and to understand explicit discrimination based on race, class, gender, language, and other differences. Further, it means to dissect and deconstruct media and other forms of representation. It means to use mathematics to examine various phenomena in both one's immediate life and in the broader social world and to identify relationships and make connections between them. (Gutstein, 2003, p. 45)

Additionally, Gutstein has appended Freire's *writing the world*—acting upon the world in critical ways—with mathematics as well. Together, he has developed a pedagogy of reading and writing the world with mathematics (RWWM) aimed at using mathematics as a lens to examine, critique, and transform inequitable relationships of power.

Gutstein's engagement of the 3 C's (Classical, Community, and Critical knowledge) has been an instrumental organizing principle in his design and implementation of social justice math projects within a RWWM pedagogy. Acknowledging that students come with vast knowledge about their lives, Gutstein has sought to develop curriculum that incorporates students' community knowledge while facilitating their access to the school-sanctioned mathematical knowledge, and enhancing their critique of sociopolitical relationships or critical knowledge (Gutstein, 2016). Through the study of sociopolitical issues, Gutstein (2006) has argued that an important goal of this work, largely absent from K-12 mathematics education, is to "connect and synthesize all three knowledge bases [community, classical, and critical], while fully honoring and respecting each, to develop liberatory mathematics education in urban schools given the current high-stakes accountability regimes and larger political climate" (p. 206). In this way, his hope has been to raise students' sociopolitical consciousness and build on students' sense of justice to become change agents for themselves, their families, their communities, and subsequently the world. The class highlighted in this chapter is based on this framing of using mathematics to understand (read) and change (write) the world through the study of social (in)justice.

Context, Methodology, and Data Sources

For this study, I interviewed 13 individuals (12 Latin@s and 1 African-American) who participated during their 12th grade year (2008–2009) in a mathematics course herein referred to as the "Math for Social Justice" class or M4SJ, for short. The participants attended a nonselective high school whose thematic focus was social justice. Although students were accustomed to discussing and learning about social justice issues across the curriculum, the M4SJ class was their first experience in which the social (in)justice contexts drove the mathematical content that was to be studied for an entire school year. Throughout their high school mathematics courses, students had been exposed to upward of 15 different justice-oriented math projects typically ranging from 1 to 2 weeks. These projects included looking at wealth inequality, the cost of war, racial profiling, and *randomness* in jury selection. Students in the study as part of their graduation requirement were obligated to take a fourth-year math class and opted into the M4SJ class among two other options. All three choices were reform-based and covered some precalculus topics. The M4SJ class stood out with respect to its primary focus on investigating sociopolitical themes that were agreed upon by the students and the teacher the year prior. These themes[1] along with the teacher's commitment to preparing students to reason quantitatively and abstractly drove the mathematics they would study in the class.

The interviews took place 2–4 years after the M4SJ course ended. Students were in different places in their postsecondary academic and career trajectories ranging from one semester of college (n=1) to a completed bachelor's degree (n=3). My overarching goal of the semi-structured interviews was to get an in-depth understanding of the personal meaning participants ascribed to using/doing mathematics to learn about social reality. While the interview transcripts were a primary source of data, I drew on data collected from the class that included teacher, student, and researcher journals and end-of-semester and end-of-year student surveys. Drawing on both an interpretive and narrative methodology, I coded (open and focused) the data by participant to gain a more complex, fuller understanding of students' experiences, worldviews, and enduring understandings that often times (not always) were corroborated across sources.

For this chapter, I focus on students' investigations of the mathematics underlying mortgages and the subprime mortgage crisis as a major subtheme of a larger unit on displacement (e.g., gentrification). I chose to focus on this aspect for several compelling reasons. First, in all the student interviews, students consistently recalled the concept/theme whereas the remaining unit themes were inconsistently recalled. Second, during the class, students were indignant about the predatory nature of the subprime mortgage lenders in their communities and across the country. My reading of their reactions was the clarity with which they saw and for some, personally experienced, the injustice of mortgages. This, in turn, incited them to want to fight back and inform their community of how to protect themselves from mortgage-related fraud. And third, related to this, I argue that students' engagement with dissecting mortgage formulas was in large part due to the sociopolitical framing that built on students' sense of social justice and fairness. Finally, while there is a substantial amount of scholarship on TMfSJ from teachers' and teacher educators' perspectives, students' perspectives and enduring understandings are sorely lacking from the literature. This chapter offers a unique contribution in this respect.

The Displacement Unit and Submortgage Crisis

The unifying theme of displacement was intended in large part to have Black and Brown students "understand the causes, mechanisms, and roots of displacement in each neighborhood…to see that both [communities] have the same larger context—a global political and financial system that plays out in particular and sometimes contradictory ways…" (Gutstein, 2013, Reflections section, para. 2). In both the Black and Latin@ communities of the study participants, families were experiencing displacement because of the predatory lending practices that targeted low-income communities. Both communities had experienced a rise in foreclosures in the previous three years (2005–2008) with some of the students in the class having first-hand experience with the struggle to manage unaffordable mortgage payments. For example, one student's grandmother had lost her home due to a subprime home equity loan and another whose mother was on the verge of losing hers (Gutstein, 2016).

The first few weeks of the displacement unit were devoted to students extrapolating and extending "linear" trends in the home sale prices that included new housing developments in the African-American community. Being able to understand the housing price trends in the context of displacement served to establish the motivation for using mathematics to determine affordability ranges in both neighborhoods. Students used the Housing and Urban Development's (HUD) guideline of affordability as represented by no more than 30% of one's household income. In other words, students engaged with the question of whether community residents (median-income households) could afford to take advantage of these new housing developments without experiencing hardship. Students asked—are these new developments designed to keep us here or push us out? Modeling affordability entailed that students study about recursive functions and Discrete Dynamical Systems (DDS). Without getting into the specifics of the mathematics, the big idea here is that interest accrues on every month that a mortgage balance is carried over creating a situation in which mortgage payments in the first 10–15 years tend to pay more interest (due to initial large balances relative to small mortgage payments) than lowering the principal balance. In part, the mortgage aspect of the displacement unit was for students to unpack and critique the disproportionately unfair advantage that a lender has over low-income borrowers. Moreover, in subprime mortgage terms, the disadvantage becomes exacerbated.

A great deal of class time in this unit was devoted to unpacking both the mathematical (interest-bearing) and sociopolitical (unfair advantage) ideas just described. Students spent several days examining a $150,000, 30-year mortgage at a 6% fixed annual interest rate and modeling it mathematically: initially by hand and eventually with a calculator program allowing them to manipulate various inputs including the monthly mortgage payment, the interest rate, and the initial loan balance. For example, they could take the template case above and change the interest rate to 5.5% or change the house price to $130,000. The ease with which students could change the terms made the calculator a valuable resource down the line when looking at balloon mortgages or negative amortization cases. Students used the template loan terms above and the calculator program to initially determine and consider several mathematical calculations:

1. the monthly mortgage payment required to pay off this debt in 30 years;
2. the amount owed if the average wage-earning person in their community were to pay only an affordable mortgage amount; and
3. the loan amount families in their communities could afford based on the median household income without hardship.

Through their collective effort at answering these questions, students established several things. For one, a family would have to pay $899.33 a month to pay off this debt in 30 years. However, if the average community resident paid the recommended 30% of their disposable income ($807.92), they would still owe $92,000 after 30 years. Students calculated that community residents from both communities (Latin@ and African-American), earning the median income and without experiencing hardship by HUD standards, could afford a home priced at $134,750 and $84,500, respectively (Gutstein, 2013). Through this investigation, students confirmed that the new housing developments cropping up around the neighborhood were not designed for the average (i.e., median income) family in their neighborhoods.

Findings

Students overwhelmingly remembered and spoke of the significance of the mortgage unit in their postclass interviews more than any other unit. While some students could not recall some of the other units all too well, there was not one student who could not recall the mortgage aspect of the displacement unit along with the enduring understanding that interest can and does create an unreasonably unfair advantage for the consumer. I share below two primary ways that students reported to have made meaning from engaging with this unit.

Connections to Real Life

In the postclass interviews, students were typically hard-pressed to find rigorous ways in which they personally engaged with mathematics in their daily life beyond basic budgetary and shopping demands. I was, nonetheless, interested in the types of connections students could make between their particular experiences in the class and their experiences in the world as it related to mathematics and social justice. I share below several instances in which students reported to have applied the mathematics they learned from the mortgages unit of the class to an authentic situation in their life after high school. I begin with Antoine.[2]

> I was kind of worried [be]cause I took out like $500 dollars [be]cause I had to pay some parking tickets [be]cause they said they were going to boot it away and I didn't want them to boot it away and I didn't have $500 dollar. So I went and put that [car title] on it [collateral for payday loan] and then afterwards I was like spending all night figuring out the math and how much I was going to pay in interest. I figured out so clearly that at a certain point when I asked the representatives how much the interest would be the next month, they didn't give me an answer. (Antoine, Postclass Interview)

Antoine, after putting up his car for collateral on a payday (i.e., high interest) loan, spent many hours figuring out how much interest he would be paying the very next month. He contended to have determined a precise amount; one that the representative was unable to produce because, as Antoine noted, he probably did not know himself.

In the next example, Gema was trying to help her parents-in-law make an informed decision on purchasing a home and comparing various mortgage scenarios.

> They were looking at different houses and then they were varying by neighborhood and prices. And then they were talking to the real estate agent and stuff and like, the older brother, he actually graduated from Prius University and he was helping them also, but he wasn't, he's not good at math so he was not really sure about the mortgages and like they had the papers and I was looking at them and I actually was like helping them and explaining it to them, like which mortgage would be better for them and cause I was like the banks are not gonna tell you, they will lie to you and everything and just so they could make money out of you. (Gema, Postclass Interview)

Gema described how she was able to look at the bank loan paperwork provided to her in-laws and help them make sense of the embedded mathematics for their particular situation; a situation, she noted, that her brother-in-law, a graduate from a very selective university, Prius University, struggled to understand.

Antoine and Gema were able to apply their mathematical learning from the class to a real situation in their lives. They described how they either still had the DDS program in their calculator and/or relied on their notes from the class to help them recall the mathematics. Hence, the relevance was explicit and formidable. Furthermore, both Antoine and Gema recounted their experiences in such a way that they felt empowered by the mathematical tools at their disposable. Antoine noted his ability to calculate the interest to a level of precision beyond the payday representative's ability whereas Gema demonstrated a sense of accomplishment for being able to interpret the loan paperwork—a mathematical situation that a university graduate struggled to examine.

Connecting the relationship between interest-bearing scenarios and students' lives as present and future consumers of credit was cogent. Renee expounded below how she came to use the calculator program to help her analyze her own credit card bill, immediately.

> The most helpful part of this unit was the dynamical systems. As soon as I really learned how to work with the dynamical systems I came home and grabbed my credit card bill and the mortgage and plugged them in the calculator. Paying the minimum balance on my credit card wasn't enough. I would have to pay double my minimum balance to get out of it in less time. Obviously, what my mother [a low-paid factory worker] is paying isn't enough to finish paying the house in 30 years. The worst part about this is that what she pays isn't 30 percent of her income, it's more. (Gutstein, 2016)

Renee made strong connections between the mathematics they learned (and were learning) in class to her own and her mother's situation.

In his postclass interview, Calvin remembered very little about the class with the exception of the mortgage aspect of the displacement unit. Calvin insisted on paying his way through community college and avoided buying a car on credit because the class learning, he confessed, scared him out of taking risks on loans and potentially acquiring bad credit. Similarly, Vanessa and Ann, having read the terms of their own student loans, conveyed to me the urgency they felt with paying more than the minimum payment while still in school so that they could avoid exorbitant amounts of interest being added on to their initial balance. The big idea that students learned was that they had to read the fine print and be watchful borrowers. This notion was one that all 13 participants were able to recall and many applied to their own lives many years after having left the class, which is quite the contrast from the inevitable question math students often raise of "when are we ever going to use this?"

Injustice to My Community!

From the onset, as part of the class syllabus, students had agreed to do two community presentations throughout the year. The year got away from them and they did not organize the mid-year presentation. Significantly, the teacher did not want to let the last one pass as that would be a missed opportunity for students to synthesize and share their learning. Nonetheless, the fore-grounded expectation (vis-à-vis the syllabus) that they were going to share their learning in the community does not dilute in any way students' over-whelming desire and commitment to want to inform, educate, and save their community from further displacement and fraud. Upon learning about the mathematics of this inequitable and ubiquitous situation, students expressed an urgency to want to take their learning to the streets.

Students' journal responses to what (content) they wanted to present in the community presentations converged around the work of the mortgages. That is, students felt strongly that illustrating the way(s) in which interest accrued and significantly impacted the loan balance in a mortgage and subprime mortgage situation was important knowledge that needed to be shared. Students believed that the mortgage knowledge could help their communities become better informed home-buyers/owners and reveal their particular disadvantage in this situation. In this way, the community presentations served as a vehicle for students to share the ways in which mathematical knowledge could serve to reveal, critique, and potentially transform an injustice—an instantiation of not only reading but also writing their world *with mathematics*.

In their penultimate journal for the year, students were asked to provide input on their goals and purposes for carrying out the community presentation. Again their responses converged around the mortgages. Mónica stated that she wanted to make the "community aware of how mortgages work and how to prevent a foreclosure." Marisol similarly stated that she believed that there were "people that are out to get people that are not well educated or well-informed so they can [get] money of them." She wanted to "show people to be wise when making their personal decisions because other educated people will not care if the person has a home or not." It is noteworthy that both Mónica and Marisol emphasized that the purpose of presenting their learning to the community was, in essence, to share information in order to prevent more foreclosures. In this way, they were writing the world with the intention of transforming it.

Ann and Antoinette wanted to share essentially the same message although they were more indignant in their tone. Ann passionately wrote that the purpose was "to flat out let our people know things are fucked up and there are reasons for things being the way they are." The predatory nature of the subprime mortgage lenders seemed to have provoked a drive to inform their community about the perilous nature of interest so that their families and neighbors could make better choices and prevent unwanted debt and loss. Possessing such critical and essential information, in students' view, contributed to their community's protection from further deceit that, in Minerva's words, was "essential to being a strong community."

Becoming aware of the power of mathematics as a direct tool for fighting against injustice was the most common claim students made with respect to the ways in which the class changed their views about math and about the world as evidenced in students' mid and end-of-year surveys. Jenny, a struggling mathematics student, asserted that being in the class made her "*more* conscious about things going on in the world" causing her to question what she is being told. I add emphasis on her use of the word *more* highlighting the fact that her experience in the class enhanced her already critical mindset. Minerva, on the other hand, maintained incredulous at the level of corruptness in the world causing her to want to "watch those in power." And Antoinette reported that she "could see the injustices happening and how math could make a difference." For Antoinette, she distinguished between the math problem and the real-to-my-life problem that math could help investigate (postclass interview). While students were impacted differently, all came to acknowledge the power of mathematics in revealing injustice.

The notion that students needed to unite and come together was also an emerging aspect of critical and collective power in their mid-year and end-of-year surveys. Several students responded to coming together and uniting (much like the community presentations) to write the world with mathematics. Calvin declared that he "believe[d] the world can change by using math and that it's going to take effort and commitment from people." In a similar vein, Monica claimed to have learned that "if we unite and work hard, then we know we can make big changes with math being a strong tool." Ellen wrote,

> The world needs a change. This world shouldn't be racist to minorities. This world should be fair. I never imagined that this world was so corrupt. We need to unite to fight for some common goals. We need to fight the cause!

In this respect, the survey data evinced students coming to see their own role in effecting change (individually but mostly collectively) and viewing mathematics as a useful tool in fighting against injustice. All of the students in their end-of-year surveys reported that their participation in the class was consequential in helping them see that they too could do something about the problems in their community and the world *with mathematics.*

Students came together in the end to create an 81-slide power-point for their end-of-year presentations to the community. I conclude this section with slide #64, the slide ending the presentation on the mortgages.

> We as a people need to inform ourselves and others about these predatory loans. We should be conscious about the decisions we make when dealing with the banking system. People need to be educated on this matter. Some ways we could make this happen is by doing workshops, understanding the fancy writing, using internet sources and mortgage calculators to your advantage.

Conclusion

I contend that students' reflections both in the postclass interviews and the class data converge around the mortgage unit being significant for several reasons. It was fundamentally a "crisis" in which lenders preyed on their families to help line their pockets despite the impact on individuals' lives and communities. It was a clear injustice that students were either experiencing personally or could see in their community with the recent upsurge in foreclosures. Understanding how mortgages work and the role of the subprime mortgages in destabilizing communities and displacing families was impactful. Politically, students could see that it was happening not only to them but that it was a structural issue at all levels (nationally and globally) that by design put neigh-borhoods and families like their own at jeopardy of financial ruin.

In my final thoughts, I turn to Skovsmose's call for an excavation of math-ematics that makes "explicit the actual use of mathematics hidden in social structures and routines" (Vithal, 2003, p. 8). His argument for revealing the *formatting power of mathematics* was based on the premise that mathematics "produces new inventions in reality, not only in the sense that new insights may change interpretations, but also in the sense that mathematics colonises part of reality and reorders it" (Skovsmose, 1994, p. 42). The hidden nature of mathematics in reordering our reality could not be more evident than in the case of the mortgage crisis that students studied. This example was an instantiation of using mathematics to expose the nature of debt and unpack how power relations benefit some at the expense of others.

For reasons of exposing the formatting power of mathematics and the ways in which it serves to reorder reality, I agree wholeheartedly with Gutstein (2016) that "it is insufficient to just teach and learn mathematics in mathe-matics class, given where humanity finds itself" (p. 34). I am inspired and reinvigorated to join critical pedagogues in our collective struggle to survive with dignity. In this assertion, I also invite others to consider how this kind of mathematical learning might also (re)invigorate Latin@s and other margin-alized groups into considering mathematics and STEM as oriented toward justice for all.

Notes

1. Throughout the year, students studied five thematic units: Voter Disenfranchisement, Displacement, HIV-AIDS Pandemic, Criminalization of Youth, and Sexism.
2. All names of students and schools are pseudonyms.

References

Frankenstein, M. (2009). Developing a critical mathematical numeracy through real real-life word problems. In L. Verschaffel, B. Greer, W. Van Dooren, & S. Mukhopadhyay (Eds.), *Words and worlds: Modelling verbal descriptions of situations* (pp. 111–130). Rotterdam: Sense.

Freire, P. (1970/1999). *Pedagogy of the oppressed* (M. B. Ramos, Trans.). New York, NY: Continuum.

Gutstein, E. (2003). Teaching and learning mathematics for social justice in an urban, Latino school. *Journal for Research in Mathematics Education, 34*(1), 37–73.

Gutstein, E. (2006). *Reading and writing the world with mathematics: Toward a pedagogy for social justice.* New York, NY: Routledge.

Gutstein, E. (2013). Whose community is this? Mathematics of neighborhood displacement. *Rethinking schools, 27*(3), 11–17.

Gutstein, E. (2016). Our issues, our people—math as our weapon: Critical mathematics in a Chicago neighborhood high school. *Journal for Research in Mathematics Education, 47*(5), 454–504.

Martin, D. B. (2003). Hidden assumptions and unaddressed questions in mathematics for all rhetoric. *The Mathematics Educator, 13*(2), 7–21.

National Science Foundation, Division of Science Resources Statistics. (2006). *S&E Degrees, by Race/Ethnicity of Recipients: 1995–2004.* January 2007. Susan T. Hill and Maurya M. Green, project officers. Arlington, VA.

Powell, A. B. (2012). The historical development of critical mathematics education. In A. A. Wager & D. W. Stinson (Eds.), *Teaching mathematics for social justice: Conversations with educators* (pp. 21–34). Reston, VA: National Council of Teachers of Mathematics.

Secada, W. (1989). Agenda setting, enlightened self-interest, and equity in mathematics education. *Peabody Journal of Education, 66*(2), 22–56. doi:10.1080/01619568909 538637

Skovsmose, O. (1994). Towards a critical mathematics education. *Educational Studies in Mathematics, 27*(1), 35–57.

Taningco, M. T., Mathew, A. B., & Pachon, H. P. (2008). *STEM professions: Opportunities and challenges for Latinos.* Los Angeles, CA: Tomás Rivera Policy Institute.

Vithal, R. (2003). *In search of a pedagogy of conflict and dialogue for mathematics education.* Dordrecht, Netherlands: Springer Science & Business Media.

13. Third Space Theory: A Theoretical Model for Designing Informal STEM Experiences for Rural Latina Youth

Rebecca Hite, Eva Midobuche, Alfredo H. Benavides, and Jerry Dwyer

Traditional formal science experiences privilege the majority male culture (Chapman, Tatiana, Hartlep, Vang, & Lipsey, 2014), failing to recognize and reflect Latinas' unique cultural context and contributions in STEM, possibly contributing to their underrepresentation at all points within the STEM pipeline (Crisp & Nora, 2012). Young girls from Latin@, Hispanic, and Chicana origin (Latinas) face specific challenges in formal STEM education due to perceptions of self-efficacy, stereotype threat, and community expectations (Britner & Pajares, 2001; Carlone & Johnson, 2007; Rodriguez, Cunningham, & Jordan, 2016). However, research has evidenced successful strategies to encourage Latinas in STEM, including single-sex instruction (Rosenthal, London, Levy, & Lobel, 2011), background-matched mentors (Syed, Goza, Chemers, & Zurbriggen, 2012), and culturally related out-of-classroom experiences (Ciechanowski, Bottoms, Fonseca, & St Clair, 2015). The latter is a promising area of research; out-of-school (informal) programs now recommend the development of participants' noncognitive factors (e.g., interest, motivation, and 21st-century skills) to enhance STEM engagement (National Research Council [NRC], 2015; P21, 2007). Research indicates that the development of these aforementioned *soft skills*, especially in the middle grades, are instrumental for STEM futures (Wingenbach *et al.*, 2007). One example where there are emergent and ample STEM opportunities are in the rurally centered agricultural sciences (Bureau of Labor Statistics, 2005); where Latin@ cultural knowledge (Saldivar-Tanaka & Krasny, 2004) has value to STEM and is accessible (locally) to Latinas. Therefore, a novel schema (curricula and pedagogies) is needed to develop Latinas' noncognitive skills through honoring Latin@ culture.

Third Space Theory, developed by Gutiérrez (2008), bridges the disconnect between what schools' value (second space) and what is important in students' lives (first space). As a curricular modality, Third Space Theory, as a framework for STEM experiences, may improve Latinas' attitudes toward an interest in STEM content, as well as foster a positive augmentation of their STEM identity, self-efficacy, and perception of garnered higher-order skills as evidenced in related empirical research (Barton *et al.*, 2012; Barton, Tan, & Rivet, 2008; Glasson, Mhango, Phiri, & Lanier, 2010). Therefore, to address the STEM participation gap, Latina-specific middle grade STEM learning opportunities in informal spaces must be targeted to STEM development (middle school), single sex (Latina only), providing hands-on experiences (noncognitive skill growth) related to an available STEM career (agricultural sciences or agrisciences), within a flexible curriculum (informal clubs) that is *also* culturally relevant (Third space). This chapter will discuss Third Space as a theoretical strategy to diversify and bolster the emergent agriscience STEM pipeline through STEM-based clubs for middle school aged, rural Latinas (Landivar, 2013).

The American STEM Workforce and Latina Underrepresentation

The United States faces an immediate shortage of STEM professionals, particularly among groups that are traditionally underrepresented, where Latinas comprise the greatest disparity (NRC, 2015; Office of Science, Technology and Innovation, n.d.). The U.S. Department of Labor (2016) has projected that Latinas will comprise 20% of the labor force and in 8 years will outpace Latino (male) job growth (Mora, 2015). Yet, Latinas face unique cultural challenges in participation in STEM careers; their connection to their cultural community (especially in rural areas) precludes them from leaving their families to engage in the centralized urban metro STEM job market (Rothwell, 2013). Per Aschbacher, Li, and Roth (2010), "gender...ethnicity and SES, seemed to play a role in under-represented minority students' aspirations and [STEM] pipeline participation...girls felt more pressure to conform to traditional Latino family patterns of staying close to home to care for and interact with family members" (p. 578). These cultural and geographic challenges are unique for Latinas, and require novel interventions to foster participation in STEM fields.

Contributing to issues of underrepresentation, the middle grades have become a renewed focus area in STEM, where students make assessments of their science abilities (Britner & Pajares, 2001) and decide on STEM as a future career (Bandura, Barbaranelli, Caprara, & Pastorelli, 2001). Middle school Latinas reported fewer school science experiences (Jones, Howe, & Rua, 2000) and extracurricular science activities (Aschbacher *et al.*, 2010). Research indicates that this impacts their perceptions of and affiliations with STEM (Jones *et al.*, 2000) and contributes to perceptions of feeling excluded from or inferior to their peers (Schmader, Johns, & Forbes, 2008; Taningco, Mathew, & Pachon, 2008). This lack of access and consequential stereotype threat is important, leading to underperformance and disinterest in STEM subjects (Keller & Dauenheimer, 2003; Shapiro & Williams, 2012). As per Schmader and Johns (2003), Latin@ students openly acknowledge and perceive this exclusion; Latinas who hold dual minority identities in STEM (Carlone & Johnson, 2007) are most vulnerable to its effects.

Connecting Curricula and Bridging Pedagogies: Third Space Theory

Third Space is a hybrid area intended "to move away from privileged, authoritative discourse by providing indigenous cultures with improved access to Eurocentric science, while at the same time validating the local communities own ways of understanding" (Glasson *et al.*, 2010, p. 128). The theory emphasizes and values the context of students' minority identities (Gee, 2000) within the majority (school science) curriculum by merging these disparate spheres into a Third Space. Third Space Theory inherently rejects the minority deficit models (Valencia, 2012). Students whose native language is not English, students of color, students in poverty, have an innate wealth of situated knowledge, skills, and understand who they are and the communities from which they come (Moll, 1990). Therefore, Third Space Theory indicates that learners, particularly those underrepresented in STEM fields, may benefit from activities in a hybrid or Third Space that theoretically exists between students' cultural heritages (first space) and the school-defined curricula (second space) (Gutiérrez, 2008).

Third Space Theory has potential to recruit and encourage Latinas to engage in STEM content and activities. Explicit connections between a group's cultural contributions to science has positive impacts on the participants' family perception of science (habitus) and their procurement and use of scientific tools and equipment (capital) (Archer *et al.*, 2012). Third Space Theory as a pedagogical modality has evidenced academic success for

Hispanic students in formal education, as well as shown promise as a curricular model in other educational contexts (Klein, Taylor, Onore, Strom, & Abrams, 2013; Skerrett, 2010) as well as in agriculture instruction (Glasson et al., 2010). Additionally, Gutiérrez (2008) found that Third Spaces appeal to the development of Latin@ students' identity within content areas. Students benefit most when science content is supported by explicit relationships to unique cultural contributions (Barton et al., 2012) and the students' daily lives (Hulleman & Harackiewicz, 2009). Moreover, research in hybrid spaces, similar to Third Space, has found promise in augmenting middle grade girls' achievement and interest in formal K–12 science education (Barton et al., 2008).

While Third Space Theory has been empirically linked to student identity, motivation, and engagement in other content areas (Gutiérrez, 2008), we hypothesize that this modality also augments other noncognitive 21st-century skills: in critical thinking, collaboration, creativity, and communication (P21, 2007). Exploration of these factors would be significant as 21st-century skills have been widely discussed as crucial and underdeveloped in the U.S. STEM workforce (Bybee & Fuchs, 2006). Third Space Theory may be used to promote engagement with an interest in STEM with Latina middle school students, (i.e., 6th, 7th, and 8th grades) when assessments of self-efficacy develop (Britner & Pajares, 2001) and science identity flourishes (Archer et al., 2010).

Latinas' Past and Future Contributions to the Agrisciences

Latinas are especially well positioned to benefit from encouragement into the rural-centered agriscience STEM industries; local (rural) opportunities provide Latinas access despite cultural pressure or discouragement to leave their families to pursue STEM careers (Rothwell, 2013).

Furthermore, the cultural relationship of many Latinas to agriculture may be a strong lever to encourage (Mayer, 2014) and empower (Counihan & Van Esterik, 2012) young women into the agricultural sciences. Hence, Latin@ culture and scientific contributions provide viability for Agriscience content connecting to the Third Space. Prior research has indicated that agricultural activity in school gardens has been shown to be impactful for Latin@ youth (Davis, Ventura, Cook, Gyllenhammer, & Gatto, 2011; Gatto, Ventura, Cook, Gyllenhammer, & Davis, 2012). Furthermore, middle grade students have evidenced gains in nutritional knowledge and choices when participating in school gardens (Blair, 2009; Leising, Pense, & Igo, 2000; Morris & Zidenberg-Cherr, 2002; Ratcliffe, Merrigan, Rogers, & Goldberg, 2011), which is important as they are susceptible to damaging health impacts of food acculturation (e.g., American-based fast foods) especially in rural areas (Batis, Hernandez-Barrera, Barquera, Rivera, & Popkin, 2011). This is especially true for Latin@ youth (Davis *et al.*, 2011; Gatto *et al.*, 2012). Latin@s need to have a historical and cultural knowledge of the agricultural contributions made by their ancestors in cultivating crops and community-based agriculture (Saldivar-Tanaka & Krasny, 2004).

Bilingual Latina STEM workers would be a boon to agribusiness be-cause of their dual languages and their potential cultural understanding of the emergent markets of Hispanics and Latin@s (Mayer, 2014). Those who are fluent in Spanish and are native to the Latin@ culture may play unique and powerful future roles as educators for Spanish-speaking farm workers regarding their pesticide risk by addressing erroneous cultural beliefs of health and safety regarding chemicals (Elmore & Arcury, 2001). Research suggests scientifically knowledgeable cultural ambassadors (Jezewski, 1990) between health professionals and farmworkers may significantly reduce ex-posure and negative health effects for the approximately 3 to 4 million mi-grant and seasonal farmworkers in the United States (Arcury, Quandt, & Russell, 2002; National Center for Farmworker Health, 2012). Through collaboration with local agriculture stakeholders, the university community, and the culturally diverse Latin@ community, Latina youth can be involved in an informal learning experience that addresses their interests by engaging the intellectual capital of those who live and work in similar agricultural areas.

Latina-Specific STEM Experiences: Informal STEM Clubs

One strategy to provide active learning experiences in STEM is informal STEM learning outside of the formal, traditional school day. Per Braund and Reiss (2006), informal science experiences are opportunities for stu-dents to engage in extended, authentic, and collaborative projects to rein-force concepts learned at school and may positively augment participants' attitudes toward science. One type of informal learning opportunity is STEM clubs—out-of-school or informal experiences that utilize hands-on activities, mentoring, and field trips to develop student knowledge and in-terest in STEM disciplines (NRC, 2015). Research conducted by Sahin (2013) found that middle grade students who had participated in STEM clubs were more likely to choose a post-secondary STEM major. In addi-tion, research by Yuen, Ek, and Scheutze (2013) found success in Hispan-ic only robotics STEM clubs, indicating informal learning environments uniquely met the cultural and linguistic needs of Hispanic students. Active learning and experiential opportunities in science "have been systematically tested and shown to reach diverse students" (Handelsman *et al.*, 2004, p. 521). Club-based outreach for K–12 students has grown as a popular and viable option for encouraging interest, motivation, and persistence in STEM (Honey, Pearson, & Schweingruber, 2014; National Research Council [NRC], 2010).

Although many clubs provide rich science experiences to school age children, most are not tailored to recruit, honor, or reflect the unique contributions of underrepresented groups. Research has explored differential attainment in K–16 science among minority groupings, finding Euro-focused, male-dominated curricula (Barton & Yang, 2000) played significant roles in increasing achievement and interest gaps between minority and majority populations. Research suggests STEM experiences that incorporated and valued underrepresented minorities' unique cultural connections to the curriculum were cited as factors for developing individuals' STEM interest, identity, and persistence (Carlone & Johnson, 2007; Espinosa, 2011). Hence, a need for innovation to restructure curricula, like Third Space, to recruit and reflect the unique cultural contributions of minorities and females to encourage their interest, motivation, and persistence in STEM disciplines. Research suggests that constructing STEM (science) identity within Latinas is unlike that of majority students; single sex STEM programs aid their sense of belonging to the sciences, which plays a major role in their STEM persistence (Rosenthal *et al.*, 2011).

Theory to Practice: Leveraging Third Space Theory to Develop Latina STEM Clubs

STEM interventions that can leverage Latinas' cultural heritage within a culturally centered framework, designed to bolster their motivation, engagement, and identity (Third Space) within a culturally relevant and geographically accessible STEM field (Agriculture), may foster a robust pipeline of Latinas into local, rural agriscience futures. Focusing on middle school aged students (ages 11–14) who self-identify as Latina, Chicana, or of Hispanic origin will aid in the development of science identity when it is most malleable (Archer *et al.*, 2010) and reflect best practices where Latinas academically benefit from single sex STEM experiences (Rosenthal *et al.*, 2011). Without the constraints of formal schooling an informal STEM club space permits modification of the curriculum to utilize Third Space Theory. Through alignment with best practices in STEM clubs for girls (Jones, 2011), and the National Research Council criteria for identifying productive STEM programs in out-of-school settings (NRC, 2015) to build interest and motivation for developing science identity (NRC, 2010), suggested club activities include:

1. identifying native plants using bilingual instruction;
2. employing sustainable methods for urban agriculture based on indigenous practices;
3. understanding Mayan astronomy strategies in planting and harvesting;
4. cultivating culturally meaningful crops (e.g., cilantro, peppers, corn, onions, tomatoes, etc.);
5. discovering the importance of pollinators on production through folk stories;
6. creating graphic presentations on plant and insect biodiversity for family gardeners;
7. investigating the biochemistry of native medicinal herbs; and
8. designing methods to distribute their harvest to their local communities.

The identification of key personnel can bring multicultural expertise to ensure that critical aspects of Third Space Theory is fully utilized to provide a culturally appropriate learning experience. The foundation of Third Space would require Latin@ scholars to underpin the cultural importance and the historical significance of Latin@ contributions to STEM in collaboration with STEM education researchers to ensure that cultural curriculum connects to authentic science experiences appropriate for middle grade students. To ensure STEM authenticity, curriculum should consist of lessons in the subject areas of the agricultural and biological sciences. Professors in all three areas should collaborate to ensure alignment of Third Space curriculum to the authentic world of STEM work. Participants should collaborate with agricultural scientists to discuss career opportunities in their discipline and interact with Latina role models (e.g., undergraduates, agriscientists) to provide mentoring and support for STEM identity development. Curricula may be supplemented with travel to a research laboratory to further explore career opportunities in STEM, specifically situated to the agrisciences. Outside of a university setting, connections to the local community are essential to vet, monitor, and reinforce the efficacy of Third Space components to support of these efforts.

Conclusion

Anzaldúa (2014) has described Latinas' traditional career choices as nun, homemaker, or prostitute. She states that "today some of us have a fourth choice: entering the world by way of education and career and becoming a self-autonomous person. A very few of us" (p. 81). Although it is questionable that all Latinas see their futures as Anzaldúa did, this fourth option provides an avenue for Latinas to demonstrate their talents and worth. It is clear from numerous governmental and educational reports that for Latinas to enter these educational futures, this will not occur organically. Otherwise, this would have transpired 20 years ago. There must be targeted programs to aid Latinas, especially those in rural areas, in cultivating their talents and worth so they may also garner all the benefits of STEM careers. To do this, we must help Latinas overcome their apprehension of science by curating uniquely tailored spaces that facilitate the cultural importance and social interactions to persist in STEM.

Recognition and accommodation of Latinas' cultural commitments through Third Space Theory may engage Latina youth in the agrisciences and agriscience futures without requiring them to leave their rural communities. By operationalizing Third Space theory through STEM Clubs is an important strategy to encourage and network middle school Latinas to opportunities and careers in STEM. To better support their development, these clubs engage Latinas in a culturally relevant curriculum that recognizes, reflects, acknowledges, and celebrates their historical contributions to an agricultural based learning environment. This empowers Latina students to grow and appreciate their cultural history and take pride in their cultural and agricultural contributions that have advanced scientific knowledge and understanding. The contemporary narrative of asking Latinas to accommodate and assimilate to the STEM disciplines needs to be challenged. Instead, preemption of STEM pipeline issues requires the creation of third spaces, in emergent STEM areas, that foster 21st-century skill development by embracing Latina talent and cultural contributions.

References

Anzaldúa, G. (2014). Movimientos de Rebeldía y las Culturas que Traicionan. In A. Darder & R. D. Torres (Eds.), *Latinos and education: A critical reader* ((2nd ed., pp. 87–92). New York, NY: Routledge.

Archer, L., DeWitt, J., Osborne, J., Dillon, J., Willis, B., & Wong, B. (2010). "Doing" science versus "being" a scientist: Examining 10/11-year-old school children's constructions of science through the lens of identity. *Science Education, 94*(4), 617–639.

Archer, L., DeWitt, J., Osborne, J., Dillon, J., Willis, B., & Wong, B. (2012). Science aspirations, capital, and family habitus how families shape children's engagement and identification with science. *American Educational Research Journal, 49*(5), 881–908.

Arcury, T. A., Quandt, S. A., & Russell, G. B. (2002). Pesticide safety among farmworkers: perceived risk and perceived control as factors reflecting environmental justice. *Environmental Health Perspectives, 110*(Suppl. 2), 233.

Aschbacher, P. R., Li, E., & Roth, E. J. (2010). Is science me? High school students' identities, participation and aspirations in science, engineering, and medicine. *Journal of Research in Science Teaching, 47*(5), 564–582.

Bandura, A., Barbaranelli, C., Caprara, G. V., & Pastorelli, C. (2001). Self-efficacy beliefs as shapers of children's aspirations and career trajectories. *Child development, 72*(1), 187–206.

Barton, A. C., Kang, H., Tan, E., O'Neill, T. B., Bautista-Guerra, J., & Brecklin, C. (2012). Crafting a future in science tracing middle school girls' identity work over time and space. *American Educational Research Journal*, 0002831212458142.

Barton, A. C., Tan, E., & Rivet, A. (2008). Creating hybrid spaces for engaging school science among urban middle school girls. *American Educational Research Journal, 45*(1), 68–103.

Barton, A. C., & Yang, K. (2000). The culture of power and science education: Learning from Miguel. *Journal of Research in Science Teaching, 37*(8), 871–889.

Batis, C., Hernandez-Barrera, L., Barquera, S., Rivera, J. A., & Popkin, B. M. (2011). Food acculturation drives dietary differences among Mexicans, Mexican Americans, and non-Hispanic whites. *The Journal of nutrition, 141*(10), 1898–1906.

Blair, D. (2009). The child in the garden: An evaluative review of the benefits of school gardening. *The Journal of Environmental Education, 40*(2), 15–38.

Braund, M., & Reiss, M. (2006). Towards a more authentic science curriculum: The contribution of out-of-school learning. *International Journal of Science Education, 28*(12), 1373–1388.

Britner, S. L., & Pajares, F. (2001). Self-efficacy beliefs, motivation, race, and gender in middle school science. *Journal of women and Minorities in Science and Engineering, 7*(4), 1–15.

Bureau of Labor Statistics. (2005). U.S. Department of Labor, *The Economics Daily*, Alternative routes to agricultural work. Retrieved from http://www.bls.gov/opub/ted/2005/jul/wk4/art01.htm

Bureau of Labor Statistics. (2016). U.S. Department of Labor, *The Economics Daily*, Hispanics will make up nearly 20 percent of the labor force in 2024. Retrieved from http://www.bls.gov/opub/ted/2016/hispanics-will-make-up-nearly-20-percent-of-the-labor-force-in-2024.htm

Bybee, R. W., & Fuchs, B. (2006). Preparing the 21st century workforce: A new reform in science and technology education. *Journal of Research in Science Teaching, 43*(4), 349–352.

Carlone, H. B., & Johnson, A. (2007). Understanding the science experiences of successful women of color: Science identity as an analytic lens. *Journal of research in science teaching, 44*(8), 1187–1218.

Chapman, T. K., Tatiana, J., Hartlep, N., Vang, M., & Lipsey, T. (2014). The double-edged sword of curriculum: How curriculum in majority white suburban high schools supports and hinders the growth of students of color. *Curriculum and Teaching Dialogue, 16*(1/2), 87.

Ciechanowski, K., Bottoms, S., Fonseca, A. L., & St Clair, T. (2015). Should Rey Mysterio drink Gatorade? Cultural competence in afterschool STEM programming. *Afterschool Matters, 21*, 29–37.

Counihan, C., & Van Esterik, P. (Eds.). (2012). *Food and culture: A reader* (3rd ed.). New York, NY: Routledge.

Crisp, G., & Nora, A. (2012). *Overview of Hispanics in Science, Math, Engineering, and Technology (STEM): K-16 representation, preparation and participation* (White paper). San Antonio, TX: Hispanic Association of Colleges and Universities, The University of Texas at San Antonio.

Davis, J. N., Ventura, E. E., Cook, L. T., Gyllenhammer, L. E., & Gatto, N. M. (2011). LA Sprouts: a gardening, nutrition, and cooking intervention for Latino youth improves diet and reduces obesity. *Journal of the American Dietetic Association, 111*(8), 1224–1230.

Elmore, R. C., & Arcury, T. A. (2001). Pesticide exposure beliefs among Latino farmworkers in North Carolina's Christmas tree industry. *American Journal of Industrial Medicine, 40*(2), 153–160.

Espinosa, L. (2011). Pipelines and pathways: Women of color in undergraduate STEM majors and the college experiences that contribute to persistence. *Harvard Educational Review, 81*(2), 209–241.

Gatto, N. M., Ventura, E. E., Cook, L. T., Gyllenhammer, L. E., & Davis, J. N. (2012). LA sprouts: A garden-based nutrition intervention pilot program influences motivation and preferences for fruits and vegetables in Latino youth. *Journal of the Academy of Nutrition and Dietetics, 112*(6), 913–920.

Gee, J. P. (2000). Identity as an analytic lens for research in education. *Review of Research in Education, 25*, 99–125.

Glasson, G. E., Mhango, N., Phiri, A., & Lanier, M. (2010). Sustainability science education in Africa: Negotiating indigenous ways of living with nature in the third space. *International Journal of Science Education, 32*(1), 125–141.

Gutiérrez, K. D. (2008). Developing a sociocritical literacy in the third space. *Reading Research Quarterly, 43*(2), 148–164.

Handelsman, J., Ebert-May, D., Beichner, R., Bruns, P., Chang, A., DeHaan, R., & Wood, W. B. (2004). Scientific teaching. *Science, 304*(5670), 521–522.

Honey, M., Pearson, G., & Schweingruber, H. (Eds.). (2014). *STEM integration in K-12 education: Status, prospects, and an agenda for research.* Washington, DC: National Academies Press.

Hulleman, C. S., & Harackiewicz, J. M. (2009). Promoting interest and performance in high school science classes. *Science, 326*(5958), 1410–1412.

Jezewski, M. A. (1990). Culture brokering in migrant farmworker health care. *Western Journal of Nursing Research, 12*(4), 497–513.

Jones, L. R. (2011). *GEMS CLUB toolkit: Creating and managing a STEM club for girls.* Retrieved from http://www.gemsclub.org/yahoo_site_admin/assets/docs/GEMS TOOLKIT.1450817.pdf

Jones, M. G., Howe, A., & Rua, M. J. (2000). Gender differences in students' experiences, interests, and attitudes toward science and scientists. *Science Education, 84*(2), 180–192.

Keller, J., & Dauenheimer, D. (2003). Stereotype threat in the classroom: Dejection mediates the disrupting threat effect on women's performance. *Personality and Social Psychology Bulletin, 29,* 371–381.

Klein, E. J., Taylor, M., Onore, C., Strom, K., & Abrams, L. (2013). Finding a third space in teacher education: Creating an urban teacher residency. *Teaching Education, 24*(1), 27–57.

Landivar, L. C. (2013). *Disparities in STEM Employment by sex, race, and Hispanic origin.* Retrieved from https://www.census.gov/prod/2013pubs/acs-24.pdf

Leising, J. G., Pense, S. L., & Igo, C. (2000). An assessment of student agricultural literacy knowledge based on the food and fiber systems literacy framework. *Journal of Southern Agricultural Education Research, 50*(1), 146–151.

Mayer, A. (2014, October 15). *Ag careers an opportunity few Latinos pursue.* Retrieved from http://iowapublicradio.org/post/ag-careers-opportunity-few-latinos-pursue#stream/0

Moll, L. C. (Ed.). (1990). *Vygotsky and education: Instructional implications and applications of socio-historical psychology.* Cambridge, MA: Cambridge University Press.

Mora, M. T. (2015). The increasing importance of Hispanics to the U.S. workforce. *Monthly Labor Review.* Retrieved from http://www.bls.gov/opub/mlr/2015/article/the-increasing-importance-of-hispanics-to-the-us-workforce.htm

Morris, J. L., & Zidenberg-Cherr, S. (2002). Garden-enhanced nutrition curriculum improves fourth-grade school children's knowledge of nutrition and preferences for some vegetables. *Journal of the Academy of Nutrition and Dietetics, 102*(1), 91.

National Center for Farmworker Health, Inc. (2012). *Demographics.* Retrieved from http://www.ncfh.org/uploads/3/8/6/8/38685499/fs-migrant_demographics.pdf

National Research Council. (2015). *Identifying and supporting productive STEM programs in out-of-school settings*. Washington, DC: The National Academies Press.

National Research Council. (2010). *Surrounded by science: Learning science in informal environments*. Washington, DC: The National Academies Press.

National Science Foundation, National Center for Science and Engineering Statistics. (2015). *Characteristics of scientists and engineers in the United States: 2013*. Retrieved from http://ncsesdata.nsf.gov/us-workforce/2013/

Office of Science, Technology and Innovation. (n.d.). *Hispanics and STEM EDUCA-TION Fact Sheet*. Retrieved from http://www2.ed.gov/about/inits/list/hispanic-initiative/stem-factsheet.pdf

P21. (2007). Partnership for 21st Century Learning. *Framework for 21st Century Learning*. Retrieved from http://www.p21.org/our-work/p21-framework

Ratcliffe, M. M., Merrigan, K. A., Rogers, B. L., & Goldberg, J. P. (2011). The effects of school garden experiences on middle school-aged students' knowledge, attitudes, and behaviors associated with vegetable consumption. *Health promotion practice, 12*(1), 36–43.

Rodriguez, S. L., Cunningham, K., & Jordan, A. (2016). What a scientist looks like: How community colleges can utilize and enhance science identity development as a means to improve success for women of color. *Community College Journal of Research and Practice, 41*(4–5), 1–7.

Rosenthal, L., London, B., Levy, S. R., & Lobel, M. (2011). The roles of perceived identity compatibility and social support for women in a single-sex STEM program at a co-educational university. *Sex Roles, 65*(9–10), 725–736.

Rothwell, J. (2013). *The hidden STEM economy*. Washington, DC: Brookings Institution. Retrieved from https://www.brookings.edu/research/the-hidden-stem-economy/

Sahin, A. (2013). STEM clubs and science fair competitions: Effects on post-secondary matriculation. *Journal of STEM Education: Innovations and Research, 14*(1), 5.

Saldivar-Tanaka, L., & Krasny, M. E. (2004). Culturing community development, neighborhood open space, and civic agriculture: The case of Latino community gardens in New York City. *Agriculture and human values, 21*(4), 399–412.

Schmader, T., & Johns, M. (2003). Converging evidence that stereotype threat reduces working memory capacity. *Journal of Personality and Social Psychology, 85*, 440–452.

Schmader, T., Johns, M., & Forbes, C. (2008). An integrated process model of stereotype threat effects on performance. *Psychological Review, 115*, 336–356.

Shapiro, J. R., & Williams, A. M. (2012). The role of stereotype threats in undermining girls' and women's performance and interest in STEM fields. *Sex Roles, 66*(3–4), 175–183.

Skerrett, A. (2010). Lolita, Facebook, and the third space of literacy teacher education. *Educational Studies, 46*(1), 67–84.

Syed, M., Goza, B. K., Chemers, M. M., & Zurbriggen, E. L. (2012). Individual differences in preferences for matched-ethnic mentors among high-achieving ethnically diverse adolescents in STEM. *Child Development, 83*(3), 896–910.

Taningco, M. T. V., Mathew, A. B., & Pachon, H. P. (2008). *STEM professions: Opportunities and challenges for Latinos in science, technology, engineering, and mathematics. A review of literature.* Los Angeles, CA: Tomas Rivera Policy Institute. Retrieved from ERIC database. (ED502063)

Valencia, R. R. (Ed.). (2012). *The evolution of deficit thinking: Educational thought and practice.* New York, NY: Routledge.

Wingenbach, S. H., Degenhart, G. J., Lindner, K. E., Dooley, J. R., Mowen, D. L., & Johnson, L. (2007). Middle school students' attitudes toward pursuing careers in science, technology, engineering, and math. *NACTA Journal, 51*(1), 52–59.

Yuen, T. T., Ek, L. D., & Scheutze, A. (2013, August). Increasing participation from underrepresented minorities in STEM through robotics clubs. In *Proceedings of 2013 IEEE International Conference on Teaching, Assessment and Learning for Engineering (TALE).*

14. "You are leaders": Latino/a College Students Learning to Act and Talk Like Engineers

Alberto Esquinca and Elsa Q. Villa

Although inroads have been made in recent decades, the science and engineering workforce is largely white and male. Similarly, Latino/a engineering graduates are scarce, with merely 7.9% of engineering bachelor's degrees awarded to them in 2011 (Landivar, 2013) compared to 64.7% awarded to Whites. This underrepresentation is even bleaker for Latinas who, according to a 2017 National Science Foundation report, earn 1.9% of engineering degrees.

While the statistics are bleak nationally, there are bright spots. Hispanic Serving Institutions (HSIs), which award 40% of all undergraduate degrees to Latinos, also award 20% of STEM degrees (Crisp & Nora, 2012). HSIs then are well positioned to play a decisive role in preparing Latina/o engineers across the United States.

This chapter reports research findings of an intervention that took place at an HSI wherein engineering undergraduates participated in a leadership institute. Using a sociocultural theoretical perspective, we utilized ethnographic methods to study the process through which young Latinas/os developed attributes needed for the 21st-century workforce in engineering (National Academy of Engineering, 2004). The focus of the study, like that of the intervention, was engineering leadership. The purpose of this chapter then is to understand how students developed engineering leadership discourse through participation in this institute. We focus in particular on the culminating activities of the leadership institute that involved participating students planning and delivering leadership workshops to undergraduate peers in engineering.

Theoretical Perspective

From a sociocultural perspective, learning is conceptualized as social practice in which learning occurs through engaged participation in communities of practice. Such situated practice is also a process of identity construction (Lave & Wenger, 1991). In this framework, identity construction involves identifying and being recognized as a particular kind of person (Gee, 1996), which in our case is an engineering leader. People signal their group affiliation to others through various meaningful signs or cues (Brown, 2004; Brown, Reveles, & Kelly, 2005), including the use of discourse and of artifacts.

Through situated practice, people learn to act and represent themselves as a particular kind of person, in part, through using discourses in ways that are particularly meaningful to their communities of practice. Being recognized as an engineer (and a special kind of engineer) is a dialogic process. Using discourses in interaction with others brings opportunities for recognition and identification in the range of social fields the learner participates in, including friendships, families, professional or university groups (Stevens *et al.*, 2008). Moreover, students must perceive an inherent value (Gee, 2005) in adopting a specialized discourse if they are to develop an identity, in this case engineering leadership.

We draw from a sociocultural theory of identity (Gee, 2000–2001; Holland, Lachiotte, Skinner, & Cain, 1998) to better understand how Latinas/os construct and enact an identity as engineering leaders discursively. Literature over the past decade has shown that identity is increasingly becoming a core issue in the study of teaching and learning, generally, and in science education, specifically (see Barton & Tan, 2010; Barton, Kang, Tan, O'Neill, Bautista-Green, & Brecklin, 2013; Carlone, 2004; Roth & Tobin, 2001; Tan & Barton, 2008). That is, we learn values, language, knowledge and skills situated in everyday practice with others and with artifacts; and what we learn creates a sense of self and identity—who we are for ourselves and in relation to others (Gee, 1996, 2001–2001). As human beings, we inherently make sense of our world in unconscious and tacit ways through our interaction with others and our environment as we engage in authentic and situated activity. In this framework, identities are constructed in social practices and are in continuous flux, or dynamic, depending on any particular situation, such as whether an individual is in a welcoming environment or in an environment where an individual senses her/himself as an outsider.

Relevant Scholarship

A National Academy of Engineering (2004) report described the attributes needed for the 21st-century workforce in engineering: creativity, good communication, business and management skills, leadership, ethical standards, professionalism, and lifelong learning. The report further encouraged educators to recognize and promote these attributes, in addition to technical and analytical skills, needed for practicing in a changing world.

Teamwork is an essential professional skill in engineering (Gilbuena, Sherrett, Gummer, Champagne, & Koretsky, 2015), and is a professional skill that is increasingly important in engineering education (Prados, Peterson, & Lattuca, 2005). In addition, teamwork is a major part of the job, with engineering graduates reporting that 60 to 80% of time is spent on teamwork (Martin, Maytham, Case, & Fraser, 2005). In a study of the competencies engineering graduates find most important on the job, Passow (2012) found that teamwork (along with communication, data analysis and problem solving) were the competencies found to be most important across 11 engineering majors. Competencies were aligned to ABET competencies; ABET is the college accreditation body for applied science and engineering. Yet, teamwork is perceived as an area of weakness or underpreparation by recent graduates (Martin *et al.*, 2005).

While teamwork is an essential professional skill, several studies have found that women's experiences in teams could potentially "recreate sexist environments already found in the university environment for undergraduate women if they are not properly managed" (Amelink & Creamer, 2010, p. 82). If not properly managed, the authors note, negative experiences in teams (such as when a student is not accepted, heard or respected by her peers) could have significant long-term impacts.

Ethnographic research methods can illuminate the subtle and complex ways teamwork can function to mediate women's participation in engineering. For instance, Karen Tonso's (2006a) work has been essential to understanding the relationship among engineering identities, campus cultures and effective teamwork, e.g., a team in which members report having a positive experience. Using a sociocultural theoretical framework, Tonso (2006b) analyzed the identity work that occurred in engineering project teams. She gathered identity terms among engineering students at a midcontinent university, and then asked students what terms, such as nerd, academic-achievers and Greek, meant to students and how the categories were related to one another. Tonso found that the categories of nerd and academic-achiever were the domain of men while women only fit into one category. Similarly, Ingram and Parker's (2002) ethnographic study at a Canadian university showed the complex ways that, even in collaborative teamwork in which students are attentive to the affective element of teamwork, gender is a factor that can potentially impact women's learning experiences. Men had higher status than the women and signaled their status by bragging about math grades. Higher status members of the team discussed technical concepts; and, at least one woman, avoided participating in those technical conversations despite being more qualified to do so than some of the men. Likewise, Meadows and Sekaquaptewa (2013) found that in presentations men were assigned (or chose) to present technical content more often than women even in teams where they were the minority. Men also answered discussion questions at the end of the presentation. Attributions of expertise were made more frequently of men. The subjective interpretation of how engineering students present themselves in teamwork is linked to gendered notions of expertise, such as expressed in gendered perceptions of ability (Wolfe & Powell, 2009).

Methodology

This study is part of a larger, four-year ethnographic study that took place at an HSI on the U.S.–Mexico border. The Hispanic Engineering Leadership Institute (HELI) was a funded project from 2011 through 2015 with the stated purpose of retaining engineering undergraduate students, particularly women and English Learners (ELs), in engineering. The project was under the direction of coauthor Villa, who is an engineering educator; and the research team who documented the experiences of HELI participants. Being comprised of language and literacy scholars, the research team focused on the mediating role of language in student socialization and mentorship.

HELI's goal was to develop leadership competencies of Latinas/os, who were engineering undergraduates, through workshops and internship learning experiences. Fifty-one undergraduate engineering students (27 males, 24 females) participated in the project with most (50/51) identifying as Latina/o. For the larger study, data were collected from semi-structured interviews, observations and focus group data over five semesters between Spring 2012 and Spring 2014.

In this chapter, we focus on the activities that took place during in the 2014–2015 academic year. During that year, as students prepared to graduate, coauthor Villa invited all active HELI participants to design and deliver leadership workshops to peers; five upper-division engineering students, identified here with pseudonyms, accepted the invitation and received stipends for their participation, including four Latina/o engineering students: Abel (mechanical), Monica (metallurgical/ materials), Andrea (computer science), and Natalia (electrical). The three women were all bilingual and transnational, having grown up in and/or schooled in Mexico; and the fifth engineering student was Roger (mechanical).

Video-recorded data were gathered at the five events: (1) workshop planning meeting with five student leaders, (2) two "Leadership Overview" workshops delivered by the student leaders to peers, and (3) two "ePortfolio Workshops." Additional artifacts were collected (e.g., emails, flyers, Power-Points, meeting agendas, handouts); and interviews were conducted with the five participants.

Discourse analysis was conducted on the video-recordings to identify literacy events and practices (Barton & Hamilton, 1998) implicit in the discourse of engineering leadership. Contextualization cues (Bloome, Carter, Christian, Otto, & Shuart-Faris, 2005), including intonation and gestures, were used to delimit literacy events. By identifying the events and interactions around texts, it was possible to analyze the values and positionalities embedded in practices. Each literacy event is identified by the use of discourse markers (e.g., "OK, let's start," "let's move on," "now, another thing is"), body positioning (e.g., students facing each other, students facing the board, leaders facing the students), and movements in the classroom space (e.g., lowering of the projection screen, lights being turned off, the classroom door opening, students moving to different chairs, tables being moved).

Our positionality in conducting this research is as follows. Coauthor Esquinca was born and raised in the same border community in which this study is set. Like some of the participants, he crossed the border daily to attend college as an undergraduate in the same HSI being studied here. Though not an engineering educator, he has been researching the experiences of undergraduate engineering students and is most interested in highlighting the cultural and linguistic assets underrepresented students bring to learning engineering and becoming engineers, with a focus on bilingualism and biliteracy. He contributed data collection and analysis to this chapter.

Coauthor Villa has been both a professional staff member and research assistant professor in the university school of engineering for over 14 years. As such, she has been working with students both in the capacity of recruitment and retention (as a professional staff member) and in research (as a research assistant professor in grant administration). Villa has and continues to use cooperative learning methods in workshops and courses, such as the workshops she led in HELI. Other than mentoring the students in the leadership activities, Villa was not involved in data collection and analysis. However, in preparation for publication and dissemination, debriefing and member checks were completed to ensure trustworthiness.

Findings

In video-recordings, participants were observed actively engaged in becoming engineering leaders; and less visible in the video, but not less engaged, was coauthor Villa. In this findings section, we begin by highlighting the activities she initiated to apprentice the engineering leaders into the discourse of engineering leadership. Next, we analyzed practices the leaders engaged in as they planned, delivered and reflected on their practice, highlighting the ways they used language and literacy practices to mediate their development of this specialized discourse.

"You are leaders": The Value of Teamwork

The leadership institute was designed to apply research in learning sciences, such as learning communities and cooperative learning to support academic success (Lave, 1998; Lave & Wenger, 1991; Johnson & Johnson, 1994; Johnson, Johnson, & Smith, 1998; Wenger, 1998), particularly for students from minority backgrounds (Villa, Kephart, Gates, Thiry, & Hug, 2013). While the range and type of learning communities may vary (Lenning & Ebbers, 1999; Price, 2005), most learning communities embody several key characteristics, including the use of smaller groups among faculty and students; the bringing together of faculty and students in more meaningful ways; curriculum integration; emphasis on the development of academic and social support networks; and a focus on learning outcomes (Shapiro & Levine, 1999). Learning communities help foster increased student engagement and is defined by Astin (1999) as "the amount of physical and psychological energy that the student devotes to the academic experience" (p. 518). For more than two decades, research has shown the benefits of student engagement on student learning, persistence, and completion at the undergraduate level (Astin, 1993; NSSE, 2014).

At the heart of the HELI learning community was the integration of cooperative learning strategies (Bielaczyc & Collins, 1999; Johnson & Johnson, 1994; Johnson et al., 1998; Slavin, 1989) where the instructor serves as a facilitator of student-generated knowledge development rather than a transmitter of knowledge. In contrast with competition- and individualistic-oriented approaches to learning, cooperative learning involves "the instructional use of small groups so that students work together to maximize their own and each other's learning" (Johnson & Johnson, 1994).

During HELI workshops, which took place in various settings for the previous three years, participants learned about teamwork, conflict resolution, and positive interdependence. These same topics and principles were again used to guide their activities during the fourth year, with an added challenge for participants. Students would have to plan and deliver the workshops to other undergraduates. Because they had learned about the aforementioned topics and principles, planning and delivering leadership workshops to fellow classmates was something that participants had been prepared to do throughout their participation in HELI.

As students geared up to plan and deliver leadership workshops in the fourth year of the institute, they were guided by the notions that had been used throughout the institute. On the day they began planning, they were provided with supportive materials, such as books on cooperative learning (Johnson & Johnson, 1994) and team building (Lencioni, 2002). Villa also communicated with student leaders in a manner that situated them as competent. She gave a few brief suggestions, directed them to key pages on team dysfunctions (Lencioni, 2002), and put the workshop in their hands. Before leaving the room, she smiled and said, "you figure it out...Because you are the leaders," signaling her trust in them.

In addition, Villa supported five participants by providing several resources: office space and equipment to include computer with shared projected display and copy machine. She provided access to a location in the engineering school where the workshops would be delivered, as well as a formal introduction to the director overseeing the space. The director in turn arranged for other undergraduates to attend the workshop, which was announced as a Leadership Overview and an ePortfolio workshop.

"We are all in charge": Artifact-Mediated Negotiation

The young leaders planned their work for over two hours one afternoon around a conference table in front of a large screen displaying the agenda they were writing together. Roger, who controlled the wireless keyboard, listened to the group and wrote down the group's ideas on how the upcoming workshop should unfold. Monica and Andrea also had their laptops open. On the table, books, handouts, notebooks, snacks and smartphones were strewn.

The values of teamwork guided the young student leaders. Through our analysis of discourse activity during the planning of the workshops, we saw that two main texts mediated the negotiation process: (1) the agenda, which was displayed for all at the table to see with Roger's key role of controlling the keyboard; and (2) the PowerPoint (PPT) to be used on the day of the workshop was being revised on Monica's laptop, which she had previously sent to the group by email. A third text, not being negotiated, was the flyer to advertise the workshops; Andrea designed it quietly on her personal laptop.

The agenda text served to establish the topics and activities to be covered, the time spent on each item and identification of the lead. For instance, they negotiated the use of a TED talk video at the start of the workshop to motivate students, as Monica had suggested via email. The excerpt below shows the use of a linguistic structure that was used to present suggestions and engaged solidarity with the group "Do you want to...?" By framing it as questions, Monica reminded the group that the agenda was a joint endeavor with collective decision-making.

> Natalia: When **do you want to** do TED talks? **Do you want** it at the end? I think it is better than the beginning.
> Roger: Yeah, 'cause it gets their interest. So, **do you want** to move it? (he types)
> Natalia: And I guess that way everyone will try to be a leader.
> Roger: It's all-motivating.

The rhetorical strategy harkens back to one of the principles of cooperative learning the student leaders would be connecting to during the planned workshop—positive interdependence and shared decision-making. As Monica stated at one point, "we are all in charge." In addition, as noted above, the agenda was not the only artifact being designed. The PowerPoint and the flier were also being designed at the meeting in Monica's and Andrea's laptops as each of them took the lead in doing that for the group.

As the agenda continued to be developed, a small conflict arose when students were planning a discussion activity. Villa had suggested a small group activity called Winter Survival (Johnson & Johnson, 1982) in which participants would rank the necessary tools they would hypothetically use to survive the aftermath of an airplane crash. Student leaders seemed unsure of how to carry out the activity, and seemed to be leaning toward not doing it.

> Roger: **Do you want** to try something else?
> Monica: There are similar [activities] in the book. So, if we don't want the Winter Survival one, we don't have to do it.

When the leaders got stuck, they asked Villa to join the group. She explained the purpose of the activity, and what participants would learn from it. After two minutes, Villa shifted topic and worked with students on the agenda. Before leaving the room again, Villa asked again if they would do Winter Survival. "We were looking at it because we hadn't like even [read] it," Natalia answered. Villa offered to take the lead in that part of the workshop and left the room. After 15 minutes, the group voted on doing the activity, with Monica and Natalia voting yes and giving ideas drawing on different meaningful resources for the PowerPoint text. Monica said "we can also just use like a dramatic video of […] things crashing," and Natalia added "And have background music and everything." With Roger, Natalia and Monica on board, a majority had voted, and the group moved on without Abel and Andrea's vote. When the majority agreed to do the activity, they moved on.

This episode shows that collective decision making was a guiding notion for the group; however, there were still some members of the group who wielded significant power over others within the group. Through their management of artifacts, members could exert power within the group. For instance, the leader who designed the flyer, Andrea, was not very vocal during negotiations, but told us that she felt included. When we asked about what she learned from the whole experience, Andrea said that the experience was very important for her. She said that at first "I didn't want to talk because I come from Mexico; I felt that I could not speak in English. I felt like everybody criticizes me, and nobody will understand me." Her participation in planning and delivering leadership workshops seemed to be crucial for her to develop the discourse of engineering leadership—in a second language. Similarly, another quiet student, Natalia, said that the experience of leading workshops seemed to be a way to be positioned in a powerful way within engineering as a whole, particularly in a male-dominated field. "In engineering there are only boys, and we need to go to speak with them to be included," she said.

Casting a Vision of Leadership

Having planned their workshops as a team, student leaders proceeded to deliver three workshops to fellow engineering students. At approximately 90 minutes each, workshops took place in a classroom in the engineering building arranged for by Villa and was attended by approximately 10–15 engineering students, in addition to Villa. The purpose of the leadership workshops was to introduce students to leadership concepts, including definition of leadership, teamwork and working through team conflicts. Student leaders took turns leading the workshop; however, a student who had a lot of experience speaking in front of groups, Monica, took on the responsibility of leading much of the discussion. Student leaders organized the agenda to include the following major activities, (a) introduction to the workshop, (b) icebreaker and personal introductions, (c) open discussion on the definition of leadership, (d) small group team-building activity, (e) debriefing on team-building activity, (f) presentation on team dysfunctions, and (g) final thoughts.

The identification of events allowed us to analyze how participants and student leaders orient toward each other to pinpoint the practices student leaders undertook as part of the culminating activities in HELI. Due to space constraints, detailed analysis is not included here.

In analyzing the discourse of the workshops, we noted the activity in which each participant was engaged. We found that student leaders participated in about half of the events, and workshop attendees participated in the remainder. This is because student leaders would ask attendees to, for instance, talk to each other or complete a survey. However, the number of events they participated in is perhaps not as important as how student leaders oriented toward attendees.

An analysis of the ways student leaders orient toward workshop attendees shows that they positioned themselves as leaders by participating as experts. Further, they used artifacts to mediate their interactions with attendees. Whereas student leaders positioned themselves as those who gave instructions, gave guidance, presented information, led discussion, formed groups and interpreted observations. Student leaders also moved freely across the physical space—sometimes standing in front of the workshop and other times circulating among the groups they had formed. The results of this analysis is shown on Table 14.1. The number of literacy events in which student leaders participated, the activity they engaged in, and the text or artifact mediating the activity, in parenthesis is summarized.

Table 14.1. Literacy events during leadership workshops

First Workshop	Second Workshop
1. Introduce themselves (n/a)	1. Introduce themselves
2. Give guidance (cards)	2. Give guidance (screen display)
3. Give guidance (n/a)	3. Give guidance (screen display)
4. Negotiate definition (screen display)	4. Give instruction (n/a)
5. Give guidance (screen display)	5. Give guidance (red dot sheet)
6. Give instruction (n/a)	6. Observe groups (n/a)
7. Give guidance (red dot sheet)	7. Lead reflection (n/a)
8. Observe groups (n/a)	8. Give guidance (screen display)
9. Give guidance (screen display)	9. Present leader types (screen display)
10. Present (screen display)	10. Present dysfunctions (screen display)
11. Lead discussion (screen display)	
12. Present on dysfunctions (screen display)	
13. Give guidance (screen display)	

Source: Authors

In contrast, attendees had a more limited range or participation in the workshop; they followed leaders' guidance and instructions, spoke to one another in small groups and answering questions from student leaders; their mobility in the physical space was also limited.

Student leaders used a leadership style that aligned to the values HELI attempted to instill in them. For instance, when defining leadership qualities, Monica used both whole-group and small group discussion. A young woman noted that leadership is not about simply ordering people around, but instead about inspiring and motivating a group people and having a vision for what the group could accomplish. Smiling, Monica echoed back "Okay, so would you say they have a goal and then you are kind of inspiring them or motivating them?" Next, Monica asked the rest of the teams to add to that definition in a way to draw a consensus around the definition. Having elicited further discussion and provided tools to arrive at a definition of leadership, Monica recapped the discussion on leadership as follows:

> So, if we say a leader is casting vision in a group and kind of being with them and helping them understand what the goals are and all of that, would you say that matches the handout pretty well? So, we all kind of have the same idea of leadership, right?

Rather than impose a definition of leadership, Monica sought to build consensus among participants through open discussion.

Discussion and Conclusion

In this chapter, we have shown how social practices in a community of practice crucially includes the process of identity construction (Lave & Wenger, 1991). Becoming a type of person occurs through participation in a community of practice, in this case of student engineering leaders. The dialogic process of becoming occurs when a person makes a bid to be recognized as a type of person and is recognized as such by the community. As we show in this chapter, a mentor recognized the group as leaders and signaled ways of belonging to the community of practice through the provision of meaningful signs and artifacts. In a dialogic process, students responded by acting as leaders and taking up the discourse of engineering leadership. They also recognized coauthor Villa as their mentor in seeking advice, resources and ideas.

Significantly, HELI was designed to include at least 50% young women in the institute. It was also designed to develop 21st-century engineering leadership skills, which the findings presented herein demonstrate. We found that in this cocurricular institute young Latinas took on the opportunity to be positioned as leaders. They sought leadership positions within the group in ways that were respectful and sought consensus, which was most clearly exemplified by the case of Monica. Other women in the group, while not seeking leadership positions within the group, quietly worked on their contribution to the group project, as exemplified by Andrea. These young women might have taken the position of leader among leaders, in part, due to the influence of Villa, who is a professional Latina and professor; however, we cannot definitively state that as a finding.

The study further suggests that opportunities to be positioned as leaders may be beneficial. Being given the reins of the project, being talked to as competent young adults, and being respected are all important values in HELI. In addition, the activity gave the young leaders the opportunity to be seen as leaders by their peers. As they were recognized as a particular kind of person, they may have experienced recognizing themselves as that kind of person. For underrepresented groups, including women and ELs, this may be especially important, as these groups are typically marginalized with little to no opportunity to participate in such activities. All these students have graduated. Some are in graduate school and the remainder are in the engineering workforce. Future research could determine whether their participation in these leadership activities contributed (or not) to their upward mobility as engineer leaders in the 21st-century workforce.

Acknowledgments

We would like to acknowledge the participation of all HELI students. We are grateful to our colleagues, especially Erika Mein, without whom this work would not be possible, and to Claudia Saldaña Corral, who contributed to this chapter as a graduate assistant.

This material is based upon work supported by the U.S. Department of Education under P120A110086. Any opinions, findings, and conclusions or recommendations expressed in this material are those of the authors and do not necessarily reflect the views of the U.S. Department of Education.

References

Amelink, C. T., & Creamer, E. G. (2010). Gender differences in elements of the undergraduate experience that influence satisfaction with the engineering major and the intent to pursue engineering as a career. *Journal of Engineering Education, 99*(1), 81–92.

Astin, A. W. (1993). *What matters in college?: Four critical years revisited* (Vol. 1). San Francisco, CA: Jossey-Bass.

Astin, A. W. (1999). Student involvement: A developmental theory for higher education. *Journal of College Student Development, 40*(5), 518.

Barton, A. C., Kang, H., Tan, E., O'Neill, T. B., Bautista-Green, J., & Brecklin, C. (2013). Creating a future in science: Tracing middle school girls' identity work over time and space. *American Educational Research Journal, 50*(1), 37–75.

Barton, A. C., & Tan, E. (2010). We be burnin'! Agency, identity, and science learning. *The Journal of the Learning Sciences, 19*(2), 187–229.

Barton, D., & Hamilton, M. (1998). *Local literacies: Reading and writing in one community.* New York, NY: Routledge.

Bielaczyc, K., & Collins, A. (1999). Learning communities in classrooms: A reconceptualization of educational practice. *Instructional-design Theories and Models: A New Paradigm of Instructional Theory, 2,* 269–292.

Bloome, D., Carter, S. P., Christian, B. M., Otto, S., & Shuart-Faris, N. (2005). *Discourse analysis and the study of classroom language and literacy events: A microethnographic perspective.* Mahwah, NJ: Lawrence Erlbaum Associates.

Brown, B. A. (2004). Discursive identity: Assimilation into the culture of science and its implications for minority students. *Journal of Research in Science Teaching, 41*(8), 810–834.

Brown, B. A., Reveles, J. M., & Kelly, G. J. (2005). Scientific literacy and discursive identity: A theoretical framework for understanding science learning. *Science Education, 89*(5), 779–802.

Carlone, H. B. (2004). The cultural production of science in reform-based physics: Girls' access, participation, and resistance. *Journal of Research in Science Teaching, 41*(4), 392–414.

Crisp, G., & Nora, A. (2012). *Overview of Hispanics in Science, Mathematics, Engineering and Technology (STEM): K-16 representation, preparation and participation.* San Antonio, TX: Hispanic Association of Colleges and Universities. Retrieved from http://www.hacu.net/images/hacu/OPAI/H3ERC/2012_papers/Crisp%20nora%20-%20hispanics%20in%20stem%20-%20updated%202012.pdf

Gee, J. P. (1996). *Social linguistics and social literacies: Ideology in discourses* (2nd ed.). New York, NY: Routledge Falmer.

Gee, J. P. (2000–2001). Identity as an analytic lens for research in education. *Review of Educational Research, 25,* 99–125.

Gee, J. P. (2005). Language in the science classroom: Academic social languages as the heart of school-based literacy. In R. W. Yerrick & W.-M. Roth (Eds.), *Establishing scientific classroom discourse communities: Multiple voices of teaching and learning in research* (pp. 19–37). Mahwah, NJ: Lawrence Erlbaum Associates.

Gilbuena, D. M., Sherrett, B. U., Gummer, E. S., Champagne, A. B., & Koretsky, M. (2015). Feedback on professional skills as enculturation into communities of practice. *Journal of Engineering Education, 104*(1), 7–34. doi:10.1002/jee.20061

Holland, D., Lachiotte, W. J., Skinner, D., & Cain, C. (1998). *Identity and agency in cultural worlds*. Cambridge, MA: Harvard University Press.

Ingram, S., & Parker, A. (2002). Gender and modes of collaboration in an engineering classroom: A profile of two women on student teams. *Journal of Business and Technical Communication, 16*(1), 33–68.

Johnson, D. W., & Johnson, F. P. (1982). Joining together (2nd ed.). Englewood Cliffs, NJ: Prentice Hall.

Johnson, D. W., & Johnson, R. T. (1994). *Learning together and alone. Cooperative, competitive, and individualistic learning*. Needham Heights, MA: Allyn and Bacon.

Johnson, D. W., Johnson, R. T., & Smith, K. A. (1998). *Active learning: Cooperation in the college classroom*. Edina, MN: Interaction Book Company.

Landivar, L. C. (2013). Disparities in STEM employment by sex, race, and Hispanic origin. *Education Review, 29*(6), 911–922.

Lave, J. (1998). Situated learning in communities of practice. In L. Resnick, J. Levine, & S. Teasley (Eds.), *Perspectives on socially shared cognition* (pp. 63–82). Washington, DC: American Psychological Association.

Lave, J., & Wenger, E. (1991). *Situated learning: Legitimate peripheral participation*. Cambridge: Cambridge University Press.

Lencioni, P. (2002). *The five dysfunctions of a team*. San Francisco, CA: Jossey-Bass.

Lenning, O. T., & Ebbers, L. H. (1999). The powerful potential of learning communities: Improving education for the future. *ASHE-ERIC Higher Education Report, 26*(6).

Martin, R., Maytham, B., Case, J., & Fraser, D. (2005). Engineering graduates' perceptions of how well they were prepared for work in industry. *European Journal of Engineering Education, 20*(2), 167–180.

Meadows, L. A., & Sekaquaptewa, D. (2013). The influence of gender stereotypes on role adoption in student teams. In *Proceedings of the 120th ASEE annual conference exposition* (pp. 1–16). Washington, DC: American Society for Engineering Education.

National Academy of Engineering. (2004). *The engineer of 2020: Visions of engineering in the new century*. Washington, DC: The National Academies Press.

National Science Foundation, National Center for Science and Engineering Statistics. (2017). *Women, minorities, and persons with disabilities in science and engineering: 2017*. Special Report NSF 17–310. Arlington, VA. Available at www.nsf.gov/statistics/wmpd/

National Survey of Student Engagement [NSSE]. (2014). *Bringing the Institution into Focus—Annual Results 2014*. Bloomington, IN: Indiana University Center for Post-secondary Research.

Passow, H. J. (2012). Which ABET competencies do engineering graduates find most important in their work? *Journal of Engineering Education, 101*(1), 95–118.

Prados, J. W., Peterson, G. D., & Lattuca, L. R. (2005). Quality assurance of engineering education through accreditation: The impact of engineering criteria 2000 and its global influence. *Journal of Engineering Education, 94*(1), 165–184.

Price, D. V. (2005). Learning communities and student success in postsecondary education: A background paper. *MDRC Building Knowledge to Improve Social Policy*.

Roth, W., & Tobin, K. (2001). The implications of coteaching/cogenerative dialogue for teacher evaluation: Learning from multiple perspectives of everyday practice. *Journal of Personnel Evaluation in Education, 15*(1), 7–29.

Shapiro, N. S., & Levine, J. H. (1999). *Creating learning communities: A practical guide to winning support, organizing for change, and implementing programs.* Jossey-Bass Higher and Adult Education Series. San Francisco, CA: Jossey-Bass Inc.

Slavin, R. E. (1989). *Effective programs for students at risk.* Needham Heights, MA: Allyn and Bacon.

Stevens, R., O'Connor, K., Garrison, L., Jocuns, A., & Amos, D. M. (2008). Becoming an engineer: Toward a three dimensional view of engineering learning. *Journal of Engineering Education, 97*(3), 355–368.

Tan, E., & Barton, A. C. (2008). Transforming science learning and student participation in sixth grade science: A case study of low-income, urban, racial minority classroom. *Equity & Excellence in \ Education 43*(1), 38–55. doi:10.1080/10665680903472367

Tonso, K. L. (2006a). Student engineers and engineer identity: Campus engineer identities as figured world. *Cultural Studies of Science Education, 1,* 273–307.

Tonso, K. L. (2006b). Teams that work: Campus culture, engineer identity, and social interactions. *Journal of Engineering Education, 95*(1), 25.

Villa, E. Q., Kephart, K., Gates, A. Q., Thiry, H., & Hug, S. (2013). Affinity research groups in practice: Apprenticing students in research. *Journal of Engineering Education, 102*(3), 444–466.

Wenger, E. (1998). *Communities of practice: Learning, meaning, and identity.* Cambridge, MA: Cambridge University Press.

Wolfe, J., & Powell, E. (2009). Biases in interpersonal communication: How engineering students perceive gender typical speech acts in teamwork. *Journal of Engineering Education, 98*(1), 5.

Contributors

Beverley Argus-Calvo, Ph.D. is an Associate Professor of Special Education at The University of Texas at El Paso. She teaches graduate and undergraduate courses in Bilingual Special Education and Assessment. She is a member of an interdisciplinary international research team that investigates how schools address the educational needs of students living in vulnerable settings along the U.S.–Mexico Border. Her research has focused on the mental health and academic-related issues that impact children and youth in schools. She holds a Ph.D. from New Mexico State University and a Master's degree from The George Washington University.

María G. Arreguín-Anderson, Ed.D. is an Associate Professor of Early Childhood and Elementary Education at the University of Texas at San Antonio. Her research explores the intricacies of cultural and linguistic factors that influence Latino students' access to education in early childhood and elementary bilingual settings, specifically in the area of science education. For several years Dr. Arreguín-Anderson has been involved in leadership positions at the state and national levels. She is current vice-president of the National Association for Bilingual Education and past president of the Texas Association for Bilingual Education.

Estanislado S. Barrera IV, Ph.D. is an Assistant Professor of Literacy Studies at Louisiana State University. His research agenda has three interrelated strands: (1) literacy studies, (2) bilingual literacy, and (3) improving teacher education and development. Within the literacy field, he gives specific attention to genre studies and their relationship to the development of comprehension and the reading, writing, and speaking reciprocal relationship. His research related to bilingual education concentrates on identifying and developing effective pedagogical approaches that maximize the students' "cultural capital" to achieve success. The roles of field experience and service-learning in developing pre-service teachers are the primary subjects of his research in regards to improving teacher education programs.

Alfredo H. Benavides, Ph.D. is a Professor of Bilingual/ESL Education at Texas Tech University. He has also held appointments at the University of Iowa and Arizona State University. He was co-editor of the *Bilingual Research Journal* from 1997 to 2006. He serves on several bilingual journal Editorial Boards. His research areas are bilingual teacher education, immigration, teacher dispositions, and multicultural education. He received the 2007–2008 Outstanding Researcher Award at Texas Tech University and a Lifetime Achievement Award from AERA in 2013.

Pranav A. Bhounsule, Ph.D. is an Assistant Professor in the Department of Mechanical Engineering at the University of Texas at San Antonio (UTSA). He received his BE degree from Goa University in 2004, the MTech degree from Indian Institute of Technology Madras in 2006, and the Ph.D. degree from Cornell University in 2012. From 2012 to 2014, he was a post-doctoral researcher at Disney Research Pittsburgh. He teaches Dynamics, Controls, and Robotics related courses at UTSA. He is interested in project-based and service-based learning approaches and use of multimedia in the classroom.

Emily P. Bonner, Ph.D. is an Associate Professor of Curriculum and Instruction at the University of Texas at San Antonio. Her work focuses on advancing equity in K–12 mathematics classrooms, and ways in which teacher preparation programs can promote culturally responsive mathematics instruction. Dr. Bonner is currently the Director and PI for the San Antonio Mathematics Collaborative, a program that provides professional development and classroom mentoring to secondary mathematics teachers that work with traditionally underserved students. Recently, Dr. Bonner was also a Co-PI/Director for the South Texas STEM Center and the San Antonio STEM Collaborative.

Marco A. Bravo, Ph.D. is an Associate Professor at Santa Clara University where he teaches courses in language and literacy development to pre-service teachers. He earned a Master's degree in Human Development and Psychology from Harvard University (1995) and a Ph.D. degree in education with a focus in Language, Literacy and Culture (2003) from the Graduate School of Education at the University of California, Berkeley. He was a post-doctoral researcher at the Lawrence Hall of Science where he was a member of the *Seeds of Science/Roots of Reading* research and curriculum development team. He was co-principal Investigator of the grant *The Role of Educative Curricu-*

lum Materials in Supporting Science Teaching Practices with English Language Learners study funded by the National Science Foundation.

Patricia Maria Buenrostro, Ph.D. is a Mexican-American Latina with an undergraduate degree in Mechanical Engineering (1997) from the University of Illinois at Urbana-Champaign and a doctorate degree in Curriculum & Instruction (2016) from the University of Illinois at Chicago. She has taught reform-based mathematics at the high school level for 20 years in low-income communities of color in Chicago and has led professional development efforts in mathematics reform for secondary mathematics teachers for over 15 years. As a graduate research fellow with the NSF-funded Center for the Mathematics of Latin@s in Education, she worked with teachers at a social justice-focused high school as a mathematics facilitator to support new teachers' implementation of reform mathematics and social justice curriculum. She currently works as a facilitator and coach across the Chicago school district promoting teachers' engagement with inquiry-based instruction. Her research interests include inquiry-based learning environments, critical mathematics, and sustainable, community schools.

Anne E. Campbell, Ph.D. is an Associate Professor of TESOL, World Languages, and Bilingual Education and Director of Bilingual Education and TESOL programs at Fairfield University, Fairfield, CT. During the grant period, she was Director of TESOL and Bilingual Education at the WSU Tri-Cities campus in Richland, WA, and she served as the bilingual member of the *Acceso la Ciencia* evaluation team from 2007 to 2012. Dr. Campbell was a Title VII Fellow and Bilingual Teacher Corps Intern in Hartford, CT. She earned her Ph. D in Curriculum and Instruction from the University of Florida. She has served as a Principal Investigator and Co-principal Investigator on numerous Title VII teacher training and National Professional Development grants. Currently, she codirects Project B.E.S.T., a five-year federally funded National Professional Development grant that offers K-12 classroom teachers certification in bilingual education, TESOL, and/or special education.

Lorena Claeys, Ph.D. is the Executive Director and Research Associate of the Academy for Teacher Excellence Research Center in the College of Education and Human Development at the University of Texas at San Antonio. Claeys' research interests include: teacher preparation, retention, and motivation for teaching culturally and linguistically diverse students, and school-community-university collaborations. Claeys has coauthored a number of peer-reviewed articles and has been successfully awarded competitive grants. Recently, the Texas Association for Bilingual Education recognized Dr. Claeys with the 2016 TABE

Honoree Award for Higher Education for the many years of commitment to bilingual education and to the linguistically and culturally diverse children of Texas.

Claudia Saldaña Corral is a doctoral candidate at the University of Texas at El Paso, in Teaching, Learning, and Culture. Her research interests are in the fields of Arts and Education and is currently conducting a qualitative study for her dissertation titled: Art as a Mediating Tool: Children Learning in an Arts-based After School Program. She holds a Master's degree in Business Administration from the Universidad Autonoma de Ciudad Juarez and an undergraduate degree in Graphic Design from the same university. She has taught both undergraduate and graduate graphic design courses at the UACJ.

Don Davis, Ph.D. is a computer science educator and researcher. He completed a doctorate in Interdisciplinary Learning and Teaching at the University of Texas at San Antonio. His current work is focused on behaviorally articulating and researching constructionist learning practices, include makerspace initiatives, in order to better provide pragmatic and measurable pathways for broadening CS participation and identity. He has utilized learning analytic and behavioral phenomenological approaches to examine computer science learning across varied contexts.

Jerry Dwyer, Ph.D. is a Professor in the College of Education at Texas Tech University. He has a background in applied mathematics and currently works in K–12 outreach and teacher education. He has obtained numerous federal grants and managed several projects related to promoting underrepresented groups in STEM. He has directed STEM centers at Texas Tech and George Washington University, most recently appointed director of the Center for the Integration of STEM Education & Research (CISER) at Texas Tech.

Alberto Esquinca, Ph.D. is an Associate Professor of Bilingual Education/ ESL in the Department of Teacher Education at the University of Texas at El Paso. An applied linguist, his publications focus on emergent bilinguals in STEM in educational contexts. In his most recent research, he studies engineering design process in elementary, dual language classrooms.

Belinda Bustos Flores is a Professor of Bilingual-Bicultural Studies and Associate Dean of Professional Preparation, Assessment, and Accreditation in the College of Education and Human Development at the University of Texas at San Antonio. Dr. Flores is the founder of the nationally recognized, award-winning Academy for Teacher Excellence at UTSA. Her research focuses on teacher personal and professional identity and beliefs. Dr. Flores has been recognized for her work by the San Antonio Women's Hall of Fame, Texas Association for Bilingual Education, and was selected as the recipient of the 2015 AERA Hispanic Research Issues SIG Elementary, Secondary, and Postsecondary Award.

Elaine Hampton, Ph.D. is a retired Associate Professor and Department Chair in Teacher Education at the University of Texas at El Paso where she taught educational research, curriculum theory, and science methods. Her long career as an educator and educational researcher includes experiences on both sides of U.S. and Mexico joining a Mexican woman as she negotiated the complexities of poverty in her quest for education; researching schools in factory communities in Mexico; and teaching middle school science in New Mexico. She is currently owner of STEM Educational Associates, a small business for educational consulting and program evaluation.

Felisha A. Herrera, Ph.D. is the Director of the Research & Equity Scholarship Institute on Student Trajectories in Education (RESISTE) and Assistant Professor of Postsecondary Education at San Diego State University (SDSU). She earned her Ph.D. and M.A. in Education at the University of California, Los Angeles (UCLA) and master's and bachelor's degrees from the University of New Mexico (UNM). Her research employs advanced statistical techniques to examine contextual factors—institutional, geographic, demographic, political and economic contexts—that impact postsecondary outcomes. Her scholarship is enhanced by 15 years of experience as a higher education professional at two- and four-year institutions, several Hispanic-Serving Institutions (HSI). She is a consummate scholar, who has published in top tier, peer-reviewed journals, has procured over $700,000 in grant funding, and serves as the PI for several large-scale research projects, including the NSF funded project ED-SYSTEMS focused on the role of HSIs and community colleges in STEM.

Rebecca Hite, Ph.D. is an Assistant Professor of STEM education in the College of Education at Texas Tech University. Her research foci involves investigating the various institutional, gender-based, and cultural barriers facilitating underrepresentation in STEM and STEM education. Thus, her research explores the efficacy of targeted interventions to augment individual and collective STEM interest, engagement, motivation, and identities. She draws inspiration from her experiences as a classroom teacher and extensive service with K–12 students in informal STEM and outreach settings.

Pei-Ling Hsu, Ph.D. is an Associate Professor of Science Education in the Department of Teacher Education at the University of Texas at El Paso and is a former high school earth science teacher. Her research interests focus on informal science learning, partnerships with scientists, discourse studies, and students' career pursuits in science. She is the recipient of 2015 Regents' Outstanding Teaching Awards from the University of Texas System. She authored or coauthored/edited 3 books, 24 refereed journal articles, 11 book chapters, 25 conference papers, and 53 presentations at international and national conferences. Her publications appeared in top journals in science education, such as the Journal of Research in Science Teaching, Science Education, Research in Science Education and International Journal of Science Education.

Olga M. Kosheleva, Ph.D. is an Associate Professor in the College of Education in the Teacher Education Department at the University of Texas at El Paso. Her areas of expertise are in mathematics education in teacher preparation, curriculum development with a focus on STEM integration and applied mathematics. She completed her Ph.D. in Computer Engineering at UTEP and holds two Master's degrees in Mathematics and Applied Mathematics from Novosibirsk University, Russia and in Computer Science from UTEP. Much of her research focuses on how students' own comprehension processes for self-evaluation and self-directed learning impacts their outcomes in STEM related fields.

Gabriela Kovats Sánchez is a Ph.D. candidate in the Joint Doctoral Program in Education at San Diego State University (SDSU) and Claremont Graduate University. She earned her MA in Latin American Studies from SDSU and her BA from UC Davis. Gabriela's research distinguishes the experiences of Mexican Indigenous students from the larger pan-Latinx student context. She specifically examines the role of colonialism and its impact on students' ethnic identity development. She is a research analyst with the Research & Equity Scholarship Institute on a large-scale NSF funded project that examines STEM pathways for students of color attending community colleges. Prior to pursuing her Ph.D., Gabriela was Director of College and Career Success at Barrio Logan College Institute, a college prep non-profit organization designed for Latinx, first generation college-bound students in San Diego, California.

Cynthia Lima, Ph.D. is a Lecturer and postdoctoral fellow at the University of Texas at San Antonio. She has a B.S. in Physics from the Universidad Nacional Autonoma de Mexico, and a Ph.D. in Science Education from the University of Texas at Austin. Her research is focused on issues of assessment for diverse cultural and linguistic populations and the design of items that are fair and equitable for all students. Some of the studies conducted within this area, include a validity study of the Texas Math and Science Diagnostic System (TMSDS), and a longitudinal study of Texas students' performance in the Mathematics Texas Assessment of Knowledge and Skills. Her research interests also include the design and implementation of science modeling activities that promote equitable and meaningful participation in the classroom.

Charles Lu, Ph.D. is an Executive Director in the Academic Diversity Initiatives portfolio at The University of Texas at Austin where he leads the largest holistic student success program for first-year students. A former middle school science and math teacher in East Los Angeles, Dr. Lu has served as an educational researcher and consultant, a school director, academic coach, and was the recipient of the Toyota International Teacher of the Year award where he created a virtual curriculum on environmental sustainability in the Galápagos Islands. Dr. Lu has published in several peer-reviewed journals and is a faculty affiliate with Project MALES (Mentoring to Achieve Latino Educational Success). Dr. Lu received his Ph.D. in Higher Education Administration from The University of Texas at Austin, his M.A. in Secondary Science Education from Loyola Marymount University, and his B.S. in Psychology from The University of Texas at Austin.

Eva Midobuche, Ed.D. is a Professor of Bilingual/ESL Education at Texas Tech University. She has been in the Bilingual/ESL Education field since 1976. Her experience as a public school teacher, administrator, and university professor has emphasized and focused her research in language and culture, teacher dispositions, student resiliency, advocacy, second language methodologies, and Latino and curriculum studies. Her publications have appeared in journals such as *the Harvard Educational Review, Educational Leadership, the Bilingual Research Journal, and Teaching Children Mathematics,* among others.

Eduardo Mosqueda, Ed.D. is an Associate Professor at the University of California, Santa Cruz and completed his Ed.D. at Harvard University. He is a former middle school math teacher and curriculum specialist. His research uses the Education Longitudinal Study (collected by the National Center of Education Statistics) and analyzes the relationship between the English proficiency of non-native English speakers, their opportunities to take rigorous courses and their achievement on standardized mathematics assessments as students prepare to take and succeed in high school Algebra. He has been involved in several large scaled studies funded by the Institute of Education Sciences and National Science Foundation.

Melissa Navarro Martell is a Ph.D. candidate in the Joint Doctoral Program in Education at San Diego State University and Claremont Graduate University. Her research interests revolve around the need to prepare critically conscious dual language educators on the sociopolitical, ideological, cultural and linguistic aspects of teacher preparation, particularly within science education. Navarro Martell is the Spanish science methods course instructor for multiple subject credential students in the Department of Dual Language and English Learner Education at SDSU. She is a research analyst with the Research & Equity Scholarship Institute on a large-scale NSF funded project that examines STEM pathways for students of color attending community colleges. Additionally, Navarro Martell served as program coordinator and data analyst for Project CORE, a program at SDSU dedicated to preparing pre-service and in-service teachers to effectively deliver Common Core State Standards and the 2012 ELD Standards to multilingual learners.

Aria Razfar, Ph.D. is a Professor of Education and Linguistics at the University of Illinois at Chicago and a faculty affiliate of the Learning Sciences Research Institute. Professor Razfar's research has been published widely in premier academic journals including *Human Development, Mind, Culture, and Activity, Anthropology and Education Quarterly,* and *Linguistics and Education.* In 2013, he was awarded the University of Illinois at Chicago's *Researcher of the Year* for the Social Sciences. For more than a decade, he has directed several federally funded programs by the U.S. Department of Education and National Science Foundation aimed at developing researchers and teachers of English learners in urban schools. His expertise is grounded in sociocultural theories of language learning and STEM education. He is author of the bestselling *Applying Linguistics in the Classroom: A Sociocultural Perspective* (Routledge Press, 2014).

Gabriela Rivera graduated from the University of Texas at San Antonio with her Masters of Arts in Education with a concentration in Special Education and Applied Behavior Analysis in December 2016. She is currently pursuing her Ph.D. in Educational Psychology at Baylor University with a concentration in Applied Behavior Analysis. Her primary research interests are severe problem behavior and verbal behavior deficits.

Sarah L. Rodriguez, Ph.D. is an Assistant Professor of Community College Leadership/Higher Education at Iowa State University. Dr. Rodriguez's research addresses issues of equity, access, and retention for Latina/o students in the higher education pipeline, with a focus on the intersections of gender and race/ethnicity. Dr. Rodriguez has coordinated large-scale interdisciplinary research projects focused on engineering and other STEM disciplines which have been sponsored by the National Science Foundation (NSF) and authored journal articles, book chapters, policy briefs, and other publications on Latina/o student success and STEM identity development. She also served as a *New*

Mathways Project Mentorship Program Coach for the Charles A. Dana Center supporting community college developmental math program implementation. She completed her PhD in Higher Education Leadership at The University of Texas at Austin and an MS from The University of Tennessee as well as a BA in English and Spanish from Texas A&M University-Commerce.

Karmin San Martin is a Ph.D. candidate in Language, Literacy, and Culture at the University of Texas San Antonio. Her research interests include the relationship of culture, language, and literacy of Latinas in STEM fields, their academic formation, influences, and struggles. She holds a master's degree in Spanish Linguistics and Literatures from The University of Texas Pan-American. She has collaborated in Secondary Science Teaching for English Language and Literacy (SSTELLA) project in Texas and California focusing in the development of academic literacy practices with second-language learners. Prior to that her research includes language pedagogy for health sciences for Spanish-speaking students along the U.S.-Mexico border.

Jorge L. Solís, Ph.D. is an Assistant Professor in the Department of Bicultural-Bilingual Studies at the University of Texas at San Antonio and holds a Ph.D. in Language, Literacy, and Culture from the University of California, Berkeley. His research interests include the development of academic literacy practices with second-language learners, preparing novice bilingual teachers, tensions and adaptations of classroom learning activity, and understanding the academic transitions of older, school-age language minority students. He is Co-Principal Investigator of the Secondary Science Teaching for English Language and Literacy (SSTELLA) study funded by the National Science Foundation.

Zayoni N. Torres, Ph.D. received her PhD in Curriculum and Instruction with a concentration in Gender and Women's Studies, from the University of Illinois at Chicago (UIC). She is a former project coordinator for the English Learning through Math, Science, and Action Research (ELMSA) Project at UIC and a former research fellow for the Center for the Mathematics Education of Latinos/as (CEMELA). She more recently served as a Peace Corps Volunteer in South Africa, where she taught English, mathematics, and computer classes to grades 5–7. Her research interests include sociocultural and feminist perspectives to explore the teaching of mathematics and science literacy for English Learners.

Michael S. Trevisan, Ph.D. is a Professor of Educational Psychology and Dean of the College of Education at Washington State University, Pullman, WA. He was the associate dean for research and external funding, and he was the lead external evaluator for *Acceso a la Ciencia* from 2007 to 2012. Dr. Trevisan has been conducting educational research and evaluation for 31 years. He is widely published in the field of evaluation. He has been Principal Investigator or Co-Principal Investigator on many grants and contracts that require evaluation, particularly evaluations of projects that serve marginalized communities. Dr. Trevisan obtained his Ph.D. in Educational Psychology from the University of Washington in 1990.

Elsa Q. Villa, Ph.D. is a Research Assistant Professor at The University of Texas at El Paso (UTEP) where she is Director of the Center for Education Research & Policy Studies in the College of Education and a member of the proposal development team in the UTEP Office of Research and Sponsored Projects. Her research interests are STEM teacher preparation, computer science and engineering undergraduate and graduate students' identity development, and communities of practice.

Angela Wall Webb, Ph.D. is an Assistant Professor of Science Education at Louisiana State University. Her research centers on the preparation and early career development of science teachers and the equitable teaching of science. In much of her research, Dr. Webb focuses on the normative and enacted identities of science teachers and students, paying specific attention not only to who teachers and students are but also who they are obligated to be in specific contexts. Spanning both of her research interests, Dr. Webb also explores the impact of simulated language learner experiences on promoting equitable science instruction for English language learners by elementary teacher candidates. Prior to joining the faculty at LSU, Dr. Webb taught biology, physical science, and Advanced Placement environmental science in North Carolina.

Timothy T. Yuen, Ph.D. is an Associate Professor of Instructional Technology at the University of Texas at San Antonio. His research investigates how learning technologies and transformative projects can lead to student success and broadening participation in computer science, engineering, and other STEM fields. He was recently a senior investigator for a Department of Education Title V grant which created STEM opportunities for Hispanic students throughout San Antonio. He is currently the project manager for a project funded by the National Science Foundation aimed at improving undergraduate engineering education at UTSA.

María-José Zeledón-Pérez is a doctoral candidate at SDSU in the Ed.D. program with a concentration in Community College Leadership (CCLEAD). Her research focuses on educational attainment for STEM students of color at two-year Hispanic Serving Institutions. Zeledón-Pérez is an Assistant Professor in the Communication Studies Department at San Diego City College and a research affiliate for the Research and Equity Scholarship Institute on Student Trajectories in Education (RESISTE). In addition, she is the secretary/treasurer for the SDSU Community College Leadership Alumni Association and one of the founders of the LatinX Alliance at San Diego Mesa College.

Index

Critical Studies of LATINXS in the Americas

Yolanda Medina and Margarita Machado-Casas
GENERAL EDITORS

Critical Studies of Latinos/as in the Americas is a provocative interdisciplinary series that offers a critical space for reflection and questioning what it means to be Latino/a living in the Americas in twenty-first century social, cultural, economic, and political arenas. The series looks forward to extending the dialogue to include the North and South Western hemispheric relations that are prevalent in the field of global studies.

Topics that explore and advance research and scholarship on contemporary topics and issues related with processes of racialization, economic exploitation, health, education, transnationalism, immigration, gendered and sexual identities, and disabilities that are not commonly highlighted in the current Latino/a Studies literature as well as the multitude of socio, cultural, economic, and political progress among the Latinos/as in the Americas are welcome.

To receive more information about CSLA, please contact:

Yolanda Medina (ymedina@bmcc.cuny.edu) &
Margarita Machado-Casas (Margarita.MachadoCasas@utsa.edu)

To order other books in this series, please contact our Customer Service Department at:

(800) 770-LANG (within the U.S.)
(212) 647-7706 (outside the U.S.)
(212) 647-7707 FAX

Or browse online by series at:

WWW.PETERLANG.COM